Big Data Analytics Framework for Smart Grids

The text comprehensively discusses smart grid operations and the use of big data analytics in overcoming the existing challenges. It covers smart power generation, transmission, and distribution, explains energy management systems, artificial intelligence, and machine learning–based computing.

- Presents a detailed state-of-the-art analysis of big data analytics and its uses in power grids.
- Describes how the big data analytics framework has been used to display energy in two scenarios including a single house and a smart grid with thousands of smart meters.
- Explores the role of the internet of things, artificial intelligence, and machine learning in smart grids.
- Discusses edge analytics for integration of generation technologies, and decision-making approaches in detail.
- Examines research limitations and presents recommendations for further research to incorporate big data analytics into power system design and operational frameworks.

The text presents a comprehensive study and assessment of the state-of-the-art research and development related to the unique needs of electrical utility grids, including operational technology, storage, processing, and communication systems. It further discusses important topics such as complex adaptive power system, self-healing power system, smart transmission, and distribution networks, and smart metering infrastructure. It will serve as an ideal reference text for senior undergraduate, graduate students, and academic researchers in the areas such as electrical engineering, electronics and communications engineering, computer engineering, and information technology.

Explainable AI (XAI) for Engineering Applications

Series Editors
Aditya Khamparia and Deepak Gupta

Explainable AI (XAI) has developed as a subfield of Artificial Inteligence, focussing on exposing complex AI models to humans in a systematic and interpretable manner. This area explores, discusses the steps and models involved in making intelligent decisions. This series will cover the working behavior and explains the ability of powerful algorithms such as neural networks, ensemble methods including random forests, and other similar algorithms to sacrifice transparency and explainability for power, performance, and accuracy in different engineering applications relates to the real world. Aimed at graduate students, academic researchers and professionals, the proposed series will focus key topics including XAI techniques for engineering applications, Explainable AI for Deep Neural Network Predictions, Explainable AI for Machine learning Predictions, XAI driven recommendation systems for Automobile and Manufacturing Industries, and Explainable AI for Autonomous Vehicles.

Artificial Intelligence for Solar Photovoltaic Systems: Approaches, Methodologies and Technologies
Bhavnesh Kumar, Bhanu Pratap and Vivek Shrivastava

Smart Distributed Embedded Systems for Healthcare Applications
Preeti Nagrath, Jafar A. Alzubi, Bhawna Singla, Joel J. P. C. Rodrigues and A.K. Verma

Medical Data Analysis and Processing using Explainable Artificial Intelligence
Edited by Om Prakash Jena, Mrutyunjaya Panda and Utku Kose

Big Data Analytics Framework for Smart Grids
Edited by R. K. Viral, Divya Asija and Surender Reddy Salkuti

For more information about this series, please visit: www.routledge.com/ Explainable-AI-XAI-for-Engineering-Applications/book-series/CRCEAIFEA

Big Data Analytics Framework for Smart Grids

Edited By
R. K. Viral, Divya Asija
and Surender Reddy Salkuti

CRC Press
Taylor & Francis Group
Boca Raton London New York

CRC Press is an imprint of the
Taylor & Francis Group, an **Informa** business

First edition published 2024
by CRC Press
2385 NW Executive Center Drive, Suite 320, Boca Raton FL 33431

and by CRC Press
4 Park Square, Milton Park, Abingdon, Oxon, OX14 4RN

CRC Press is an imprint of Taylor & Francis Group, LLC

© 2024 selection and editorial matter, R. K. Viral, Divya Asija and
Surender Reddy Salkuti, individual chapters, the contributors

ISBN: 978-1-032-39290-5 (hbk)
ISBN: 978-1-032-66538-2 (pbk)
ISBN: 978-1-032-66539-9 (ebk)

DOI: 10.1201/9781032665399

Typeset in Sabon
by Apex CoVantage, LLC

Contents

8 Big Data for Smart Grid: A Case Study   142

TAHA A. TAHA, MOHD KHAIR HASSAN, HUSSEIN I. ZAYNAL, AND NOOR IZZRI ABDUL WAHAB

Preface

In our always-connected, data-centric culture, the concept of a "smart grid" has emerged as a revolutionary force within the energy sector. The growing use of sensors, intelligent devices, and robust data analytics is transforming our electrical grids into intelligent networks that provide greater efficiency, reliability, and sustainability. At the heart of this revolution is the promise of big data analytics, a potent framework that enables utilities to utilize the massive amounts of data produced by smart grids. These significant insights support utilities' decision-making and operational optimization.

This book, *Big Data Analytics Framework for Smart Grid*, delves into the fascinating realm of data-driven intelligence in the context of smart grids. It is an in-depth examination of the most recent studies and innovations on the particular needs of electrical utility grids, including operational technology, information technology, storage, processing, and communication systems, as well as technical and financial solutions for implementing a future electric smart grid model. It is envisaged that by incorporating a big data framework into smart grid technologies, a variety of possible issues and hazards pertaining to grid design, interface, standardization, security, dependability, communication, grid optimization, and sustainable smart grid strategies would be addressed. It serves as a thorough guide for professionals, researchers, students, data science engineers, system operators, transmission and distribution utilities, energy managers, grid operators, smart grid engineers, power engineers, power industries, power testing industries, etc. who want to fully comprehend the potential impacts of big data analytics in transforming our energy systems. Explore big data analytics' foundational ideas, methodology, and real-world applications in the context of smart grids in this book. Explore the many phases of the analytics framework, starting with data collection and preprocessing and moving on to modelling, analysis, and decision-making. Give a comprehensive view of how big data analytics may spur innovation and efficiency in the operation of smart grids by referencing real-world case studies, cutting-edge research, and industry best practices.

Key topics explored in this book:

- Introduction to Smart Grids: Laying the foundation for the use of big data analytics by examining the fundamental ideas, innovations, and benefits of smart grids.
- Big Data Acquisition and Management: Learn about the difficulties and strategies associated with gathering and archiving the enormous amounts of data produced by smart grid devices and systems.
- Data Preprocessing and Integration: Examining the crucial step of putting together data for analysis, which includes tasks like filtering, cleaning, and merging various data sources.
- Data Modelling and Visualization: Investigating various modelling approaches and visualization strategies that let us glean important information from complicated smart grid data, spot trends, and arrive at useful conclusions.
- Advanced Analytics Techniques: Investigating cutting-edge analytical methods, such as machine learning, statistical analysis, and optimization, and demonstrating how these might be used in smart grid situations.
- Applications of Big Data Analytics in Smart Grids: presenting a real-world case study that exemplifies how big data analytics may alter a variety of industries, including grid optimization, asset management, demand response, and predictive maintenance.
- Challenges and Future Directions: In order to provide helpful insights into the future of this quickly developing profession, this article will discuss the challenges, ethical issues, and upcoming trends in the field of big data analytics for smart grids.

We genuinely hope that readers will find this book to be a priceless tool for navigating the complex world of big data analytics in the context of smart grids. We have the chance to build smarter, more effective, and sustainable energy systems by understanding and using the potential of data, paving the path for a brighter and more environmentally friendly future.

About the Editors

R. K. Viral is presently working as Associate Professor in the Department of Electrical & Electronics Engineering, Amity School of Engineering & Tech., Amity University, Noida, UP, India. Additionally, he has more than 16 years of teaching experience at UG and PG level in various engineering institutes/universities.

He was awarded a doctoral degree from Indian Institute of Technology Roorkee, Roorkee in the area of Distributed Generation in 2016. He also received his postgraduate degree in Energy Systems from IIT Roorkee in 2010 and graduated in Electrical Engineering (with honors) from MJP Rohilkhand University, Bareilly in 2003. His research interests include distribution system planning and optimization, renewable energy system, soft computing techniques in power systems, small hydropower design, development and applications, smart grid, big data analytics and cyber security in power system. He is guiding five Ph.D students and supervised many M.Tech dissertations.

He has filed more than 16 patents in various multidisciplinary areas. He has also published more than 150 research publications in various international/national journals/conferences/book chapters of repute and peer reviewed. He has one edited book of CRC Press, Taylor & Francis, and two are in the process in Elsevier/CRC. He has served as TPC member of several international conferences held worldwide. He is also an active member of professional societies, namely IEEE, PES, ISTE, IEI, IDES, ACEEE, and a contributing editorial board member (IJORCS, IJESCE, IJBST, etc.) and reviewer of various international journals.

Divya Asija is Assistant Professor in the Electrical and Electronics Engineering Department of Amity School of Engineering and Technology at the Amity University, Noida, India, where she has been a faculty member since 2012. She has more than 16 years of teaching experience at various prestigious institutions/universities. She completed her PhD at Amity University, Noida and her postgraduate studies at YMCA, Faridabad. Her research interests include power systems, ranging from congestion management to renewable energy resources, distributed generation, smart grids and electric vehicles. She has filed five patents and applied various funded projects of different government and private agencies. She is also the author and coauthor of over 75 research papers and book chapters in several international journals of repute. She is also an active reviewer of international journals (*Energy* (Elsevier), the *International Journal of System Assurance Engineering and Management* (Springer), the *International Journal of Emerging Electric Power Systems* (Degruyter), the *International Journal of Electrical and Computer Engineering* (Institute of Advanced Engineering and Science), the *Journal of Electrical Engineering & Technology* (Springer) and the *International Journal of Renewable Energy Research*). In the interim, she was also awarded for her outstanding contribution in reviewing *Energy*, Elsevier for the academic years 2017–18 and 2018–19. She was also a winner of the gold award for courseware creation using Moodle for outcome-based education and ethical commitment.

Surender Reddy Salkuti is working with Woosong University, Republic of Korea as Associate Professor in the Department of Railroad and Electrical Engineering since April 2014. He received the Ph.D. degree in electrical engineering from the Indian Institute of Technology Delhi (IITD), India, in 2013. He was Postdoctoral Researcher at Howard University, Washington, DC, USA, from 2013 to 2014.

His research interests include power system restructuring issues, smart grid development with the integration of wind and solar photovoltaic energy sources, battery storage and electric vehicles, demand response, power system analysis and optimization, soft computing techniques application in power systems and renewable energy.

He has published two edited volumes with Springer (LNEE) and more than 250 research articles in peer-reviewed international journals and conference proceedings. He has served as, or is serving as, Guest Editor for various international journals. He is also an editorial board member for many journals. He is the recipient of the 2016 Distinguished Researcher Award from Woosong University Educational Foundation, South Korea, and the POSOCO Power System Award (PPSA) 2013, India. He is listed in the top 2% of scientists published in a study conducted by researchers of ICSR Lab, Elsevier BV and Stanford University, USA. He is a member of IEEE and IEEE Power and Energy Society.

Contributors

Divya Asija
Amity University Uttar Pradesh
 Noida,
Noida, Uttar Pradesh, India

Aniruddh Atrey
Amity University Uttar Pradesh
 Noida,
Noida, Uttar Pradesh, India

Devyanshi Bansal
Amity University Uttar Pradesh
 Noida,
Noida, Uttar Pradesh, India

Madhulika Bhatia
Amity University Uttar Pradesh
 Noida,
Noida, Uttar Pradesh, India

Vishal Kumar Gaur
Department of Electrical &
 Instrumentation Engineering,
Thapar Institute of Engineering &
 Technology, India

Mohd Khair Hassan
University Putra Malaysia
 (UPM),
Serdang, Selangor, Malaysia

Ramgopal Kashyap
Amity University
Chhattisgarh, Raipur, India

Jameer Kotwal
Amity University
Chhattisgarh, Raipur, India

Sumit Kushwaha
University Institute of Computing,
 Chandigarh University,
India

Anita Devi Ningthoujam
Amity University Uttar Pradesh
 Noida,
Noida, Uttar Pradesh, India

Subho Paul
Washington State University, Pullman,
WA, USA

Pathan Shafi
MIT-ADT University,
Pune, India

Sachin Sharma
Amity University Uttar Pradesh
 Noida,
Noida, Uttar Pradesh, India

Sudiksha Sharma
Amity University Uttar Pradesh
    Noida,
Noida, Uttar Pradesh, India

Taha A. Taha
Putra Malaysia (UPM),
Serdang, Selangor, Malaysia

R. K. Viral
Amity University Uttar Pradesh
    Noida,
Noida, Uttar Pradesh, India

Noor Izzri Abdul Wahab
University Putra Malaysia (UPM),
Serdang, Selangor, Malaysia

Arun Kumar Yadav
National Institute of Technology,
Hamirpur, H.P., India

Hussein I. Zaynal
Computer Engineering Technology
    Department,
Al-Kitab University, Altun Kupri,
    Kirkuk, Iraq

Chapter 1

Necessities of Big Data in Smart Grid

*Anita Devi Ningthoujam, Divya Asija,
and R. K. Viral*

1.1 INTRODUCTION

With rapid advancement in digital technology and cloud computing, an increasing amount of data is generated by digital devices and sensors, including smartphones, computers, improved measuring infrastructures, etc., as well as through human activity and communications. For instance, exabytes (1018) and zettabytes (1021) are now used for measuring data on the Internet [1]. The rational and efficient analysis of these data has a significant positive impact on our day-to-day life. Introduction of big data has a large opportunity for the processing and analysis of these vast volumes of data. However, the amount of data being stored is increasing exponentially, resulting in a more complex structure of this data. The Indian government has been planning to implement a national grid since early 1990, which was later utilized.

Similar to traditional grids, smart grids are also made up of several moving components. But in terms of efficiency, smart grids excel the existing grid system with improved designed and functionality [2]. Several intelligent components have also been introduced that can decide energy consumption based on the preset user preferences. Several smart substations data have been implemented which can control the critical and non-critical operations, such as power factor performance, battery, breaker, and transformer status.

Smart generation is another essential component of a smart grid. Based on feedback generated from various grid multi points, it can study the distinct behavior of power generation resources to optimize energy production and automatically maintain voltage, power factor, and frequency standards. Affordable low-carbon methods of generating and storing electricity are also made accessible for the public in general [3]. Thus, the implementation of a smart meter, an essential component of smart grid into the system, allows two-way communication between the consumer as well as service provider. This made both the utilities and consumers detect power consumption, outages, billing, and collection of real-time data a lot easier and faster [1]. In addition, smart distribution uses superconducting cables for long-distance

DOI: 10.1201/9781032665399-1

transmission, automated monitoring and analytical tools, self-healing, self-optimization, and self-balancing.

1.1.1 Indian Old Grid

The Indian government has been planning to implement a national grid since early 1990 which was later utilized in the 1960s. First, it was established on a regional basis, where each state grid had been interconnected individually across the country [2]. Thus, it came into operation forming five regional grids, namely Northern, Eastern, Western, Northeastern, and Southern Grids. This created the possibility of transmitting surplus amounts of electricity within the states [2]. Earlier, the regional grids had been interconnected using asynchronous HVDC links in a back-to-back manner. This limited exchange of power has been regulated [1]. It was later improved using high-capacity synchronous links which made the exchange much more convenient and made a higher amount possible.

In October 1991, two grids were interconnected at first, Northeastern and Eastern grids [2]. It was further expanded when Western grids were interconnected in March 2003 [2]. Later, the Northern grids were added in August 2006. With this interconnection, a Central Grid has been formed which is operated synchronously at one frequency. The Central Grid was later interconnected with the Southern grid on 31st December 2013 with the introduction of 765 kV Raipur-Solapur transmission line, which resulted in the formation of the National Grid [1].

1.1.2 New Progression in Grids

The Indian National Grid is the largest high-voltage energy transmission network, linking major substations and various power plants to avail the electricity generated, meeting its requirements throughout the country. [2] The Power Grid Corporation of India, a state-owned corporation, owns, operates, and maintains the National Grid. The Power System Operation Corporation is a state-owned corporation. As of 30 June 2020, it had an installed power generation capacity of 371.054 GW, making it one of the largest functioning synchronous grids in the entire globe [1].

The grid in India is linked as a wide-area synchronous grid that typically operates at 50 Hz. As of September 17, 2012, the permitted frequency band range is 49.5–50.5 Hz. The frequency of this grid is regulated by the Union Government by charging states extra whenever the states draw power at low frequency. Additionally, there are asynchronous connections with Bangladesh, Myanmar, and Nepal as well as synchronous connections to Bhutan [1]. There has also been a connection integrated to Sri Lanka (the India-Sri Lanka HVDC Interconnection). All the BIMSTEC countries might trade with one another and create a power pool in the future with the proposed connection between Myanmar and Thailand [3].

1.1.3 Smart Grid Present and Future Drift

In the twenty-first century, the rise in demand for electricity led researchers to find a way to improve power efficiency as well as its supply, which led to the introduction of smart grid. It can automate and manage the grid to meet rising energy demands if fully implemented with enabling of renewable energy. It generates power and can transmit and distribute automatically with the help of modern technologies with improved techniques and methods [3]. The system aims to integrate and promote the use of alternative energy sources like solar, wind, and hydropower, give users access to real-time data on their energy use, and help utility companies cut down on outages.

Present Drift: Use of smart grid also lessens power surges and blackouts and can lower the price of energy generation as well as consumption [3]. But more importantly, this technology enables widespread charging of electric vehicles and allows users almost real-time control over their energy expenses.

Future Drift: According to research, customers are more likely to take the necessary steps to reduce their energy use when they are fully aware of how much energy they are using. In the future, consumers will be able to provide a financial edge with improved power management and adoption to greener technology through implementation of smart grid. It will save nearly $600 in direct bill savings in an average household [1, 3]. The overall energy consumption can be reduced from 5% to 10% with the access of real-time information on energy consumption.

To encourage innovation in smart grid technology, the Department of Energy has already invested a total of $3.5 billion from the year 2016 up to 2026 [4–6]. Machine learning, plug-and-play technologies, self-healing grid, and complete grid automation are some of the research areas coming up soon.

1.1.4 Brief Description for the Necessity of Big Data in Smart Grid

Nowadays, big data plays an important role in the smart grid. It helps consumers in understanding the behavior of electricity consumption, improves services, and provides them customized services [4]. It encourages them to save energy and reduce the emissions of hazardous gases in the world.

Numerous data acquisition devices and information management systems are needed to make the modern power system more intelligent, including smart meters, remote terminal units (RTU), power distribution management systems (DMS), phasor measurement units (PMU), customer management systems (CMS), energy management systems (EMS), and power generation management systems (GMS) which have been proposed widely. These smart meters and sensors can store and analyze the data which is collected as information from the transmitted and distributed electricity [4]. Big data for the smart grid is primarily produced by these systems, which generate a lot of data. Data analysis technology is an essential component for developing a smart grid and plays an important role in the modern industrial system. The flexibility, safety, reliability, and efficiency of the electricity system can all be improved by making the best decisions possible for grid control and operation.

With advanced and improved technology of information and communication technology, huge amounts of information have been adapted to conventional electricity transmission. With the adoption of big data, the present power system has many advantages by utilizing vast volumes of data from the electricity network, geographic information system, and meteorological information system, etc. [4]. This will also improve customer service and societal welfare. To progress big data analytics applications in actual smart grids, however, other challenges must be resolved, including those relating to methodologies, awareness, synergies, etc.

1.2 NOTION FOR TODAY'S ELECTRICITY GRID

1.2.1 Scenario of Today's Grid

The Indian grid is made up of a combination of power plants and a huge network of transmission and distribution systems.

Power Grid Corporation of India Limited (POWERGRID), which operates under the Ministry of Power, is responsible for bulk transmission of power with EHVAC (up to 765 kV level) and ±800/±500kV HVDC transmission network. This company falls under the listed companies which hold up to 51.34% of the power of Government of India and is kept balanced by public and institutional investors [3].

As recorded on 30th June 2021, POWERGRID has a total operating EHV transmission line up to 172,154 km across the country. It also owns 262 EHV AC and HVDC substations with a transformation capacity of more than 446,940 MVA. This huge network has been made available with proper infrastructure and management of state-of-the-art operation and maintenance techniques in accordance with global standards.

As of FY 2020–21, POWERGRID faced a major turn of about Rs. 40,823.53 crore and net profit of Rs. 12,036.46 crore along with the total fixed assets reaching up to Rs. 2,41,498.22 crore as on 31.03.2021 [3]. The current inter-regional power transfer capacity of the National Grid is about 105,050 MW, which was enhanced to 1,18,000 MW as of 2022. Moreover, POWERGRID is responsible for upgrading of distribution reforms under various national schemes under GoI such as Deendayal Upadhyaya Gram Jyoti Yojana (DDUGJY) and Integrated Power Development Scheme (IPDS) [7–9].

Currently, interconnections have been extended between India and Bhutan, India and Nepal, and India and Bangladesh. Moreover, these interconnections of the previously said regions have been reinforced for widespread exchange of power across the borders. POWERGRID is also responsible for providing consultancy services across several national and international clients, which include most of the South Asian, African, and Middle East countries.

1.2.2 Determination of Operating Challenges

The Indian grid constantly balances the energy that is supplied and demanded that powers everything from industry to household appliances. Most people seem to be concerned for grids only when significant failures occur, such as power blackouts, that bring it to the public's notice.

Extreme weather conditions with climate change have always been a major challenge for grid operation. Power theft and cyberattacks have also been a concern for the grid's reliability.

With introduction to renewable energy and distributed generation systems, most of the traditional grids have been replaced for household and industrial uses. This urges private companies and individual homes to produce power of their own, which poses a threat to the traditional ones [1, 3]. At the same time, a number of consumers have opted for new and advanced grids, which causes great loss to the previous customers. Moreover, from time to time, most of the grid's infrastructure gets depleted with weather exposure, which requires a major and expensive overhaul.

Figure 1.1 shows the overall grid interconnection comprising of generation, transmission, and distribution systems. In generation, electricity is generated by either burning fossil fuels or using renewable energy sources, which is then sent across long distances using high-voltage transmission lines in the transmission system. There are local facilities known as substations present in the distribution system where the transmitted high-voltage power has been converted to a lower voltage (by a process called "stepping down") and then distributed to local homes and businesses through distribution lines [3]. Electricity transmission and distribution is seen as a "natural monopoly" due to the increase in its costs of construction for infrastructure, meaning that only a company that is capable of controlling a huge market can afford

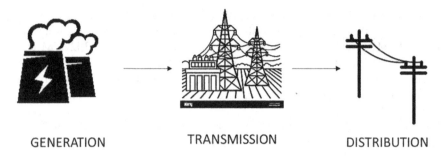

GENERATION   TRANSMISSION   DISTRIBUTION

Figure 1.1 Components of electric grid [7].

the necessary investments. As a result, the majority of energy utilities are given monopoly power over a local market which is necessary for providing provide low-cost, reliable energy as a public good [4]. Utilities that are either publicly owned or, more frequently, regulated by state regulatory bodies that can determine the prices of utilities are allowed to charge customers for carrying out their responsibility.

1.2.3 Example of Challenges like Blackouts and Cyber Theft

1.2.3.1 Blackout

Blackout occurs due to extreme climatic conditions such as hurricanes, blizzards, floods, heat waves, wildfires, and even solar flares with aging of power lines. Most of the power transformers installed in substations and electrical grids are probably older than 40 years old, despite the fact that the average age of power plants is over 30 years old. Also, the majority of the grid infrastructure is constructed aboveground, which is less expensive to install but more prone to disaster. The demand for energy continuously rises as a result of variability in climate changes, which proves to be less efficient for production and transmission of energy.

One of the major blackout cases detained happened in India was on July 30 and 31, 2012 in the northern and eastern part of India due to grid malfunction [10, 11]. The exact reason for the failure is unknown, but it surely affected more than 620 million people, which is half the population of India. Power Minister Sushil Kumar Shinde estimated that power failure might be due to some states trying to draw power more than permitted with increase in demand. Spokesperson for Power Grid Corporation of India Limited (PGCIL) and the Northern Regional Load Dispatch Centre (NRLDC) even stated the states responsible for the overdraw were Uttar Pradesh, Punjab, and Haryana [10]. A senior director for an Indian power company also commented on the outage to be a huge breakdown with an estimated shortage of 32 GW, which resulted in huge technical faults in India's grid. The effect of the outage was so severe that it even led to the failure of backup systems.

To prevent future disasters, utilities will need to harden grid infrastructure like burying of power lines and ensuring that poles aboveground are fire-resistant. The costs of installations are high, but blackouts are estimated to have cost the state more.

1.2.3.2 Cyber Theft

Additionally, the introduction of smart digital systems on grids increases the possibility of cyberattacks. Recent reports have warned the national grids of the growing vulnerability of the grid's generation, transmission, and distribution systems to cyber invasions [3, 4]. Grid operators have relied on electronic industrial control (IC) centers since the 1970s, yet these systems are typically unprotected against malware. One of the recent examples of cyber theft in India was reported on October 30, 2022. Tata Power, a leading power generation company in India, has confirmed it was hit by a cyberattack [1].

1.3 FUTURISTIC SMART GRIDS AND OTHER ENERGY SYSTEMS

The current grid technology we are adopting proves to be less advanced; hence, electric grid systems are inefficient and unreliable. With further research, researchers are trying to cope with this problem by implementing smart grids over the traditional grids [12]. It can considerably reduce greenhouse gas emissions by up to 211 million metric tons and is very efficient in terms of reliability [12]. Industries aimed to bring a valuation of over $400 billion in 2020.

Figure 1.2 represents the futuristic overview of smart grid. Some of the improved functionalities over the conventional grid are mentioned in the following points [13, 14].

1. It allows integration of renewable energy sources, which solves global climate change.
2. It enables healthy participation of the customers by making them aware of their energy usage and allowing them to remotely control their smart appliances and temperature settings.
3. It has highly secured cybersecurity communication systems and ensures the system safety from end to end by providing two-way secure communications for improving energy conservation.
4. It promotes the use of existing resources for long-term sustainability.

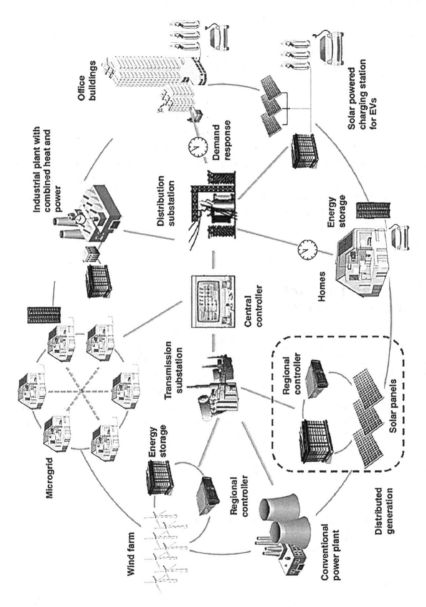

Figure 1.2 A futuristic overview of smart grid [12].

5. It permits optimum energy flow with reduced losses and saving energy costs.
6. It helps in integrating the control and communication of energy systems with safe and flexible system operation.

As discussed earlier, smart grid does not necessarily mean a complete replacement of the traditional present grid, but rather an improvement of the infrastructure for more utilization of power available [13]. As of today, large-scale energy generation has been focused more on solar and wind plants which constitute a major component of smart grid. With two-way accessibility and secure communications, the consumers can also facilitate real-time operations and their energy usage. Controlling and monitoring of the utility becomes easier with the future smart grid [14]. The integrated system modeling, along with advanced tools, will allow detection of system failure and reduce the maintenance costs. Remotely controlled equipment and distributed generation with energy sources are major necessities in managing the smart grid.

1.3.1 Need of Smart Grid

Smart grids met the needs and demands of recent times, and these impacts are expected to last for a very long period [15]. This technology will modernize and overhaul the dated equipment, resulting in the reduction for occurrence of blackouts, burnouts, and power surges which will drop the price for both energy consumption and production [15]. If fully implemented, smart grids will enable renewable energy and prepare the grid to meet rising energy demands. This technology allows customers to control their energy bills in real time and facilitate electric vehicle charging.

1.3.2 Practices to Overcome the Active Challenges

The main aim of smart grid is all about giving consumers financial advantages, not only in the betterment of power management but also in implementing environmentally friendly technology. It is expected to save an average household nearly $600 in direct bills while successfully adopting this technology, and force it to limit energy consumption by 5–10% with the involvement of real-time technology [15]. Studies by different researchers suggest that the total energy savings regarding this technology is estimated to be $42 billion after a year, and $48 billion will be saved annually in the next five years. Over $65 billion can be saved in 15 years and $102 billion in 30 years [15].

The main goal of smart grid is to increase electricity consumption at a lower cost to improve the living standard of all people. So power affordability should also be considered with this aspect [16]. The capacity factor of the electric system is expected to improve over time through more efficient supply and demand management. By incorporating cutting-edge controller intelligence into the current system, it will enable effective reuse of existing hardware infrastructure [16]. Smart grid utilities should be able to minimize peak demand and lower capital and O&M costs by understanding the risks and consumer effects of using the available resources optimally. The cost effectiveness of smart grid components must be both at the individual level and at the system level.

1. Education: Utilities, service providers, and universities must produce educated customers as well as a new generation of electrical engineers knowledgeable in computer sciences and systems engineering.
2. Enable to incorporate advanced technologies available.

1.3.3 Comparison Table of Existing Grid and Smart Grid

With the use of advanced modern communications and technologies, smart grids can digitally enhance power systems in terms of robustness, efficiency, and flexibility.

Table 1.1 shows the comparison of smart grid with an existing grid that is operated in today's power systems [17].

Table 1.1 Comparison Table of an Existing Grid and Smart Grid

Existing Grid	Smart Grid
Most technologies used are electromechanical	Mostly digital in nature
It provides only one-way communication	It supports both one-way and two-way communication
Generation is mostly centralized	Distributed generation
Sensors are not widely used	Sensors are widely used
It is lacking in monitoring; only manual	It is digital self-monitoring
Failures and blackouts often occur	Adaptive and intelligent techniques are adopted
Lack of control	Robust control
Less energy-efficient	Energy-efficient
Usually not possible to integrate RE	Possible to integrate large-scale RE
Customers have less scope to modify uses	Customers can check uses and modify

1.3.4 Future Direction in Operation of Smart Grid

The Department of Energy proposed an investment of $3.5 billion for innovating smart grid technologies from the year 2016 to 2026 [15]. It mainly focuses on adopting newly advanced techniques that can enhance the performance of smart grid and make it more efficient in the near future [15]. Some of the futuristic techniques that can enhance the operation of smart grid are as follows [16–18]:

a) Machine Learning – Through this method, utility companies will be able to utilize power that is updated on the cloud as well as in big data. Power outages can be significantly reduced by enhancing grid security.

b) Plug and Play – This smart grid technique allows consumers to redistribute the power generated to other customers in need through personal means such as solar cells and wind turbines.

c) The Self-Healing Grid – It comprises sensors and has advanced software for use in a real-time distribution system, and data transferred can be detected automatically. It can also analyze faults and isolate the faulty part from the remaining functional components so as to configure the distribution network and minimize the customer's impact.

d) Total Automation – With the advancement in smart grid, futuristic smart grids aim for total automation of the smart grid, from power generation to distribution and overall control in its service management.

1.3.5 Inclusion of Renewable Energy and Other Energy Systems

Renewable energy sources (RESs) and other energy storage systems (ESSs) are the essential technologies that play a huge role in smart grid applications. It offers numerous advantages in improving the urban areas with decarbonizing to enhance the grid operation. It can facilitate power grids in frequency regulation and voltage deviations [14]. It mainly focuses on bringing smart and healthy power transmission as well as distribution which is sustainable, reliable, and climate friendly. Integration of renewable energy with power networks can be made possible through smart grid. Traditional grid systems cause major greenhouse effects and global warming [15]. They have environmental impacts, with the use of fossil fuels such as burning of coal. Alternately, renewable energy (RE) encourages the use of environmental-friendly solutions that are pollution-free and are sustainable. Power plants are mostly integrated with REs, mainly solar and wind energy.

For example, mechanical gears used in wind farms need each link for supporting numerous sensors. Each sensor records the environment's and the climate's current state. The utility then gets information in case of any faults, which increases the quality of services and level of safety.

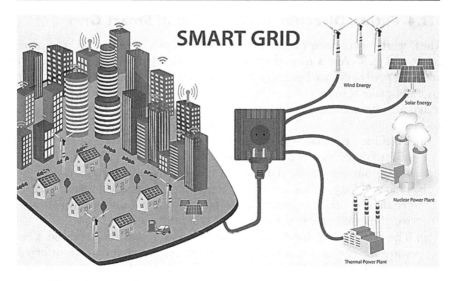

Figure 1.3 Applications of renewable energy in smart grid systems [16].

Figure 1.3 shows the representation of the possible contribution of renewable energy-based power plants in smart grid systems. It integrates various distributed energy resources with the power grid [19]. The implementation of IoT (Internet of Things) with the smart grid allows the grid to collect data and detect any service failure in real time through continuous self-healing techniques [20]. This helps the utilities be aware without involving the customer's concern and report the outages due to instant faults.

1.4 ENERGY IN NUMBERS

1.4.1 Need of Energy Analysis

Data analysts can generate real-time data and weather conditions for applications in smart grid so as to obtain an improved and optimized system operation [21]. Energy analysis is necessarily carried out for reducing the operational costs and enhancing the grid's reliability along with customizing energy services for customers [21]. The main reason for adopting big data analytics is to obtain valuable information from data recorded previously and future advancement in the operation and maintenance of the smart grid.

1.4.2 Energy and Data

Smart meters are used in smart grids for data collection and transmission of energy-related information between the two ends (consumers and utility companies or DSO) [22]. As consumers' energy consumption also increases, anticipation of smart meters readings for a power utility company rises to 220 million a day from 24 million a year [23]. With the advancement of artificial intelligence and the trend towards electrification in the transportation sector, electric cars (EVs) and plug-in hybrid EVs (PHEVs), there is a huge demand in the emerging component in the power market and smart grid. For normal operation of the distribution system, the traditional DSO depends on the measurements taken in the primary substation of the MV feeder, where the protection mechanisms are typically installed [23]. A typical smart meter will measure things like load demand, total harmonic distortion and power factor, active and reactive power, as well as consumed energy over a period of time.

Table 1.2 includes a list of the smart grid's AI technique used for data collection [22].

Table 1.2 Intelligent Devices for Data Collection in Smart Grid

Intelligent Device	Technology	Application
Advanced metering infrastructure (AMI)	Bidirectional contact between customers and utilities through the integration of smart meters, communication networks, and data management	Used for local control, dynamic tariffs, power quality monitoring, and remote meter configuration
Phasor measurement unit (PMU)	Employing a single time source to synchronize several distant points in real time (30 to 60 samples per second)	Used to measure electrical waves of power grid
Wide area monitoring system (WAMS)	A server that handles software that processes information from PMUs	Used for dynamic stability of the grid
Remote terminal unit (RTU)	Devices for transferring telemetry data that is microprocessor-controlled	Used for collecting status information collection of system operation
Supervisory control and data acquisition (SCADA)	Both manual as well as automatic	Used in system monitoring and for event processing and alarm
Intelligent electronic device (IED)	Records changes and monitors the substation and outgoing feeders	Combining various monitoring, recording, and protection functionalities for relays

1.4.3 Huge Data Generation in Grid

With rapid depletion of fossil fuels and increase in decarbonization, power systems are to decrease the carbon emission for the power grid. Smart grid and super grid are efficient ways to expand electrification of human society with high use of renewable energy sources [22]. The intermittent nature of wind and photovoltaic energies provides a huge challenge in a low inertia power system for a safe and stable operation, despite the growing awareness of sustainable development being the driving force behind their use. Data analytics is important research in this case for smooth regulation and dispatching of energy when integrated with renewable energy-based forecasting methods [22]. As in the traditional grid, the amount of data collected from electricity meters for analyzing billing purposes is mostly manual and is difficult. With huge data generated and stored from two-way communication smart grids, advanced data analytics becomes a must for billing as well as maintaining the network status. For example, the generated data can be used in predicting a customer's behavior, forecasting electricity demand, and optimizing electric generation [24].

1.4.4 Data Analysis Requirement in Grid

Data analytics plays an important role in the modern, advancing world. Electricity has become a necessity in industries [25]. Various improved data analytics techniques have been adapted so far. The data collected from smart grids using smart meters and sensors are so huge that data analysis becomes a vital role. Some methods adopted in the electricity transmission and distribution networks are big data analytics and machine learning algorithms [25]. With these, collecting, storing, and analyzing of data can be processed by predicting the data and forecasting it along with maintaining the system. These techniques not only deliver energy at lower costs but also aim in improving customer service with social welfare.

1.5 SELF-HEALING AND ADAPTIVENESS

Traditional electricity grids are unable to respond to the needs of the twenty-first century. The use of information technology is imminent in electrical energy generation, transmission, and distribution technologies for today's needs and for providing sufficient energy. Nowadays, significant challenges like energy demand, commercial losses, and power supply quality are being faced by the electricity sector [26]. To overcome these obstacles, energy must be delivered to consumers in a secure, reliable, and high-quality manner.

Smart grid technology has come into the picture for providing sustainable energy by integrating energy systems and new developments in data and communication technologies [26].

There are two basic ways in which self-healing control ensures a reliable and consistent power supply:

a) In normal operation, the primary goals of self-healing control are to improve performance and eliminate hidden issues.
b) Another option is to correct the defect as quickly as possible; in the control area, the fault can be either external or internal.

The important aim is to quickly eliminate and recover from defects in the control regions, minimizing the outage area and operational loss to the system. The fault network should be disconnected from the external network when an irreversible fault develops outside the control area [26]. The system relies on the operation of distributed power supply and energy storage devices in the region that maintains the uninterrupted power supply.

1.5.1 Smart Grid Major Advantages

According to supply and demand, smart grids can measure and send data to automatically adjust electricity flow using sensors in it. Using this information, energy managers can adjust the grid and respond in real time, thereby making the managing task simple and efficient and improving fault detection [27].

Communicating through smart power meters, the grid can also connect customers' homes. This means that smart grids can perform the following operations [27]:

a) Reducing emissions and fuel costs.
b) Integrating various sources of renewable energy into a single grid.
c) Providing real-time feedback on energy production and consumption.
d) Creating seamless fault detection.
e) Providing more efficiency to a customer's demand according to user needs.

A smart grid is made up of different technologies, including communications systems, smart power generation devices, smart meters, sensors and measurement devices, phasor measurement units and power system automation technologies, and some artificial intelligence included.

1.5.2 Self-Healing Purpose

A smart grid provides solutions for an extensive range of information technology resources, allowing for both old as well as advanced grids to reduce electricity waste and energy costs [28]. Smart meters help customers analyze their used energy based on price signals given as rates fluctuate.

In order for smart grid to allow real-time troubleshooting for unforeseen events, self- healing grid has its significant purpose [28]. With smart grids having the capability of self- healing, it can easily identify faults, shorten the frequency, and quicken the duration of outages. It can also recover the grid fast in case of the occurrence of any faults.

1.5.3 Smart Grid Adaptiveness in Operation

With the advancement of technology, system complexity increases, which results in increasing the cost and difficulty fixing the system's fault and restoring it to its default operating state. In order to achieve the previous challenge, self-healing systems must be used [29]. Figure 1.4 summarizes the aim of self-healing systems utilized in smart grid [26]. In case of a fault occurrence, system performance should not be affected. The system must be resilient and reconfigured so that it can cope with any disturbances that might occur. To be effective against grid faults and to take protection against grid propagation are the main goals in self-healing. The smart grid must realize the following to be able to achieve self-healing [25, 26]:

a) Fast and accurate fault analysis for systems protection from harmful effects.
b) Positive or negative situations should be provided.
c) Minimization of the service's self-healing period.

1.5.3.1 Transmission Grid in Smart Grid Using Self-Healing

For continuous determination and monitoring the transmission line parameters, developed sensors, signal processors, and communication networks

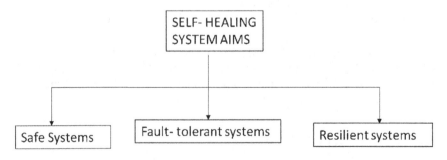

Figure 1.4 Goals of self-healing system [24].

must be created in all the transmission grids in a smart grid [26]. Therefore, the sensors will provide crucial information such as the conductors' sagging on the overload line, their temperature, and their current carrying capacity in relation to their thermal capacity. In addition, the intelligent transmission transformer station must return to its default state following blackout failures. Optimal voltage control based on genetic algorithms is one of the solutions. Fast and effective solutions can be obtained by inserting prior phenomena into the system's genetic learning algorithm while controlling the voltage. We need to obtain a comprehensive and planned system for the self-healing of the grid [23–26]. To guarantee this, it needs to optimally locate the grid elements, energy storage sources, and compensation systems. The mode of data transfer between these systems may be either wired communication or wireless communication, and the self-healing procedure will be generated by sending a warning to the system center in case of any fault.

Researchers suggest that by adopting the United Power Flow Controller (UPFC) and obtaining a steady power flow under network faults, a self-healing method for the smart grid can be started [26]. In this method to execute the control algorithm, inverse current grid is applied instead of the iterative algorithm; the node analysis method is applied instead of the optimization method, and the power flow is rearranged.

1.5.3.2 Distribution Grid in Smart Grid Using Self-Healing

Self-healing plays an important role in smart distribution grid systems. A common method based on travelling waves has been proposed for this self-healing system [30, 31]. Here, faults can be detected easily when the threshold of measured travelling wave is found greater than its threshold value. The faults are then calculated using the least squares method. Then the system is kept for healing itself by proposing this algorithm and thus providing a smooth and uninterrupted energy. Another method generally proposed is the analytical method, where the Markov method has been used for ensuring electrical distribution system reliability [32]. With the help of this method, smart electric distribution systems have been improved to a great extent. It has been tested and is practically applicable with huge economic benefits.

1.5.3.3 Micro Grids in Smart Grid Using Self-Healing

Micro grids play a significant role in the smart grid. It can be connected into the network and can also feed loads that are connected in island states. Energy sources from micro grids can be classified broadly into solar panels, fuel cells, and wind turbines. For a more secure and robust smart grid, the micro grids should be capable of self-healing. Taking into consideration the availability of renewable sources and stored energy, the power flow time can be maximized using advanced methods that are essential for building micro grids in island conditions [33]. Accordingly, electricity reliability depends on ensuring proper maintenance of micro grids.

1.6 MAJOR NECESSITIES OF BIG DATA IN SMART GRID

There have been numerous publications stating that IT departments should invest in big data for managing smart grids. Big data has very interesting heterogeneous characteristics, which differ in resolution, mainly asynchronous, and are saved in different formats such as raw data or processed data at different locations in the world. For instance, the data collected by a normal smart meter for energy consumption for every 15 minutes are stored in billing centers [33]. One million smart meters generated from utilities results in nearly 3 TB data of energy consumption every year.

Some applications of big data in smart grid [33]:

a) PMU's (Phasor Measurement Unit) can detect high resolution voltage and current in the smart grid and can report the data collected in real time at 30–60 times per second rate. The time synchronized from phasors to phasors and data concentrators are located at every substation or at control centers, resulting in around 40 TB of new data recorded per year for a common utility [34].

b) Big data carries a huge amount of information that allows information-driven control algorithms in bridging revolutionized and improved ways of smart grid that are well planned and operated [35, 36].

c) It innovates the operation and planning of existing grids for all levels (from generation to transmission to distribution and end users) [37].

d) Big data also provides opportunity in maintaining the grid assets, energy consumption at user's end, and distributed energy resources (DER) at real time which is not possible in traditional grids due to certain limits of control and measurements.

Figure 1.5 shows the main characteristics of big data in a smart grid. It is highly characterized with huge volume (in terms of TB), wide varieties such as structured/unstructured and synchronous/asynchronous, changing velocity (for real time, that is, in seconds/minutes/hours resolution), veracity (for identifying inconsistencies, redundancies, lost data, and other information) and values (for identifying economic, technical, and operational) [38]. So a huge volume of data in both real time as well as historical records are required for getting precise information for making data-driven decisions. So it has been clear that big data analytics play an incredible role for both operating of futuristic grids efficiently as well as

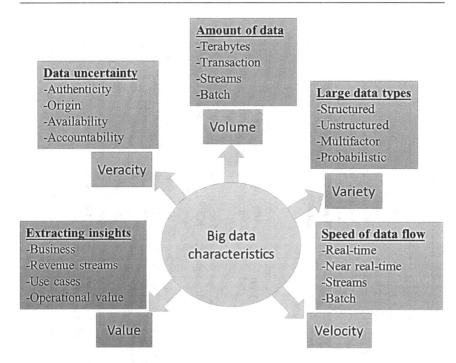

Figure 1.5 Key characteristics of big data in smart grid [31].

for developing of business models properly for the main stakeholders (like electric utilities, consumers, system operators, and aggregators) [39, 40].

1.6.1 Cyber Security and Privacy

Self-Healing in Cyber Security – With advancement in communication technologies and improved reliability of the power industry, connectivity has increased drastically, which becomes more critical to cyber security of power systems. It covers all ITs and communications problems that might affect the operation and management of various utilities. There is a need for securing the grid for prevention against unwanted cyberattacks [41].

Table 1.3 shows the cyber security issues on smart grid [42].

1.6.2 Edge Analytics Involvement

Self-Healing in Edge Analytics – It is the process of analyzing data and finding solutions at the edge, where data is collected through smart devices and IoT sensors. A smart grid is an electricity supply network that uses digital

Table 1.3 Cyber Security Issues on Smart Grid

Topics	Cyber Security Issues		
	Key Words	Potential Problems	Possible Solutions
Devices	Smart meter	Customer tariffs vary depending on individuals, and meter breaching of database can result in alternate bills. Physical damage of meters due to battery change, removal, and modification.	· Ensures the accuracy of meter data. · Securing and maintaining meter · Detects faults on meter. · Authorize all accesses to/from AMI networks.
	PHEV	Can be charged at different locations. Inaccurate billing or unwarranted service will disrupt operations of the market [3].	Establish electric vehicle standards [3].
Networking	Internet	Different applications can be built on the Internet. Problems such as malicious malware and denial of service (DoS) attacks are threats to the grid operations.	· Adopt TCP/IP for smart grid networks. · VPN (IPSec), SSH, SSL/TLS. · Intrusion detection and firewalls.
	Wireless network	Layer 2/3 can be easily attacked with traffic injection and modification. Not reliable without routing security, traffic on these layers.	Security features in 802.11i, 802.16e, and 3GPP LTE. Safeguard routing protocols in layer 2/3 networks.
Dispatching and Management	SCADA/EMS	Every SCADA decision comes with analyzing the raw data using an appropriate model. Improper models can cause malfunctioning actions [3]. In addition, different vendors using distinct SCADA models will disrupt the consistency of the grid.	· Verify the accuracy and security of all commands and log files. Employ a GPS time stamp as a common time reference to synchronize the time. · Use multilayer intrusion detection.
	Real-time operation	Some applications (e.g., real-time process) must meet limited time constraints. Increasing interoperability may cause unbounded and uncontrollable delays of the power system.	Minimize and make predictable timing impacts of security protections.

communications technology to react to usage changes [43]. With the rising numbers of households and energy usage, there is also a rising interest in monitoring data related to energy production, usage, or storage to maximize the customer experience, often using cloud computing-based applications. However, the cloud has certain limitations. For example, an electricity company and/or the government may not want systems controlling the supply of electricity to be processed in a data center outside their country. Secondly, several sensors must be used for data collection so as to track supply and demand in real time and utilize the knowledge to predict both of these in advance. Processing this in the cloud would be inefficient as it would raise the possibility of latency in the processing time and significant costs from data transport. Edge computing poses an alternative by bringing computing closer to users and the source of the data.

Within a smart grid, there are grid users, who could be energy generators or storage owners, as well as end users. Market operators oversee power markets and communicate with providers of energy services, whereas system operators control the physical power system. The edge acts as an intermediary that facilitates storage and communication between computing resources and the smart grid that controls the center of things.

There are many benefits associated with using edge computing to power the smart grid [44]:

a) Low Latency – The role of smart grids within this context is to facilitate smooth frequency control to ensure stable conditions within the network, checking for any imbalance between generations and loads. Edge computing can guarantee low latency, which helps to monitor the frequency of the grid in real-time and proactively make any decisions to mitigate power factor penalties.

b) Data Privacy – With the rise of smart homes and smart metering, smart grids are dealing with an increasing volume of private and sensitive information on their end users. The possibility of leaking such information is unthinkable for both energy providers and end users. Edge computing's ability to process data locally can help in the selection of which data needs to go through the cloud and which data can stay local. Consequently, the data risk is reduced.

c) Reduce Bandwidth, Collect More Data – The biggest incentive within the renewable market for commercial and household users is the possibility of saving money. If there is more power generated than necessary, users can sell it back to the grid. In this way, an energy market is created in which unused energy is traded to save or earn money. However, to do this, users must ensure that they can predict or forecast their energy generation or usage. With high demand for renewable energy, the ability to build such models will be extremely complex, and users will prefer to buy it rather than building it themselves. Edge computing can enable these accurate forecasts and models, accounting for weather, location, or roof angle when using solar panels.

1.7 RECOMMENDATIONS AND FUTURE DIRECTIONS

The consumer-to-utility privacy impact assessment (PIA) of the smart grid has been reported [3] from NIST [42]. To solve problems of smart grid, some of the proposed principles have been listed as follows:

a) A company must ensure that the policies and procedures for information security and privacy are in practice and recorded. All data accesses and changes should be observed by audit functions.
b) A specific notice should be announced before collecting and sharing personal information and energy consumption data.
c) Only the required minimum amount of personal data necessary for fulfilling certain purposes should be gathered from people. These privacy guidelines should be followed in sharing information.
d) Consumers should be able to examine their corresponding personal information and inquire about the organization in case of any discrepancies. Data subjects should be informed of any third parties with whom their personal information has been shared.
e) Personal information should be used in the reasonable way for which it was collected. Apart from the parties listed in the notice or with the service recipient's consent, no other parties should receive access to personal information.
f) It is necessary to safeguard all forms of personal data against unauthorized modification, duplication, disclosure, access, use, loss, or theft.
g) DSOs shall make sure the data usage information is correct, up-to-date, and relevant for the stated purposes in the notice.

In general, to enhance the grid security, three areas should be further researched [42]:

a) Integrity and confidentiality of the transmitted data.
b) Developing a strong and effective SCADA system dispatching and management model.
c) Establishing a global policy and standard for secure communication technology.

Smart grid's privacy is a big concern. To eliminate leakage of a consumer's personal information, state-of-the-art approaches like accountability, access control, and anonymity might be the solution to these problems.

1.8 CONCLUSION

As a result of traditional power plants, there has been a significant increase in environmental awareness, which has led to more research into the creation of current smart grid technology and its integration with environmentally friendly renewable energy. By adapting proper management of the system, the implementation of smart grid operations enables wider penetration of variable energy sources. Considering the current situation, significant research, planning, and development efforts have been made globally, particularly in Europe, the USA, and Australia. The United States articulates that its objective is to link everyone to an affordable, clean, reliable, and efficient electric power network by the year 2030, or "Grid 2030." Analyzing the effects of integrating renewable energy sources widely into smart power networks, it provides an integrated platform to monitor the effects of RE throughout time. The technical, security, and legal challenges in implementing big data in a smart grid have been analyzed for better understanding of smart grid system. It has been pointed out how utilities might use big data analytics for generating new revenue streams and business models. Furthermore, the utilities can make the best operational and investment choices at the appropriate times and locations through big data analytics in smart grid.

REFERENCES

[1]. https://en.wikipedia.org/wiki/Category:Electric_power_transmission_infrastructure_in_India (accessed December, 2022).

[2]. https://en.wikipedia.org/wiki/National_Grid_(India)#:~:text=The%20first%20interconnection%20of%20regional,aforementioned%20grids%20in%20March%202003 (accessed December, 2022).

[3]. https://engineeringonline.ucr.edu/blog/the-future-of-smart-grid technologies/#:~:text=A%20smart%20grid%20can%20help,valuation%20of%20over%20%2400%20billion (accessed December, 2022).

[4]. https://iopscience.iop.org/article/10.1088/1742-6596/1639/1/012043/pdf (accessed December, 2022).

[5]. https://energyinformatics.springeropen.com/articles/10.1186/s42162-018-0007-5#Abs1 (accessed December, 2022).

[6]. https://powermin.gov.in/en/content/power-grid (accessed December, 2022).

[7]. www.cfr.org/backgrounder/how-does-us-power-grid-work (accessed December, 2022).

[8]. https://en.wikipedia.org/wiki/2012_India_blackouts (accessed December, 2022).

[9]. https://techcrunch.com/2022/10/14/india-power-company-tata-power-cyber-attack/ (accessed December, 2022).

[12]. https://engineeringonline.ucr.edu/blog/the-future-of-smart-grid-technologies/ (accessed December, 2022).

[13]. www.researchgate.net/figure/Smart-grid-A-vision-for-the-future_fig1_32525040 (accessed January, 2023).

[14]. www.ijert.org/research/smart-grid-the-future-of-the-electric-energy-system-IJERTCONV9IS04031.pdf (accessed January, 2023).

[15]. www.researchgate.net/publication/276494143_Smart_Grid_for_a_Sustainable_Future (accessed January, 2023).

[16]. https://innovationatwork.ieee.org/smart-grid-transforming-renewable-energy/#:~:text=Smart%20grid%20technology%20is%20enabling,assets%20to%20the%20power%20grid (accessed January, 2023).

[17]. Pilkington, B. "The role of semiconductors in clean energy." *AZO Clean Tech-Web Article*, 4 September 2019. Available at: https://www.azocleantech.com/article.aspx?ArticleID=965 (accessed January, 2023).

[18]. Castagna, R. "How smart grid technology is driving renewable energy." *IoT World Toda-Web Article*, 29 August 2019. Available at: https://www.iotworldtoday.com/iiot/how-smart-grid-technology-is-driving-renewable-energy (accessed January, 2023).

[19]. https://link.springer.com/chapter/10.1007/978-981-15-0135-7_38#:~:text=The%20principal%20job%20of%20big,maintenance%20for%20future%20%5B24%5D (accessed January, 2023).

[20]. Zhang, Y., Huang, T., and Bompard, E. F. "Big data analytics in smart grids: A review." *Energy Informatics* 1, no. 1 (2018): 1–24.

[21]. Sagiroglu, S., Terzi, R., Canbay, Y., and Colak, I. "Big data issues in smart grid systems." In *2016 IEEE International Conference on Renewable Energy Research and Applications (ICRERA)*, pp. 1007–1012. IEEE, 2016.

[22]. Tu, C., He, X., Shuai, Z., and Jiang, F. "Big data issues in smart grid–A review." *Renewable and Sustainable Energy Reviews* 79 (2017): 1099–1107.

[23]. Daki, H., El Hannani, A., Aqqal, A., Haidine, A., and Dahbi, A. "Big data management in smart grid: Concepts, requirements and implementation." *Journal of Big Data* 4, no. 1 (2017): 1–19.

[24]. www.researchgate.net/publication/329979410_SelfHealing_In_Smart_Grid_A_Review (accessed February, 2023).

[25]. www.intelligentbuildingeurope.com/en/smart-building-news/what-are-the-advantages-of-a-smart-grid.html (accessed February, 2023).

[26]. https://www.eesi.org/briefings/view/smart-grid-how-does-it-work-and-why-do-we-need-i (accessed February, 2023).

[27]. Ghosh, D., Sharman, R., Raghav Rao, H., and Upadhyaya, S. "Self-healing systems—Survey and synthesis." *Decision Support Systems* 42, no. 4 (2007): 2164–2185.

[28]. Arefifar, S. A., Yasser Abdel-Rady, I. M., and El-Fouly, T. K. M. "Comprehensive operational planning framework for self-healing control actions in smart distribution grids." *IEEE Transactions on Power Systems* 28, no. 4 (2013): 4192–4200.

[29]. Qianqian, L., Zeng, X., Xue, M., and Xiang, L. "A new smart distribution grid fault self-healing system based on traveling-wave." In *2013 IEEE Industry Applications Society Annual Meeting*, pp. 1–6. IEEE, 2013.

[30]. Ahadi A., Ghadimi N., and Mirabbasi D. "An analytical methodology for assessment of smart monitoring impact on future electric power distribution system reliability." *Complexity* 21 (2015): 99–113.

[31]. https://doi.org/10.1049/iet-stg.2018.0261 (accessed February, 2023).

[32]. Zhou, K., Fu, C., and Yang, S. "Big data driven smart energy management: From big data to big insights." *Renewable and Sustainable Energy Reviews* 56 (2016): 215–225.

[33]. Yu, N., Shah, S., Johnson, R., Sherick, R., Hong, M., and Loparo, K. "Big data analytics in power distribution systems." In *2015 IEEE Power & Energy Society Innovative Smart Grid Technologies Conference (ISGT)*, pp. 1–5. IEEE, 2015.

[34]. Kim, Y.-J., Thottan, M., Kolesnikov, V., and Lee, W. "A secure decentralized data-centric information infrastructure for smart grid." *IEEE Communications Magazine* 48, no. 11 (2010): 58–65.

[35]. Garrity, T. F. "Getting smart." *The IEEE Power & Energy Magazine* 6, no. 2 (2008): 38–45 (accessed February, 2023).

[36]. Zinaman, O., Miller, M., Adil, A., et al. "Power systems of the future." *The Electricity Journal* 28, no. 2 (2015): 113–126. https://doi.org/10.1016/j.tej.2015.02.006.

[37]. Stimmel, C. L. *Big Data Analytics Strategies for the Smart Grid.* CRC Press, 2014 (accessed February, 2023).

[38]. Chen, S., Wei, Z., Sun, G., et al. "Identifying optimal energy flow solvability in electricity-gas integrated energy systems." *The IEEE Transactions on Sustainable Energy* 8, no. 2 (2017): 846–854.

[39]. http://dx.doi.org/10.1109/SURV.2011.122111.00145 (accessed March, 2023).

[40]. Grid, NIST Smart. "Guidelines for smart grid cyber security: Vol. 2, privacy and the smart grid." *Guideline*, 6 August 2014. https://doi.org/10.6028/NIST.IR.7628r1.

[41]. Kasar, A. B., Joshi, R. P., and Dushing, P. L. "Survey paper on power system blackouts in India & Around Globe." *Journal of Seybold Report* 1533: 9211.

[42]. https://doi.org/10.1016/j.adapen.2020.100006 (accessed March, 2023).

[43]. Pidd, H. "India blackouts leave 700 million without power." *The Guardian* 31 (2012).

[44]. Brown, M. A., Zhou, S., and Ahmadi, M. "Smart grid governance: An international review of evolving policy issues and innovations." *Wiley Interdisciplinary Reviews: Energy and Environment* 7, no. 5 (2018): e290.

Chapter 2

Challenges and Opportunities in the Development of a Smart Grid System in India

Sumit Kushwaha

2.1 INTRODUCTION

A grid, commonly known as an electrical grid or power grid, is a network that facilitates the transfer of energy from generators to consumers. It comprises a comprehensive system of local distribution lines and high-voltage transmission lines, serving as both a transmission and distribution network. In contrast, a smart grid is a modernised version of the electrical grid that incorporates automation, communication, and IT systems to manage power flow between generating and consuming locations. Typical household activities such as lighting, cooking, heating, cooling, and Electric Vehicle (EV) charging are among the functions performed by an average family. The standard power supply lacks the necessary infrastructure, called Advanced Metering Infrastructure (AMI), to monitor and measure electricity consumption. Moreover, dealing with electrical network issues and power outages should not rely on lengthy and inconsistent energy management approaches. The development and implementation of smart grids offer advantages to various stakeholders in the smart grid industry, including governments, utilities, power plant owners, and electricity distribution companies. These benefits are realised through improved grid operations and optimised energy utilisation that benefits both the grid and consumers [1, 2].

A smart grid links up every component of the electrical system at several stages, including energy generation, transmission, storage, and distribution. By connecting each gadget to the internet and becoming online, an integrated data and energy grid is established. A smart grid can rapidly divert electricity in the event of a malfunction or outage due to its two-way communication. A broad and extended blackout, for instance, can be prevented by finding and isolating an outage. More customer engagement and faster demand response are possible with a smart grid than with a conventional grid. A smart grid uses smart metering to monitor, measure, and transmit data about specific homes, businesses, and other entities, such as energy use [3].

DOI: 10.1201/9781032665399-2

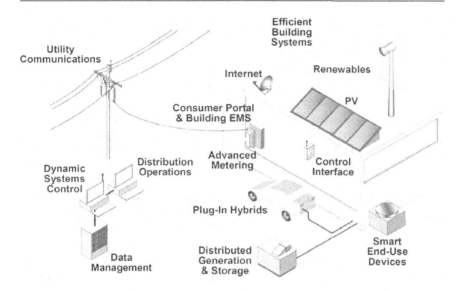

Figure 2.1 Smart Grid System (SGS) concept.

Figure 2.1 shows the Smart Grid System (SGS) concept. Today's Smart Grid System (SGS) has developed into a massive global network to handle the rising demand for power. According to research by the Global Smart Grid Federation (GSMART GRIDF), the capacity of current electricity grid networks is insufficient to satisfy twenty-first-century requirements for quantity, quality, efficiency, dependability, ecology, and economy [4]. These caused the centralised power generation-based electric grid to modify its paradigm in favour of decentralisation [5]. The current power scenario is beneficial for the smart grid since it takes efficiency, dependability, economy, and other important factors into account in addition to making the best use of the existing power supplies [6, 7].

Smart grid initiatives being piloted all around the world show that stakeholders, consumers, regulators, and others may look forward to a bright future with the technology. By June 2012, peak demand and power consumption in Queensland, the smart city of Australia, had decreased by 46% [8, 9].

Demand response (DR) contribution to peak load reduction has grown by 10%, per studies of ISO/wholesale markets in the US, since 2006 [10]. The state of California plans to reduce peak load by 100 MW by using smart metres for demand response and variable pricing schemes. According to the smart grid 2013 worldwide report, a survey of 200 smart grid initiatives found that 70% of pilots have improved dependability of up to 9% [9].

Studies have shown that the smart grid may be made robust and self-healing. According to Yu et al.'s [11] analysis of the economic benefits of smart grid, upgrading to it rather than expanding conventionally will save the UK £19 billion in net show value on smart grid resources between 2012 and 2025. Additionally, smart grid has the ability to sustain 12,000 jobs per year in the UK alone.

In Ohio, Duke Energy has claimed annual savings of $10.18 per customer for special metre readings and an additional annual savings of $3.5 per customer for non-labour costs including metre testing, mending, and replacement. According to the Smart Grid Consumer Collaborative (SGCC), the Time of Usage tariff offers benefits ranging from $2 to $19.98 per customer per year.

All types of power producers and storage units may be planned, scheduled, and maintained optimally with the help of the smart grid, which lowers both operating and capital expenses. Along with immediate cost reductions, smart grids enable the integration of backup power sources including distributed generation, thermal energy, renewable energy, and electric vehicles. Customers directly benefit from smart grid through savings through restructured tariffs, reduction in the length and frequency of power outages, capability to become more energy self-reliant, benefits in terms of home automation and electric vehicles.

India's situation is comparable to the rest of the world's [12–14]. With a planned growth to 900 GW by 2032, India would have the largest single synchronous grid in the world, with an installed capacity of roughly 300 GW [15, 16]. India is implementing the National Smart Grid Mission, the Nehru National Solar Mission, and other smart grid initiatives to improve the grid's performance and dependability as well as to advance the nation's technological, economic, and social development [17, 18].

2.2 COMPONENTS OF A SMART GRID

A knowledgeable audience will understand that a smart grid has the potential to connect numerous transmission lines to supply electricity to an entire country. This advanced grid design integrates various elements to enhance stability, resilience, reliability, and efficiency. Additionally, the smart grid enables comprehensive management, empowering consumers and facilitating cost savings. Embedded systems play a vital role in the smart grid by enabling the processing and communication of information across different applications [19].

2.3 SMART GRID (SG) TECHNOLOGIES

A smart grid gives clients real-time control over electricity generation, transmission, and distribution by utilising a wide range of technologies and communication networks. Here are the main smart grid technologies that make it possible to manage energy more effectively, make the most use of available resources, and enhance overall performance [20].

i.   **Autoregressive Integrated Moving Average (ARIMA):** ARIMA and other statistical methods are used to produce forecasting reports utilising advanced demand forecasting, which also makes use of data analytics and machine learning (ML) approaches. ARIMA forecasting foretells yearly power usage and hourly electricity pricing as a crucial part of smart grid management. In order to identify cyber intrusion assaults on the smart metres installed to assess the power consumption of residential and non-residential users, ARIMA forecasting also offers an extra layer of verification.

ii. **Advanced Metering Infrastructure (AMI):** AMI is a comprehensive system that combines transmission networks, DMS, and smart metres. Its primary goal is to enhance customer satisfaction, upgrade to good production, and control costs effectively. The implementation of AMI leads to the development of a smart grid, which offers numerous benefits such as accurate consumption estimates, efficient cash collection and theft detection, identification of faults and outages, measurement of losses, and the option of time-based pricing. One of the key features of AMI is its ability to facilitate two-way communication between consumers and utilities, further enhancing its functionality and advantages.

iii. **Big Data:** The smart grid generates a significant amount of data that varies in type and flows at a high pace. Effectively managing this large-scale data within the limitations of available resources poses a major challenge. Utilising big data analytics can significantly contribute to optimising power utilisation, efficiency, system consistency, stability, and customer satisfaction within the smart grid. Without the application of big data analytics, the analysis of petabytes of data generated by smart grid devices would be impossible. Big data enables the collection and analysis of unstructured data from various endpoints in the smart grid, while also facilitating efficient resource allocation, cost reduction, and improved customer service.

iv. **Distributed Energy Resources (DERs):** DERs increase local dependability and enhance system stability and on-site fuel consumption. Examples of controlled loads include solar panels, small natural gas-powered generators, electric vehicles, and controlled loads like air conditioning and electric water heaters. Effective DER integration improves the reliability and service level of a grid. The main advantage of using PVs is lower utility costs due to using less power from the grid.

   v. **Non-intrusive Load Monitoring (NILM):** NILM gauges each build-
       ing's unique energy use, including residences and commercial estab-
       lishments. It could be useful to break down the total energy utilization
       (of active appliances) into its individual components in order to find
       energy-consuming or damaged appliances. Additionally, customers
       may monitor their energy expenses and regulate them in line with
       their power consumption by scheduling the most cost-effective times
       to utilise equipment that consumes a lot of energy.
   vi. **Vehicle-to-Grid (V2G):** V2G technology enables the transfer of unused
       vehicle power to the smart grid. An EV (electric vehicle) battery is a
       cost-effective technique to store energy. V2G lowers grid overload
       and balances increases in power usage during peak hours. By adding
       energy (unused battery capacity) from an electric car's battery back
       into the power system, for example, V2G may maximise the benefits
       of renewable energy and boost grid stability.

2.4 TRADITIONAL ELECTRICITY GRID SYSTEM VS. SMART GRID SYSTEM

Table 2.1 shows the key differences between a traditional electricity grid
system and smart grid system.

Table 2.1 Key Differences between a Traditional Electricity Grid System and Smart Grid System

S. No.	Traditional Electricity Grid System	Smart Grid System
1	Electromechanical System	Digital Smart Grid System
2	Unidirectional Information and Power Flow (One-Way Communication)	Bidirectional Information and Power Flow (Two-Way Communication)
3	Centralised Power Generation	Distributed Power Generation
4	No Real-Time Monitoring	Real-Time Monitoring
5	Manual Restoration during Outage Recovery	Automatic Restoration during Outage Recovery
6	There is a High Risk of Blackout and Failures	There is a Low Risk of Blackout and Failures
7	Absence of Energy Storage	Energy Storage Available
8	Low Energy Efficiency	High Energy Efficiency
9	Low Sensor Deployment	High Sensor Deployment (Full Grid Coverage)

Centralised electricity production from power plants has evolved through time into a distributed energy resource in order to adapt to a dynamic energy market and enhance the experience of energy customers [21].

2.4.1 Traditional Electricity Grid System

The conventional electrical grid system is shown in Figure 2.2. Since there is minimal local control and communication, there is a lot of dispersion in this system. In essence, it fulfils the role of a demand-based load energy supplier. There are several losses, including transmission and distribution losses, and the efficiency of thermodynamic cycles, like those in fossil fuel power plants, is sometimes limited to 30% or less. High-voltage transmission lines make up conventional electric power grids, which transport generated electricity to distribution networks for consumption in a "one-way network." Every stage—generation, transmission, and distribution—has unique engineering difficulties that must be overcome. Cascade effects might develop as a result of the dependency between the components of the electrical grid; for instance, a huge blackout could happen when a number of little incidents take place at or around the same time and cause the system to collapse. Smart grids were created as a result.

2.4.2 Smart Grid System

Renewable energy was first produced using a random process. Smart grids have been created to produce more energy in order to solve this problem.

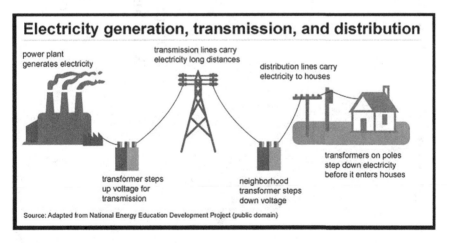

Figure 2.2 A traditional electricity grid system.

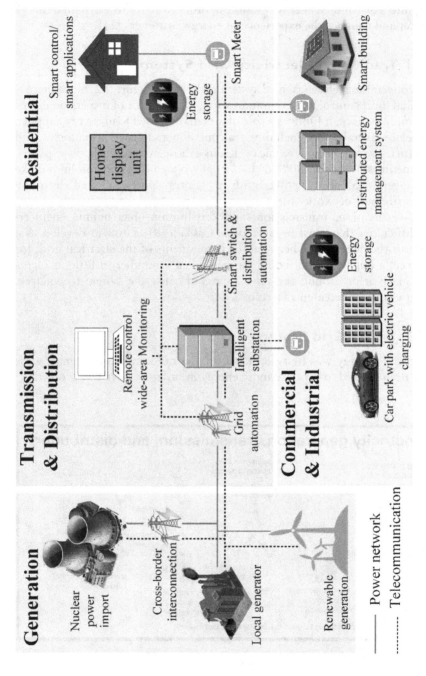

Figure 2.3 A Smart Grid System.

The acceptance rate of smart grids is adopted by a number of factors. Firstly, there are currently very few non-renewable energy sources on the planet. Renewable energy sources are becoming increasingly important for the future energy supply. Secondly, environmental pollution is on the increase and is the result of almost all energy consumption and production. The main objectives of a smart grid are to generate and transfer energy efficiently across various nodes, increase energy generation, streamline energy distribution, and ensure consistency between consumer energy consumption and energy consumption. As shown in Figure 2.3, SGS consists of several modules, each of which performs a certain duty to complete the process. The information supplied by the user may be used to set the period of energy consumption in the bright equipment, and intelligent sensors can control the greatest load energy and cost. Due to two-way communication, smart power measures allow you to collect invoices and find system issues anywhere. The management and oversight of the power function and standing is the responsibility of smart substations. At the stations, different voltages are converted in order to split the energy stream in different ways and to reach the customers. Combination communication, a crucial component of smart grid interaction, needs to be quick in order to provide outputs right away. There are several technologies that should be used depending on the situation when it comes to smart grid interaction.

Figure 2.4 shows the main applications of smart grid system. The IEA created a technological road map for constructing smart grids for regions

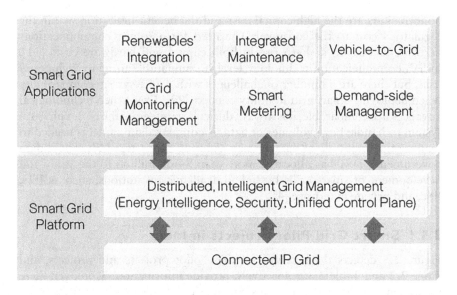

Figure 2.4 Main applications of Smart Grid System.

and developing nations in order to meet these problems; nevertheless, the latter confronts more difficulties. The most significant ones are the following: increasing energy demand, energy theft, integrating renewable energy sources into the system, ageing infrastructure, increasing demand (electric transport), and lowering peak demand, etc.

2.5 DEVELOPMENT OF SMART GRID IN INDIA

India's electrical industry has a lot of untapped potential. The government and industry leaders have highlighted the importance of Smart Grid and Micro-grid for India. This has opened up huge business opportunities. By 2019, India's key objectives are to electrify all households, provide enough electricity for agriculture, and ensure that every citizen has access to electricity 24 hours a day, seven days a week. The disadvantage of renewable energy sources is that they are intermittent, meaning that they can only be used during certain times of the day (e.g. during the day when solar energy is available or in windy conditions), and these variables are not controllable. As the grid is powered by these intermittent energy sources, a highly flexible grid is essential. India has a huge potential to develop smart grids at both the distribution and transmission level. The goal of India's smart grid is to transform the Indian power industry into a safe, resilient, sustainable, digitally connected ecosystem that provides reliable and quality electricity to all with active stakeholder involvement.

Smart grid technologies face several challenges. The main challenges for policymakers are the high capital cost and the benefit limitation within the regulator's cost to the consumer. The need for a robust communications network has led to a sharp rise in both capital and hardware costs [11]. India's communication technology level is comparable to many rich countries, but there are a number of challenges with device/system compatibility when deploying smart grid in utility context [22]. Even when technological advances are comparable, it is always difficult to integrate the entire physical system to handle huge volumes of data. A complex data model is needed to manage the multitude of data formats entering the system [23]. The Indian government's DST has allocated more than $46.5 million to the study and development of smart grids by Indian academic institutions, such as IITs, IISc, and private enterprise [4].

2.5.1 Smart Grid Pilot Projects in India

Figure 2.5 depicts the locations of these pilot projects and projects, and Table 2.2 and Table 2.3, respectively, provide information. Moreover, there have been more than 4.4 million smart metres installed (NSGM website).

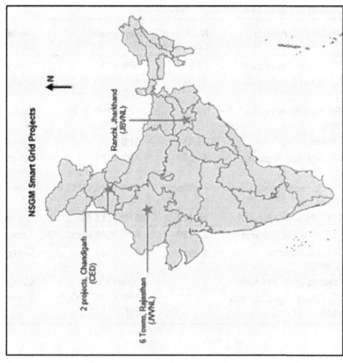

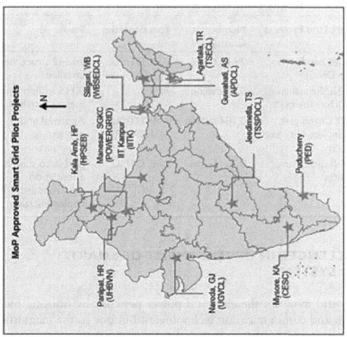

Figure 2.5 (a) Smart grid pilot projects in India and (b) smart grid projects in India.

Table 2.2 Details of the Smart Grid Pilot Projects in India

S. No.	Smart Grid Pilot Projects	Number of Consumers	Functionalities	Status
1	APDCL, Guwahati, Assam	14,519	AMI, PLM	Completed
2	CESC, Mysore, Karnataka	21,824	AMI, OMS, PLM, MG/DG	Completed
3	HPSEB, Kala Amb, Himachal Pradesh	1335	AMI, OMS, PLM	Completed
4	PED, Puducherry	33,499	AMI	Completed
5	TSECL, Agartala, Tripura	45,290	AMI, PLM	Yet to be submitted
6	TSSPDCL, Jeedimetla, Telangana	11,906	AMI, PLM, OMS, PQ	Completed
7	UHBVN, Panipat, Haryana	10,188	AMI, PLM, OMS	Completed
8	UGVCL, Naroda, Gujarat	22,230	AMI, PLM, OMS, PQ	Completed
9	WBSEDCL, Siliguri, West Bengal	5,265	AMI, PLM	Completed
10	IIT Kanpur, Uttar Pradesh	–	Smart city	Completed
11	SGKC, Power Grid, Manesar, Haryana	–	AMI, OMS, MG/DG, EVCI	Completed

Table 2.3 Details of the Smart Grid Projects in India

S. No.	Smart Grid Projects	Number of Consumers	Functionalities	Status
1	CED, Chandigarh (Sub Div-5)	29,433	AMI, DTMU, SCADA	24,149 smart metres installed
2	JVVNL, Rajasthan (6 Urban Towns)	0.15 million	AMI	0.115 million smart metres installed
3	CED, Chandigarh (Complete City Excl. SD -5)	0.184 million	AMI, DTMU, SCADA, ERP	Approval under process
4	JBVNL, Jharkhand (Ranchi)	0.36 million	AMI, DTMU	JBVNL to submit a report on the proposed implementation

2.6 CHALLENGES IN DEVELOPMENT OF SMART GRID SYSTEM

The smart grid modifies the electrical power network by utilising modern information and communication technologies. But due to the magnitude of the electricity network and the substantial prior investment made over the years to establish the conventional grid system, a valid rationale for any adjustments would require careful consideration.

2.6.1 Sociocultural

Many problems will emerge when social and cultural factors are integrated, mostly consumer-related problems like the existing issue of consumers' misunderstanding about the goal, scope, and drawbacks of smart grids. Users should not be charged for energy consumption education or evaluation. The potential cost reductions from implementing automatic pricing mechanisms made feasible by smart grids in preservation chains should be made known to consumers. When gas costs are low, consumers are generally not motivated to cut back on their consumption or even think about the cost of energy per hour. The success of energy and power projects depends on the engagement and comprehension of customers; thus, it is essential to address all consumer-related concerns during the construction process. This will allow for the early consideration of new ideas and the resolution of problems [24, 25].

2.6.2 Collaboration of Stakeholders

The core concept of smart grids is largely dependent on technological challenges, but integration and research is gradually bridging the gap between theory and real-world, successful smart grid deployments. While several smart grid initiatives, such as the BESCOM projects in India, have been launched, they are not succeeding due to the significantly increased industrial barriers of recent years. All energy network developments in the last few years have followed a linear integration model. For smart grids to work, multiple types of associations must be interconnected via a more robust, bidirectional network. The implementation of the strategy must involve as many interested parties as possible through close association to build a bidirectional, interactive network during the initial stages, which will drive the further development of smart grids. The execution division that is most likely to face challenges in the smart grid development process could be improved by a new structural structure of smart grid stakeholders [26].

2.6.3 Role of Government

Electrical pricing and profits from smart technology must be under control by government authorities, despite the fact that smart grid systems clearly outperform conventional electricity networks. While it is necessary to alter secondary policies that will indirectly support the growth and development of smart grids, such as promoting renewable energy, boosting energy security, and enhancing energy efficiency, there is also a need to alter primary policies that will directly support the development of smart grids. While the value of smart grid initiatives will come from the whole electrical network, from generation to distribution, the major emphasis of investments will be on this most costly component: distribution. The public and private sectors must work together to attain this level of growth. A plan for effective energy management with smart communication processes to enable bidirectional communication networks is required for variable sources of renewable energy; as green energy consumption rises, smart grid initiatives are becoming less and less important [2, 19, 25, 26].

2.7 CONCLUSION

The goal of this chapter is to understand the many SGS elements and their potential for growth in India. The challenges of smart grid adoption such as high investment cost, need for infrastructure development, high cost of smart products, and user ignorance have hindered the development of smart grid systems. Using a range of SGS tools such as the rich picture, and conceptual model, the stakeholders were able to visualise the issue and have a collaborative discussion on how to solve it. During the meetings, there were many positive comments which helped to explain the steps needed to bring about change. Participants discussed their involvement and limitations, as well as their roles, morality, and expectations of different stakeholders. The study highlighted the importance of all stakeholders, particularly CEOs and public servants, to be involved in developing improvement and management strategies. This study demonstrated that due to technological developments, environmental pressures, and human sensitivities, soft issues need to be addressed. Methodologically, this study is remarkable in that it recognises and reports on issues that affect a wide range of stakeholders that may not have had the chance to collaborate on common concerns around the smart grid before. It also examines the context, addresses all stakeholders fairly, and takes a holistic approach. This study also raised awareness that smart grid stakeholders are interdependent and the need to develop a collaborative solution that addresses each stakeholder's specific interests. The complex and problematic nature of the situation makes it extremely difficult for a single stakeholder to tackle such issues. Stakeholders may see the difference between the real and standard world. This strategy helped in the development of a collaborative relationship between researchers and participants.

REFERENCES

[1] R. Athawale and F. A. Felder, "Overbuilding transmission: A case study and policy analysis of the Indian power sector", *Energy Policy*, Volume 174, p. 113437, 2023.

[2] *Electric Power System*, 2023, Available at: https://en.wikipedia.org/wiki/ Electric power system.

[3] *Power Sector at a Glance All India*, 2023, Available at: https://powermin. gov.in/en/content/power-sector-glance-all-india.

[4] Smart Grid Canada, Global Smart Grid Federation Report, 2012.

[5] Smart Grid Bulletin, Indian Smart Grid Forum 2 (1), 2015.

[6] M. E. El-hawary, "The smart grid—State-of-the-art and future trends", *Electric Power Components and Systems*, Volume 42, Issue 3–4, pp. 239– 250, 2014.

[7] US DOE, US, Report on "Understanding the Benefits of the Smart Grid". National Energy Technology Laboratory, 2010.

[8] US Department of Electricity, "Demand reduction from application of advance metering infrastructure, pricing programs, and customer-based systems – initial results", In *Smart Grid Investment Grant Programme*, Report of Department of Energy, 2012. Available at: https://www.smart-grid.gov/document/demand_reductions_application_advanced_metering_ infrastructure_pricing_programs_and_custome.

[9] Available at: www.behance.net/gallery/11990517/VentyxABB-Smart-Grid-Global-Impact-Report 2013.

[10] *EPRI, Smart Grid Resource Center*, 2023, Available at: https://smartgrid. epri.com/Index.aspx.

[11] X. Yu, C. Cecati, T. Dillon and M. G. Simões, "The new frontier of smart grids", In *IEEE Industrial Electronics Magazine*, Volume 5, Issue 3, pp. 49–63, 2011.

[12] V. S. K. M. Balijepalli, S. A. Khaparde and R. P. Gupta, "Towards Indian Smart Grids", In *TENCON 2009–2009 IEEE Region 10 Conference*, Singapore, pp. 1–7, 2009.

[13] V. S. K. M. Balijepalli, S. A. Khaparde, R. P. Gupta and Y. Pradeep, "Smart grid initiatives and power market in India", In *IEEE PES General Meeting*, Minneapolis, MN, pp. 1–7, 2010.

[14] R. Kappagantu, S. A. Daniel and N. S. Suresh, "Techno-economic analysis of Smart Grid pilot project-Puducherry", *Resource-Efficient Technologies*, Volume 2, Issue 4, pp. 185–198, 2016.

[15] S. Madan, S. Manimuthu and S. Tiruvengadam, "History of electric power in India (1890–1990)", In *IEEE Conference on History of Electric Power*, Newark, NJ, 2007.

[16] M. Manas, "Development of self-sustainable technologies for smart grid in India", In *IEEE International Conference on Computational Intelligence & Communication Technology*, Ghaziabad, 2015.

[17] Available at: https://indiaesa.info/buzz/news/industry-news/855-national-smart-grid-mission-in-line-with-emerging-reality.

[18] June 2015. Press release on "Revision of cumulative targets under National Solar Mission from 20,000 MW by 2021–22 to 1,00,000 MW". MNRE, GoI.

[19] M. Albano, L. L. Ferreira and L. M. Pinho, "Convergence of smart grid ICT architectures for the last mile", *IEEE Transactions on Industrial Informatics*, Volume 11, Issue 1, pp. 187–197, 2015.

[20] *NSGM Website*, 2023, Available at: www.nsgm.gov.in.

[21] T. Reynolds and A. Mickoleit, "ICT application for the smart grid: Opportunities and policy implications", In *OECD Digital Economy Papers No. 190*, Paris, 2012. https://doi.org/10.1787/5k9h2q8v9bln-en.

[24] *Grid Modernization and the Smart Grid*, 2023, Available at: www.energy.gov/oe/activities/technology-development/grid-modernization-and-smart-grid.

[25] *International Smart Grid Action Network (ISGAN)*, 2023, Available at: www.iea-isgan.org/.

[26] R. Kappagantu and S. Arul Daniel, "Challenges and issues of smart grid implementation: A case of Indian scenario", *Journal of Electrical Systems and Information Technology*, Volume 5, Issue 3, pp. 453–467, 2018.

Chapter 3

Why Big Data for Smart Cities?

Sudiksha Sharma and Sachin Sharma

3.1 INTRODUCTION: BIG DATA

"Big data" is a phrase that is used to describe massive and complicated data sets that are too vast and varied to be effectively handled using standard techniques of data processing. These types of data collections are referred to as data lakes. Typical characteristics of these data sets include a large amount of data, a rapid rate of data transit, and a wide diversity of data kinds and points of origin.

Big data is a term for very large collections of data. It is often used to describe how hard it is to process and understand large amounts of data, as well as the tools and technology that are needed to manage and work with these large amounts of data. Distributed computing systems, cloud computing platforms, and machine learning algorithms are examples of the kinds of tools and technologies that fall under this category.

In general, when people talk about "big data," they are referring to massive data sets that have been collected by companies and governments. These data sets are so vast and complicated that typical data processing techniques are unable to cope with the computations that are required to make sense of the data [1].

Big data can be used in many different fields, like finance, healthcare, marketing, social media, and many more, to find insights and patterns that would be hard or impossible to find with traditional data analysis methods.

Big data refers to large data sets with a lot of different complex structures that make it hard to store, analyse, and show the results. We discover hidden patterns and secrets by researching these massive data sets. This critical information assists. This important information helps businesses make money and get a competitive edge by giving them deep insights. Needs to be analysed and used as accurately as possible.

When talking about big data, the word "power" can refer to a number of different things, such as the following:

Big data requires a lot of computer power because it is based on processing and analysing huge amounts of data. Powerful hardware and software

DOI: 10.1201/9781032665399-3

systems are needed to handle the amount, variety, and speed of data that comes from many different sources, like sensors, social media, and transactions. Because to advances in processing capability, there is no longer a problem with data storage, despite the fact that the amount of data acquired from customers and by government agencies is always increasing [1].

We can see that big data has several traits and aspects by looking at the preceding Figure 3.1. These attributes are referred to as the Vs of big data management.

Power in big data may also refer to the analytical capabilities of the system that are being used to analyse the data. This is another meaning of the term analytical power. To extract insights and patterns from the data, sophisticated analytic tools and processes, including machine learning, natural language processing, and data mining, are used. Businesses may be able to gain a competitive edge if they can find useful information in huge amounts of data.

The collection and analysis of massive amounts of data can also provide a company with enormous economic power. This power can be gained via big data. Businesses that have access to huge volumes of data may make use of that data to acquire insights about the behaviour of their customers, the trends in the market, and other forms of business intelligence. This information can be used to make smart decisions, which can help the business make more money and get a bigger share of the market.

When it comes to big data, the word "power" may also refer to the social and political effects of how it is used. The public's opinion, political

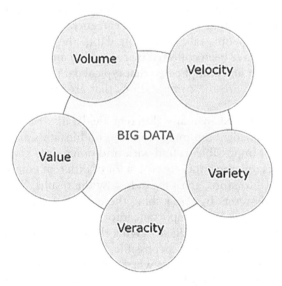

Figure 3.1 Big data traits.

campaigns, and the conduct of individuals may all be influenced and monitored with the use of data. The ability to manage and control the flow of information via Big Data and the Internet of Things (IOT) are inextricably linked concepts because the IOT generates massive amounts of data that must be processed and analysed in a sophisticated manner in order to yield relevant insights. It has huge repercussions for both society and politics. While working with large amounts of data, it is crucial to keep in mind the ethical and legal implications of one's actions.

Big Data and the Internet of Things (IOT) are inextricably linked concepts because IOT generates massive amounts of data that must be processed and analysed in a sophisticated manner in order to yield relevant insights. IOT is a network that consists of networked physical devices, sensors, and machines that are able to gather and share data through this information and can come from many different places, such as wearables, smart home devices, industrial machines, cars, and more.

"Big Data" is shorthand for very big and intricate data sets that are collected from a variety of sources, including the Internet of Things. Because of how big they are, these data sets can't be handled and evaluated with the usual data processing methods.

IOT and big data are intertwined due to the fact that IOT creates a vast number of data points in real time. This data can then be examined to provide insights into a variety of topics, including customer behaviour, machine performance, and other areas. This data may be put to use to increase the quality of client experiences, as well as to improve the efficiency of company operations.

Also, putting IOT and Big Data together could open up new ways to do preventive maintenance, control supply chains, and manage energy. By using the data that is produced by the devices connected to the Internet of Things, businesses are able to make educated choices, discover new possibilities, and propel innovation.

In a nutshell, the Internet of Things (IOT) creates huge amounts of data that must be processed and analysed using big data technologies. As a result, the two technologies work very well together. The combination of the Internet of Things with big data has the potential to provide companies and society with new insights, possibilities, and value.

As shown in the picture, Figure 3.2 describes that data analytics can be used in many different ways in smart cities, such as for public health, energy efficiency, public awareness, and water and waste management. Data science is the practice of dealing with huge volumes of high-quality data in order to draw specific and logical conclusions as well as patterns from the data. These applications are made possible by the conclusions we draw from data analytics in smart cities [2]. It also shows how the city becomes smarter than a typical environment, such as by having smart transportation, a smart economy, and a smart environment, by teaching people how to live smarter lives.

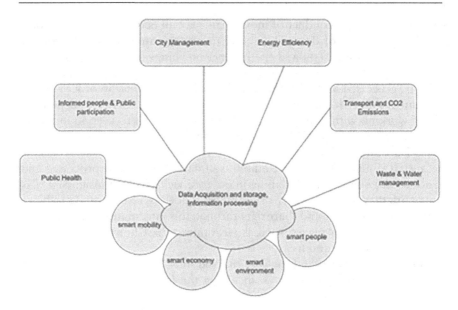

Figure 3.2 Various uses of data analytics.

3.2 IOT – INTERNET OF THINGS

IOT is a network that is growing quickly. It is made up of physical devices, vehicles, buildings, and other things that are connected to each other and have sensors, software, and other technologies that let them collect and share data. This network connects physical devices, vehicles, and buildings, among other things. The Internet of Things technology is already being used a lot in a wide range of business areas, such as healthcare, transportation, agriculture, and manufacturing. Concerns have been raised, though, about privacy, security, and the possibility that connected devices could be used for bad things. This is because the number of connected devices keeps growing. Because of this, it is very important that we create and use IOT technology in a responsible and proactive way.

The Internet of Things (IOT) as well as big data analytics are allowing smart city projects, which are reinventing cities by enhancing their buildings and mobility systems, decreasing the amount of movement in traffic, offering garbage collection, and enhancing their standard of life [3].

"Big data analytics" is the process of analysing huge data sets to find patterns, correlations, and insights that were not known before. These can be used to make better decisions and create economic value. They use advanced analytical techniques and tools to process, organise, and make sense of huge amounts of data that can't be evaluated with standard data processing methods. This requires a significant investment in time and resources. Big data analytics is a broad term for a number of different ways to analyse data, such as data mining, machine learning, predictive analytics, and natural language processing. The phrase "Internet of Things" often refers to situations in which network connection and computing power extends to objects, sensors, and other ordinary things that are not traditionally considered computers. This gives these devices the potential to create, trade, and consume data with minimum interaction from a human being. However, there is not a solitary definition that applies everywhere [4].

With traditional methods of analytics, businesses would have a much harder time, if not an extremely difficult time, seeing trends and patterns than they might with the help of these tools and methodologies. The analysis of large amounts of data may be put to a variety of different uses, such as predicting how consumers will act, making the public safer, making supply chain management more efficient, and coming up with custom healthcare solutions. In general, big data analytics gives businesses a powerful tool that helps them learn more about their operations and their customers, which in turn helps them make better decisions.

IOT and big data are two types of technology that are becoming more interwoven with one another. Many IOT devices, such as environmental sensors that measure temperature and humidity and wearables that monitor our physical activity and health, create massive volumes of data. Tools for analysing large amounts of data can use this information to help us learn things that will help us make better decisions. For instance, shops may use the data from IOT devices to monitor client behaviour and improve their store layouts, and manufacturers can use the data from sensors installed in their machines to identify and avoid equipment breakdowns using the data from those sensors. The combination of the internet of things and big data has additional consequences for users' rights to privacy and safety. As the amount of data that is collected and processed keeps going up, it is very important to make sure that people's personal information is safe and that the systems that are used to store and process this data are safe. In general, IOT and big data have the potential to revolutionise many facets of our lives; yet, it is essential to approach these technologies with prudence and a responsible attitude towards data privacy and security.

The ability of the Internet of Things to reach its full potential is contingent on the development of tactics that respect the individual privacy preferences of users over a wide range of expectations. The data streams and personal specificity that IOT devices provide may unleash extraordinary and one-of-a-kind value for IOT users, but worries about privacy and the potential for damage may prevent the Internet of Things from gaining widespread usage. This indicates that protecting users' privacy rights and adhering to the standards that users have set for their own privacy is essential to fostering users' trust and confidence in the Internet, linked devices, and other associated services.

The proliferation of big data and the creation of systems centred around IOT have made significant contributions to the improved functionality of smart city initiatives. Big data offers cities the opportunity to discover valuable information from an enormous quantity of data gathered from a wide variety of sources, and IOT makes it feasible to employ massively distributed services to link sensors, RFID, and Bluetooth to the real world. Big data also gives cities the opportunity to gain valuable information from an immense volume of data obtained from a wide variety of organisations. The huge volumes of data acquired from a diverse range of sources may also provide cities with the knowledge that is of service to the cities. The majority of these new problems are related to commercial and technological concerns that enable cities to achieve the goals, ideals, and demands of smart city projects by establishing the essential components of smart environments. This may be accomplished by setting in place critical elements such as smart lighting and smart traffic management. IOT and big data together constitute a brand new and intriguing study field that has introduced a number of new and interesting difficulties to the overall objective of developing smart cities in the future. These brand new issues have surfaced as a direct result of recent shifts that have taken place in both business and technology. In order to make the vision, concepts, and needs of smart city applications a reality, it is necessary to put into practice the essential qualities of smart settings. We take a look at the ways in which big data analytics might assist smart cities, with a particular emphasis on the ways in which big data has the potential to alter the lives of people living in cities in a variety of different ways. Cities. We take a look at the opportunities that big data analytics provide for developing smart cities, with a particular emphasis on how big data has the potential to alter the lives of people living in cities in a variety of different ways. A future business model for smart cities that is built on big data is also presented, along with the challenges that are faced by the corporate sector as well as the area of technological research. In the future, academic institutions and private companies could look to the findings of this research as a benchmark for the establishment and expansion of smart cities.

The Internet of Things, sometimes known as IOT, has recently emerged as a major subject of discussion in the technology sector, as well as in engineering and policy circles. It has also been a hot issue in both the specialised press and the mainstream media. This technology is implemented in a broad range of networked goods, systems, and sensors. These networked products, systems, and sensors take use of developments in processing power, electronics downsizing, and network connectivity to provide new capabilities that were not before feasible [5].

The next generation of computing will take place away from the typical setting of desktop computers. Under the concept of the "Internet of Things," a significant number of the things that are all around us will be connected to the network in one way or another. RFID and sensor network technologies will be created to solve this new problem, in which communication and information systems will be hidden in the world around us. This will be done in order to address the issue. In order to overcome this obstacle, information and communication technology will need to be integrated into the environment in which we find ourselves. Because of this, tremendous amounts of data are generated, all of which need to be preserved, analysed, and presented in a manner that is streamlined, efficient, and easy to comprehend. Under this strategy, the provision of commodities will be carried out in the same way that it is currently done for commodities. Cloud computing could provide the virtual infrastructure that this type of utility computing needs.

The Internet of Things relies heavily on intelligent connections with pre-existing networks and computations that are aware of their surroundings and make use of network resources. The shift towards pervasive data and communication networks can already be seen, thanks to the expanding availability of wireless Internet connections through Wi-Fi and 4G-LTE. In order for the Internet of Things to become a reality, the way computers are used must change beyond the typical mobile computing scenarios that use smartphones and portables. Only then will the vision of the Internet of Things be able to become a reality. Instead, the computer paradigm needs to change so that common things are linked together, and intelligence is built into our surroundings. For the Internet of Things to be able to process and send information based on context, it needs to know about its users and the devices they use, as well as have software structures and communication networks that are everywhere. This will enable the user's awareness to become less preoccupied with the technology. Even though it is still in its infancy, the Internet of Things will have an impact on a wide variety of application domains. Applications are separated into several categories according to the characteristics of the networks on which they run, which might include the networks' availability, coverage, size, heterogeneity, repetition, impact, and user involvement. The applications may be classified as personal and home, business, utility, or mobile. These are the four categories that are available.

3.3 SMART ENVIRONMENT

A physical space that is equipped with sensors, devices, and other technologies that can collect and analyse data to optimise the operations of the environment and improve the quality of life for those who live or work within it is referred to as a smart environment. A smart environment can be defined as a physical space. Intelligent environments can be found in many places, such as homes, offices, public spaces, and even hospitals. In these settings, both hardware and software are used to collect information about things like temperature, lighting, air quality, and energy use. The collected data is then used to make automated modifications that increase the environment's efficiency as well as its level of comfort. In a smart building, if sensors find that a space is empty, the temperature and lighting can be changed automatically to save energy. Smart environments may also use artificial intelligence and machine learning algorithms to do data analysis and create forecasts about the future. The goal of the idea of "smart environments" is to make places that are more responsive, efficient, and sustainable while also improving the overall quality of life for the people who use these places.

When you look at a "smart city" from a human perspective instead of a technological one, it means different things. This is evident when nations launch programs to transform into smart cities, since they offer diverse viewpoints on the subject. Even though smart cities are happening all over the world, it's not clear what they are. "Without a widely accepted definition, the smart city sector is still in the "I know it when I see it" phase." In other words, there isn't a common idea of what a "smart city" is, and it's been hard to find a description that everyone agrees on. The bulk of definitions, however, focuses on typical traits and elements that could define the perspectives of smart cities.

According to the definitions given, a smart city is an integrated living solution that brings together different parts of everyday life, like electricity, transportation, and buildings, in a creative and efficient way to improve the quality of life for its citizens. The criteria also put a lot of weight on the future by emphasising how important it is for future generations that resources and applications are sustainable. No matter the size, location, or amount of resources, we found these things in every smart city plan. Due to different financial situations and a lack of both natural and human resources, governments around the world worry most about how much it will cost to build a smart city. The quantity, availability, and capabilities of such resources may be challenging to manage, which is one of the challenges associated with developing and maintaining a smart city. Another problem comes from the regulatory frameworks, which, if put into place, could have a big effect on the success rates. In addition to everything else, there are technical issues that need to be fixed using the most advanced technology currently available. On the other side, cutting-edge technology has the potential to aid in transforming challenges like these into opportunities.

3.4 SMART CITIES

Several cities are in a race to become "smart cities" so that they can get some of the economic, environmental, and social benefits that come with this title.

Because of this, a lot of people are interested in what big data analytics can do for smart city applications. Investing in human and social capital, both conventional and cutting-edge information facilities, and democratic governance are the hallmarks of smart cities. They are dependent on highly developed constructions as well as leading-edge technology for networking and information [5].

Because of this, in the following part, we will talk about some of the advantages and prospects that may play a role in the choice to convert or redesign a city so that it may become a smart city. By making such a choice, it is possible to increase the levels of sustainability, resilience, and governance that are present in an organisation. In addition to enhancing the standard of living of the populace, the implementation of intelligent infrastructure and the management of natural resources are also included. The following are some of the advantages of having a smart city:

- **Coherent resource utilisation:** It is very necessary to include solutions that allow for better and more tightly managed resource use when an increasing number of resources become either limited or excessively costly. It will be to your advantage to begin with technology solutions such as ERP. When monitoring systems are in place, it will be much simpler to locate waste spots and improve resource distribution, all while keeping expenses under control and reducing the amount of energy and natural resources that are used. In addition, the interconnection and data gathering capabilities included into smart city apps are one of the most crucial components of their design. These capabilities may help improve the level of cooperation that exists across different applications and services.
- **An enhanced standard of living:** Residents in smart cities will have a superior quality of life because of increased waste reduction, enhanced public services, and more productive work and living arrangements (both time and resources). This is because of improvements in the design of living and working spaces and places, in the efficiency of transportation systems, in the quality and speed of services, and in the availability of adequate information to make choices in an educated manner.
- **Greater transparency and openness:** Increased interoperability and openness will be driven by the need for more effective administration and control of the myriad of smart city elements and applications. The exchange of information and use of shared resources will become the standard. In addition, everyone engaged will be better off as a result of enhanced information openness. This would foster cooperation and communication among the many organisations in the smart city, as well as the creation of new services and apps to increase the

functionality of the smart city. The United States federal government has collected and made available a vast assortment of information, publications, and material under the guise of promoting openness and transparency. They created the potential for individuals and government institutions to successfully share and utilise data in a variety of contexts.

3.5 NEW FORMS OF URBAN COMMUNICATION: THE RISE OF THE SMART CITY

Most big data applications for smart cities need the use of smart networks in order to bring together all of the components of the city. This includes the technology that the citizens of the city utilise, such as autos, technologies for smart homes, and smartphones. This network needs to have the capability of transmitting data received from sources to locations where large amounts of data are gathered, stored, and analysed. In addition to that, it needs to have the capability of sending responses back to the various firms in the smart city that want them. When there is a low number of events that are currently being generated and there are no constraints imposed on the network resources that are used to communicate these events, the centralised technique is preferable. This is the case even if there are no limitations placed on the network resources. When it would be wasteful and maybe even impossible to transfer all of the newly created events to a single site within an acceptable length of time and within the restrictions of acceptable performance, it is better to utilise the scattered approach. This is one of the instances in which the dispersed technique should be used. In this situation, filtering and aggregation will be vital, especially for smart cities, because of their potential to lower the amount of network traffic that is created and speed up the processing of data. This is because filtering and aggregation may reduce the amount of network traffic that is produced. This may be performed by using either an open-loop or a closed-loop strategy at the event sources and the intermediate locations, respectively. Both methods have their advantages and disadvantages. Closed-loop systems allow for the establishment of filtering and aggregation criteria in a manner that is dynamically driven by current events and user decisions, as well as system and network resources, or external smart city application regulations. On the other hand, open-loop techniques have these regulations defined before they are implemented. There should not be any exceptions to the rule that the integrity, accuracy, and correctness of the data that is being aggregated should not be compromised when event filtering and aggregation are used together. This is an essential step to take in order to maintain the same high degree of decision-making quality in real-time, large-data systems.

The vast majority of big data applications for smart cities need smart networks to link their numerous elements, including devices owned by inhabitants, such as vehicles, smart home gadgets, and smartphones. This network should be ready to effectively transmit data acquired from its sources to the location wherein big data is gathered, stored, and analysed, and it should also be able to send replies to the various organisations in the smart city that need them [6].

The technologies that are found in smart cities are shown in the picture earlier via the usage of this diagram. Technology is integrated into every aspect of smart cities, from organisational systems and security networks to geographic sensor networks and network security. These technologies are often combined, and their synergistic effect contributes to an improvement in both the efficiency of municipal operations and the standard of living enjoyed by the people who live there. IOT and big data analytics are entangled in this scenario due to the fact that sensors in the Internet of Things gather massive amounts of data from a variety of sources all throughout the city. These sources include things like traffic, air quality, and energy consumption. These data are then analysed and examined using methodologies for big data analytics in order to find patterns and trends that could influence the decision-making process of the municipality. In a similar fashion, the other characteristics are interconnected; however, for the time being, we will focus our attention on big data and conduct an analysis of how it influences the many facets of smart cities and how it helps to the expansion of the city as a whole.

Figure 3.3 describes the different technologies that are present in the emerging smart cities.

3.6 HOW BIG DATA IMPACTS SMART CITIES

A physical space that is equipped with sensors, devices, and other technologies that can collect and analyse data to optimise the operations of the environment and improve the quality of life for those who live or work within it is referred to as a smart environment. A smart environment can be defined as a physical space. Intelligent surroundings may be found in a variety of locations, including private homes and workplaces, public places, and even hospitals. These settings employ a mix of hardware and software to gather data on parameters such as temperature, lighting, air quality, and energy use. The collected data is then used to make automated modifications that increase the environment's efficiency as well as its level of comfort. For the purpose of reducing energy consumption, the settings for the room's temperature and lighting may be automatically adjusted in a smart building if sensors determine that a particular space is vacant. Smart environments may

Figure 3.3 Technologies in smart cities.

also use artificial intelligence and machine learning algorithms to do data analysis and create forecasts about the circumstances of the future. Utilising sensors that can detect whether a portion of a cooling tower is empty allows designers to create rooms with improved usefulness. As a result, these sensors set off automated temperature and lighting adjustments, resulting in energy savings and better customer service. Energy services are crucial in helping companies function better, which may result in higher earnings and a more powerful market position. On the other side, advances in the healthcare system may be beneficial for a number of areas, including patient care, medications, preventative care services, and diagnostic and treatment equipment. The use of big data may assist transportation systems in optimising their routes and timetables, adapting to fluctuating levels of demand, and being friendlier to the environment.

A strong information and communication technology infrastructure is needed to run applications that deal with large amounts of data. ICT is good for smart cities because it makes it possible to use new and helpful solutions that would not be possible without it. For example, it makes transportation planning easier by making it easier to manage their services from different areas and places. This helps cut down on transportation costs. This helps minimise overall transportation expenditures. Additional examples include the more effective management of water and waste through the use of technologies that are designed to handle these services in a more efficient manner. ICT solutions can be used to handle different parts of trash management, like collecting, getting rid of, recycling, and recovering trash, which are all examples of trash management tasks. Other examples include the development of innovative building construction and structural techniques for enhanced building health and the environment, risk management, safety and security, and the quality of the air and the pollution that it causes.

Sensors and connected devices are used in smart cities to collect and analyse data. This data is used to improve city operations, manage resources, and improve residents' daily lives. Smart cities, among other things, use technology to improve public transportation, traffic management, water and electricity supply, law enforcement, schools, and hospitals. Every community is concerned about its citizens' safety, and it is critical to protect them in any situation. Predictive analysis could be used to look at historical and geographical data to find out when and where crimes are most likely to happen in the city. This could help people avoid problems. When the right information makes a city safer, it will be clear that a lot of progress has been made.

In recent years, big data has had a big impact on both how smart cities are made and how they are run. Cities that are intended to employ technology and data to enhance the quality of services and infrastructure for their residents are referred to as "smart cities." Big data has become an important part of making smart cities a reality, thanks to the growth of data sources and the development of new technology for collecting, storing, and analysing data. The following is a list of some of the impacts that big data has had on smart cities:

Traffic management: Big data enables smart cities to better control traffic flow by analysing data collected from traffic sensors, cameras, and GPS devices. This results in improved traffic management. This information may be put to use to improve the timing of traffic lights and to redirect cars so that congestion can be avoided.

Energy efficiency: Efficient use of energy may be accomplished by analysing patterns of energy use and locating chances to cut down on that consumption with the help of big data in smart cities. Analysing the data collected by smart metres, sensors, and other Internet of Things devices is one way to achieve this goal.

Public safety: The analysis of crime data may assist enhance public safety by identifying trends and predicting where crimes are likely to occur. This can be done with the use of big data. Because of this, law enforcement authorities may be able to more efficiently deploy their resources.

Waste management: Better waste management is possible with the use of big data, which may assist smart cities in optimising their waste management systems via the analysis of data on the amount and kind of garbage produced in various parts of the city. This may help boost recycling rates and decrease the amount of garbage that is sent to landfills. It can also help reduce the amount of waste that is sent to landfills.

Healthcare: Big data may be used in the analysis of healthcare data in order to uncover patterns and trends, which can then assist healthcare practitioners in making more informed choices about patient care. This results in better healthcare. In addition to this, it may be used to track the progression of infectious illnesses and identify locations within the city where public health interventions may be required.

In general, big data plays an essential role in making smart cities more effective, sustainable, and liveable for the people who live there. Big data could improve the quality of life in smart cities, and this possibility will only grow as more data becomes available and as new technologies are developed.

In a smart city, big data applications have the ability to benefit several industries. "Big data" refers to the huge and complicated data sets that sensors, social media, and transactional data in the city create. By looking at this data, municipal authorities and other interested parties may be able to learn things that can be used to change decisions and improve services in all areas. Here are a few instances:

Transportation: Big data analytics may be used to monitor traffic trends and enhance transportation services in the transportation sector. This may include the identification of traffic bottlenecks, the prediction of congestion, and the optimisation of public transport routes.

Energy: Big data may be used to monitor energy use in buildings and throughout the city, finding places where energy efficiency can be improved and decreasing energy waste.

Public safety: Big data may be used to enhance public safety by examining crime trends and identifying places where more patrols are needed. Also, it may be utilised to identify possible security concerns and react more effectively to crises.

Healthcare: Big data may be used to monitor public health trends and identify regions where more healthcare services are required. Moreover, it may be used to evaluate patient data in order to build individualised treatment plans and enhance healthcare results.

Environment: Big data may be used to monitor air and water quality and identify locations with high levels of pollution. This may be used to guide policies and efforts aimed at enhancing environmental sustainability.

These are just a few examples of how big data applications in a smart city may benefit many industries. By using the power of "big data," city leaders can make better decisions and improve services for their citizens.

3.7 SUSTAINABLE DEVELOPMENT IN SMART CITIES AND BIG DATA

Sustainable development is an important part of smart cities, and large amounts of data could help cities reach their sustainability goals. Big data, information, and the IOT might influence smart city implementation worldwide. This paper provides an automobile congestion-based dynamic intuitive algorithm to estimate total volume at different multi-day and all-out scenarios. Transportation may be managed or rerouted to reduce carbon emissions. Computational experiments examined effective leadership [7].

In smart cities, big data may help sustainable development in a number of different ways, including the following:

Energy efficiency: Smart cities may use big data to find possibilities to minimise energy consumption and maximise the usage of renewable energy sources. This can be accomplished through the use of big data. Monitoring energy use and finding areas for improvement may be accomplished via the collection of data from smart metres, sensors, and other Internet of Things devices.

Waste management: Big data may assist smart cities in optimising their waste management systems by evaluating data on the amount and kind of garbage created in various locations of the city. This can be accomplished through the use of data collected from big data. This may help boost recycling rates and decrease the amount of garbage that is sent to landfills. It can also help reduce the amount of waste that is sent to landfills.

Water management: Using big data to monitor and manage water resources in smart cities is one use of smart city technology. Sensors and other types of equipment may be used to gather data that can then be used to monitor water quality and consumption, locate leaks, and improve water distribution.

Transportation: Using big data to improve transportation systems in smart cities could help reduce the number of cars on the road and increase the use of public transportation, bicycles, and other ways to get around that are better for the environment.

Urban planning: The use of big data may contribute to the development of more environmentally friendly urban design by illuminating the ways in which people interact with and navigate a city. This knowledge may be utilised to design structures and infrastructure that are more energy efficient and sustainable, as well as to create urban places that are more habitable.

In general, big data has the potential to provide smart cities with the knowledge they need to make educated choices about the sustainable development of their communities. Smart cities are able to maximise their use of resources, decrease waste and emissions, and create an environment that is more livable and sustainable for the people who live there by doing data analysis on data gathered from a broad variety of sources.

3.8 ENERGY MANAGEMENT IN SMART CITIES

The management of energy in smart cities entails the use of cutting-edge technology and data analytics in order to maximise the efficiency with which energy is used and minimise the negative effects of urban energy systems on the surrounding environment. This means putting together smart grid technology, energy storage systems, and renewable energy sources to make a more efficient and long-lasting energy infrastructure. When smart city technology is used, transportation systems can be made to work better and be better for the environment. As a result, emissions and energy consumption from cars both decreases. Smart metres and other data collection technologies can be used to monitor and evaluate energy use in homes and businesses. This will allow for the identification of potential opportunities for energy savings. Also, real-time data analysis could be used to help predict and manage energy demand, which could cut down on the need to make extra energy and make the grid more stable. In smart cities, energy management aims to build a more efficient and long-lasting energy infrastructure. This reduces the impact that urban energy systems have on the environment and improves the quality of life for the people who live in the city.

Due to the intricate nature and significance of energy systems, urban energy administration represents one of the biggest challenges. Thus, this issue requires major focus. Planning and training are the main techniques used to examine the technical and policy consequences of smart solutions and design the most effective approaches to transition to smarter cities [8].

Cities use a lot of energy and are responsible for a big chunk of the world's greenhouse gas emissions, so it's important for them to be able to manage their energy use. Smart cities use cutting-edge technology and data analytics to maximise the efficiency of energising resources while minimising negative impact on the surrounding environment. To build an energy infrastructure that works better and lasts longer, smart grids, different types of renewable energy sources, and different types of energy storage devices need to be used. For example, smart metres could be put in homes and businesses to track how much energy is being used. The data from these metres could then be used to figure out where energy efficiency could be improved. Integrating renewable energy sources like solar and wind power into the smart grid is one way to lessen dependency on fossil fuels and bring down emissions. Batteries and other energy storage devices can be used to store extra energy from renewable sources so that it can be used when demand is high. This extra energy can then be used to meet the demand. Furthermore, smart city technology has the potential to enable more efficient and sustainable transportation systems, lowering both the amount of energy consumed by cars and the amount of emissions produced. When cities use these energy management strategies, they can have less of a negative effect on the environment around them and build cities that are more sustainable and easier to live in.

The term "smart city" refers to a metropolitan area that is good for the environment and the economy and gives its residents a good quality of life by making good use of the resources it has. Energy management is one of the hardest things to do in big cities because the energy systems are so complicated, and they are so important. As a direct consequence of this, a significant amount of attention and work is required. Modelling and simulation are two of the most common ways to evaluate the technical and policy implications of smart solutions and to plan the best ways to move from existing cities to smarter ones. The switch to smart cities is very important right now because people are facing big problems like a rise in the average global temperature and a rise in the world's population. Even though there are many good things about building smart cities, there are also a number of problems that must be solved first. As a result, it is necessary that appropriate planning and regulations be implemented. Smart cities need to manage their resources, like energy, transportation, and building infrastructure, with care. This is another requirement for smart cities. In this respect, the use of renewable energy sources plays a significant role in maintaining the comfort and wellness of the populace.

Cities of all sizes are beginning to use a variety of technology to operate more intelligently in order to support an ever-increasing population. Cities of all sizes are starting to use a variety of technologies to run smartly and keep up with the needs of a growing population. This is done in order to provide enough housing for the growing population. Some of these technologies are advanced data analytics, wireless communication networks, sensors that don't cost much, and devices that can be controlled by data. People think that this plan will help them grow and improve the quality of life for the people who live in their community. In order to speed up the process of creating smart cities, technological advances are being made at a rate that is higher than at any other time in history. Five-gigabit wireless networks (5G), cloud computing, artificial intelligence (AI), and edge computing are some examples. Moreover, the use of technologies such as the Internet of Things is fruitful in the monitoring of energy consumption, the determination of CO_2 and nitrogen levels, the measurement of pH levels and sulphur oxides, the exact tracking of transportation systems, and the enhancement of the lighting schedule.

3.9 ENERGY STORAGE IN SMART CITIES

Cloud storage online in smart cities is needed for the vast volume of data analysis. Cloud data systems have solid-state discs, get rid of unnecessary data, and send and receive data in a secure way. Cloud-based solutions often provide more versatile payment alternatives than on-premises data centres. With edge computing, data can be processed close to where it was first created. If data is streamed to a remote storage location and then sent to the relevant local authorities, the cost might be higher than if it were computed at the edge of the network and then delivered. In the past, researchers have explored one of the features of edge computing, the use of AI for traffic management, in a few specific locations. In AI traffic management, intelligent automation is used to find accidents and traffic jams and find good solutions to a wide range of problems.

The end goal of energy storage is to store energy so that it can be used efficiently at a later time. Power quality and reliability can be improved in a number of ways, such as by using technologies that store energy. Due to the worsening energy situation, energy storage has lately drawn a lot of interest from both business and academia. There are a wide variety of ways to store energy, including mechanical, electrical, chemical, electrochemical, and thermal methods. The output characteristics of renewable energy sources make energy storage devices the best option. One type of energy storage system is thermal energy storage. When compared to other forms of energy storage, thermal energy storage is affordable and has a straightforward construction. Systems for storing thermal energy are frequently employed in daily life. It is primarily used for heating and hot water in domestic applications. This chapter talks about how solar thermal systems work and how to store thermal energy in different ways. The technologies for storing thermal energy have been put into two groups: those that use sensible heat and those that use latent heat. Some of these methods are thermal storage using subsurface systems, thermal storage using liquids, and thermal storage using air.

3.10 RENEWABLE ENERGY SOURCE IN SMART CITIES

Renewable energy sources are a very important part of building smart cities, which are supposed to be good for the environment and save money on energy use. However, in order to accomplish a greener approach and greater environmentally friendly growth, efficiency concerns will need to be solved first. Renewable energy sources are a viable answer for cities that are smart [9].

Figure 3.4 represents a list of some of the most prevalent forms of renewable energy that may be used in smart cities, and it is explained later.

Solar energy: Solar energy is the renewable energy source that is employed the most often and extensively in today's smart cities. Solar panels, which are used to produce power, may be mounted on the roofs of buildings as well as on the façades of buildings and other public areas. This energy may be put to use for a variety of purposes, including but not limited to lighting, powering electrical appliances, and charging electric cars.

Wind energy: The generation of wind energy may be accomplished via the installation of wind turbines in open areas, such as parks or the outskirts of a city. These turbines have the capability of generating

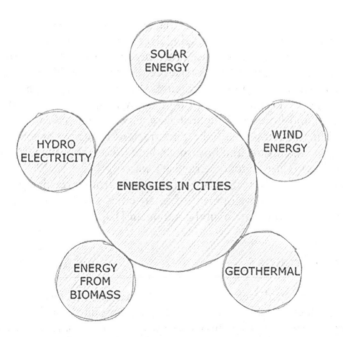

Figure 3.4 Types of energies in smart cities.

energy, which may then be utilised to power the public services and infrastructure of the city.

Hydroelectric energy: It is produced by converting the kinetic energy of moving water into electrical energy. This technique may be used by smart cities can get energy from rivers, streams, and canals, as well as the energy in wastewater.

Geothermal energy: Geothermal energy is produced by drawing heat from the earth's interior by tapping into the earth's heat reservoir. This energy has the potential to be used to heat and cool buildings, in addition to providing hot water for public facilities like swimming pools.

Energy derived from biomass: Energy derived from biomass is produced by burning organic waste and then using the heat that is produced to create power. This energy has the potential to be put to use in the operation of public utilities and infrastructure inside the city.

By using renewable energy sources, smart cities could become less dependent on fossil fuels, reduce their carbon emissions, become more environmentally friendly, and increase their energy efficiency.

3.11 ELECTRICITY CONSUMPTION IN SMART CITIES

One of the most important problems that smart cities have is that they use a lot of electricity. On the other hand, big data analytics could be a key part of managing and making the best use of energy in smart cities since the growing usage of technology and infrastructure demands a significant amount of it. On the other hand, big data recognises the opportunity to play a critical role in energy. By keeping track of how many people are in a building, its temperature, and how much light it uses, city officials can make changes to the building's energy use. By keeping track of how many people are in a building, its temperature, and how much light it uses, city officials can make changes to energy use so that energy isn't wasted.

The study presents a technique to find trends from large data sequences, which is vital for the development of smart cities since energy expenditure tendencies of structures are a vital component [10].

3.12 SMART GRIDS

The term "smart grid" refers to an integrated system of energy producers, wires, and plugs capable of delivering energy produced in both centrally distributed areas and individual user-owned items. Smart solutions keep track of and control everything, from the manufacturing process to how the product is used in the end. This enables modification to suit certain ecological and social criteria. A smart grid may include a power exchange that works in both directions, allowing utilities to engage customers in power production on both commercial and personal levels. In order to give the appearance that these grid elements are "smart," large volumes of data are sent back and forth between these pieces and the business systems that monitor them. Regardless of the application, the information that is exchanged here between the utility and its customers provides the most financially optimum flow of electricity in both directions. The smart grid is a cutting-edge communication and data network that has the ability to increase fuel efficiency at every level of the generation, transportation, redistribution, and preservation processes. This improvement may be achieved in a number of ways. Some of the other benefits are being able to simplify system management, make better-informed planning decisions, spend less time and money, and have a more stable energy system [11]. The capabilities of smart grids have an effect on every level of the power system, from the producers and energy providers to the final consumers of electricity. Smart grids make it easier for customers to get involved and make it easier to use a variety of options for making and storing electricity. When seen from one angle, the smart grid is shown as a single entity that is composed of several different domains.

3.13 CONCLUSION

In conclusion, the incorporation of big data into the design and construction of smart cities is an extremely important step. Cities have the ability to make choices that are better informed, optimise the allocation of resources, improve services, and generally increase the quality of life for their residents if they harness the power of data. Big data has the potential to make smart cities more resilient, sustainable, and efficient while also fostering economic development and innovation. The use of big data in smart cities makes it possible for a variety of applications to be developed, including, but not limited to, the control of traffic, public safety, waste management, energy management, and citizen involvement. Smart cities can gather useful insights and make data-driven choices to solve urban issues and enhance urban planning and governance because they collect, analyse, and interpret massive volumes of data from a variety of sources, such as sensors, devices, social media, and other digital platforms. This allows smart cities to improve urban planning and governance.

Having said that, it is essential to point out that the use of big data in smart cities also raises concerns about issues of equality, privacy, and security. It is imperative that appropriate measures be put into place to preserve the data privacy of individuals and to guarantee that data is utilised in an ethical and responsible manner. Additionally, efforts should be made to bridge the digital gap and guarantee that access to data and the advantages of smart city programmes are inclusive and equitable for all people, regardless of their socioeconomic background or location. This is something that can be ensured by ensuring that efforts are made to bridge the digital divide.

In conclusion, the use of big data has the potential to radically alter the way cities are run and to significantly enhance the quality of life enjoyed by residents living in smart cities. Nonetheless, it is necessary to find a middle ground between data-driven innovation and the safeguarding of the rights and privacy of the general public. Big data has the potential to be properly used in order to develop cities that are more intelligent and more sustainable in the future. This will need good governance, legislation, and inclusive methods.

REFERENCES

[1]   A. Lyons and J. Grable, "An introduction to big data," *Journal of Financial Services Professionals*, vol. 72, no. 5, pp. 17–20, September 2018.

[2]   K. Suriyan and N. Ramalingam, "Chapter 6 — Recent challenges, opportunities, and issues in various data analytics," in *Data Science for Genomics*, A. K. Tyagi and A. Abraham, Eds., Cambridge: Academic Press, pp. 99–105, 2023, doi: 10.1016/B978-0-323-98352-5.00012-4.

[3]   Y. Mehmood, F. Ahmad, I. Yaqoob, A. Adnane, M. Imran and S. Guizani, "Internet-of-things-based smart cities: Recent advances and challenges," *IEEE Communications Magazine*, vol. 55, no. 9, pp. 16–24, 2017, doi: 10.1109/MCOM.2017.1600514.

[4]   R. H. Weber and R. Weber, *Internet of Things: Legal Perspectives*. Berlin, Heidelberg: Springer, 2010, doi: 10.1007/978-3-642-11710-7.

[5]   S. M. A. Group et al., "Internet of Things (IOT): A literature review," *The Journal of Computing and Communication*, vol. 03, no. 05, Art. no. 05, 2015, doi: 10.4236/jcc.2015.35021.

[6]   Y. Qian, D. Wu, W. Bao and P. Lorenz, "The internet of things for smart cities: Technologies and applications," *IEEE Network*, vol. 33, no. 2, pp. 4–5, 2019, doi: 10.1109/MNET.2019.8675165.

[7]   E. Al Nuaimi, H. Al Neyadi, N. Mohamed and J. Al-Jaroodi, "Applications of big data to smart cities," *Journal of Internet Services and Applications*, vol. 6, no. 1, p. 25, 2015, doi: 10.1186/s13174-015-0041-5.

[8]   J. Chang, S. Nimer Kadry, and S. Krishnamoorthy, "Review and synthesis of Big Data analytics and computing for smart sustainable cities," *IET Intelligent Transport Systems*, vol. 14, no. 11, pp. 1363–1370, 2020, doi: 10.1049/iet-its.2020.0006.

[9]   C. F. Calvillo, A. Sánchez-Miralles and J. Villar, "Energy management and planning in smart cities," *Renewable and Sustainable Energy Reviews*, vol. 55, pp. 273–287, 2016, doi: 10.1016/j.rser.2015.10.133.

[10] A. T. Hoang, V. V. Pham and X. P. Nguyen, "Integrating renewable sources into energy system for smart city as a sagacious strategy towards clean and sustainable process," *The Journal of Cleaner Production*, vol. 305, p. 127161, 2021, doi: 10.1016/j.jclepro.2021.127161.

[11] R. Pérez-Chacón, J. M. Luna-Romera, A. Troncoso, F. Martínez-Álvarez and J. C. Riquelme, "Big data analytics for discovering electricity consumption patterns in smart cities," *Energies*, vol. 11, no. 3, 2018, doi: 10.3390/en11030683.

Chapter 4

Big Data for Smart Grid
A Way Forward

Sachin Sharma and Devyanshi Bansal

4.1 INTRODUCTION: CONCEPT OF SMART GRIDS

A smart grid is a modernized electrical grid that uses advanced communication and control technology to make the processes of making, moving, and delivering energy more efficient, reliable, and long-lasting. In the past, power grids were thought to have a one-way flow of energy, with power being made at centralized power plants and then sent to users over long distances. But new developments in technology have made it possible for energy to flow both ways through power grids. Electrical networks that can intelligently integrate the activities of all connected users, such as generators, consumers, and those who do both, are what the European Union refers to as "smart grids." Smart grids are designed to successfully provide environmentally friendly, cost-effective, and safe power supplies.

In a similar way, the US has said that the smart grid of the future will be a fully automated system that uses distributed generation, information exchange, and storage resources to make the electric system more reliable, secure, and efficient. As part of its financial aid package, the American Recovery and Reinvestment Act of 2009 set aside \$4.5 billion for smart grid projects. In order to encourage the development of smart grids, the Department of Energy has also hired help and given grid operators more tools and information. This is being done in order to support the progression of smart grids. Because of these things, the smart grid project in the United States has made a lot of progress in the past few years. The people in charge of the grid have also used cutting-edge technology to make the system for making, moving, and storing power more efficient and reliable.

Smart grids are made possible by the installation of sensors, meters, and other devices that track how much electricity is being used, as well as the use of complex analytics and algorithms to analyze this data and improve the way the grid works in real time. This makes it possible for utilities to better control the quantity and demand for electricity, cut down on waste, and react more swiftly to power failures and other problems.

DOI: 10.1201/9781032665399-4

In addition to making the power grid more efficient and reliable, a smart grid may make it easier to use renewable energy sources like solar and wind power. This is because a smart grid makes it easier for power production and demand to be better coordinated. A smart grid plays a vital role in the use of renewable energy sources. Renewable energy sources like solar and wind power tend to be spread out and inconsistent, which makes it harder for the traditional power grid to stay stable and reliable. Still, renewable energy sources could be added to the power system with the help of a smart grid, which makes the grid more flexible, cost-effective, and long-lasting.

Portable generators are becoming more and more popular as a way to meet the rule that renewable energy sources must be used. Because of this, huge centralized power plants are losing their significance. This means that the old form of centralized control is less successful than it would have been since there is only one route that electricity may travel from the units. The ability to link to the grid system is necessary for power production that is on a smaller scale, typically between 3 kW and 10 kW. So distribution systems need to be able to be run and managed both ways. It is expected that both the traditional electro-mechanical power grid and the electronic knowledge and networking systems will be made better. This will help cut down on the cost of power outages and problems with the reliability of the system, which can cost millions of dollars each year.

4.2 SMART GRID ARCHITECTURE MODEL (SGAM)

A smart grid is a more modern electrical power system that includes digital technology and communication infrastructure. This allows for improved power grid monitoring, control, and optimization.

Unified computational modeling that is influenced by SGAM may be used to assist in the development of interconnected complicated system scenarios for the purpose of merging various smart grid elements, pertaining to models of communication, oversight, estimating, and data analytics features [1].

A framework that offers an organized method for planning, developing, and putting into action smart grid systems is called the Smart Grid Architecture Model (SGAM). In Figure 4.1 we see that the Smart Grid Architecture Model (SGAM) outlines the essential parts of a smart grid and the connections between them. In this model, the smart grid system is shown as a five-layered structure [2]. Each layer represents a different part of the system:

Business Layer: The laws, regulations, and business models that control the functioning of the smart grid system are included inside this layer of the architecture.

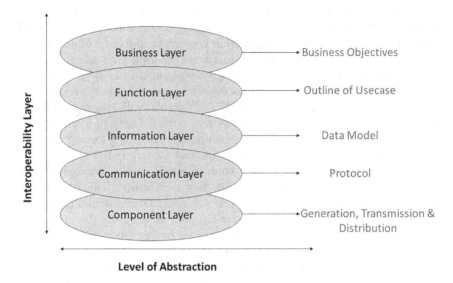

Figure 4.1 Smart Grid Architecture Model.

Function Layer: This layer is responsible for defining the functions and services that are made available by the smart grid system. Some examples of
these functions and services are demand response, energy management,
and distribution automation.

Information Layer: This layer covers the communication and information systems that support the tasks of the smart grid. Some examples
of these systems are metering systems, monitoring systems, and control
systems.

Communication Layer: This layer is responsible for defining the communication protocols and networks that make it possible for various components of the smart grid to share information with one another.

Physical Layer: This layer consists of the physical components of the smart
grid system, such as the equipment for electricity production, transmission, and distribution. It also contains the devices that are used to communicate with the grid, such as smart meters.

SGAM gives everyone in the smart grid environment a common language
and a framework for how to work. These parties include companies, legisla-
tors, software vendors, and end users. The paradigm helps to make sure that
all users have a complete understanding of the system's parts and how they
work together. This makes it easier for people to communicate and work

together. In addition, it gives a starting point for making smart grid recommendations and standards.

4.3 NEED OF DATA ANALYTICS IN SMART GRID

The smart grid collects data from many different sources and stores it so that analytics can use it. Advanced machine learning approaches are required for managing smart grids to deliver smart energy. The right data must be collected, decisions must be made, and local and global events must be controlled by these techniques. In smart grids, there are many sources of data about markets, machines, geography, and the electrical system that can be used to predict states, give situational awareness, evaluate stability, find problems, and send out warnings. So analytics, which includes big data analytics, machine learning, and artificial intelligence, is very important for making the grid smarter, more effective, and more productive. Analytics can be used for signal, seventh, state, engineering operations, and customer analytics. These can be given for the smart grid. For example, for demand response programming, descriptive models describe how customers act. Diagnostic models are used to analyze specific customer behaviors and power-related decisions. Each type of model can give useful information to models that try to predict what customers will do in the future and, as a result, how much power will be needed. Lastly, prescriptive models can give high-level analytics that can be used to change smart grid marketing, engagement strategies, and decision-making.

Neural networks, k-means, and support vector machines may retrieve important characteristics from unstructured data and create safe and economical operating techniques. Modern ICT technology needs faster analysis of data structures, cybersecurity, and safeguards for privacy. The social services and electricity industries need a reliable data analysis system. The analysis of data in smart grids demands collaboration between professionals from diverse industries and tactical ideas for top solutions [3].

As was already said, energy systems must change to take into account distributed power generation as well as the dynamic processes of managing demand, controlling load, and managing energy storage. Changes in regulatory frameworks and policies related to sustainability are causing big changes in the energy system now. This has led to a big jump in the amount, variety, and speed of data, as well as a big jump in the number and types of stakeholders and new business opportunities that are more reliable and cost-effective. Everyone with a stake in the energy system knows how important data analytics and new technologies are. This includes the system operator, the market operator, the regulator, the service provider, the customer, the transmission and distribution system operators, the service providers, and the generators. A big dataset will be used to build a smart grid. This set will include information about how customers use power, how the weather has been in the past for the area, and details about current supply and demand.

The use of big data analytics in banking, health care, the Internet of Things (IoT), communication, smart cities, and transportation has shown enormous promise for innovation and corporate success. Power grids now use a wide range of monitoring, regulation, communication, and computer science technologies to run energy systems that provide cheap, reliable, sustainable, and high-quality energy to end users. The grid will be powered by data retrieved from storage. By analyzing these inputs in real time and getting new information from them, the smart grid may get smarter.

4.4 CURRENT USE OF DATA ANALYTICS IN THE SMART GRID

The use of data analytics in smart grids is becoming more widespread in the present day with the goal of enhancing energy efficiency, dependability, and overall performance. Smart grids are contemporary electrical power networks that make use of cutting-edge technology to maximize the production, distribution, and consumption of electrical power. Some examples of these cutting-edge technologies include sensors, automation, and data analytics.

The appropriate use of big data analytics in conjunction with visualization may result in improved knowledge of the situation and more accurate prediction [4]. The following is a list of the many applications of data analytics that may be found in smart grids:

Demand Response: Data analytics are being used to monitor and analyze patterns of energy use. This enables utilities to detect periods of peak demand and offer customers incentives to cut their consumption during these times. This helps to relieve pressure on the system, prevent power outages, and cut down on overall energy expenditures.

Predictive Maintenance: Smart grids are outfitted with sensors that monitor the health and operation of different pieces of equipment. Data analytics is used to evaluate the sensor data, find prospective problems before they exist, and plan maintenance in accordance with those problems. This strategy helps to increase the stability of the system while also reducing downtime.

Fault Detection: Data analytics is used to examine the large quantity of data created in real time by the smart grid. This helps to find faults and abnormalities in the system. This makes it easier for utilities to swiftly react to problems and restore service more quickly.

Energy Forecasting: Data analytics are used in energy forecasting to provide predictions about future energy demand and production, which enables utilities to maximize energy supply and distribution efficiency. This helps to bring down costs and improves the reliability of the grid.

Integration of Renewable Energy: Smart grids are intended to allow for the integration of various forms of renewable energy, such as solar and wind power. Data analytics is used to predict the amount of energy that will be generated by various sources and to optimize how they will be integrated into the grid. This helps to keep the system stable and cuts down on carbon emissions.

Implementation of the technologies that make up the smart grid is required so that consumers will have an easier time connecting to the grid and will continue to have trust in the service (ICT). A self-sufficient electricity distribution network is referred to as a "smart grid system." The supply chain may be monitored, controlled, and analyzed with the help of the digital automation technologies that are included in its construction. A "smart grid" is another name for this kind of electrical distribution system.

This kind of electricity distribution system also goes by the label "smart grid," which is another name for it [5]. It is a network-based system built with digital automation technologies that is used to track, control, and study supply networks. Related phrases include supply chain management, supply chain analysis, and supply chain management. This system can find problems in the current system that could lead to a sharp drop in the number of employees, and it will do everything it can to make sure that all customers have reliable, safe, and high-quality electricity. It gets its electricity from many different sources that are not all in one place. These sources may be located in many different locations. These sources can come from a wide range of technologies, such as solar panels, wind turbines, and even plug-in hybrid electric vehicles (PHEVs). Technology in the area of communication is what enables the smart grid to work correctly, reduce the amount of energy that is used, and coordinate all of its components, from power plants to consumers. This is made possible by the advancement of technology. All of these things can be accomplished if you put your mind to them. As smart grids continue to evolve, it is likely that more advanced data analytics techniques will be developed and implemented to further improve energy efficiency, reliability, and sustainability.

4.5 BIG DATA CHARACTERISTICS IN SMART GRID

Smart grids are updated electricity supply grids that use new technology like detectors, communications infrastructure, and big data analysis to make power generation, transmission, and distribution more reliable and sustainable.

Table 4.1 Description of Properties of Big Data Analytics

S.No.	Characteristics	Description
1.	Volume	Because there are so many datasets, traditional database systems can't store or work with them all. The smart grid is made up of a lot of smart meters, and a lot of new sensor technologies analyze them because the datasets themselves are too large.
2.	Velocity	The speed at which data is created and moved is called its "velocity." The need for the sharing of data in real time is only expected to increase.
3.	Variety	We need to employ big data technology to manage many kinds of unstructured data, such as communications like social network discussions, digital pictures, sensor data, and video or audio recordings, and mix them with more conventional forms of structured data.
4.	Veracity	The degree to which you can trust the information given is called its veracity. The quality and accuracy are less trustworthy as a result of the enormous volume of big data, which makes it harder to create. These systems need to be able to automatically get accurate data, make decisions, and control what happens both locally and globally.
5.	Value	Finding the important information and really understanding what it means takes a level of knowledge that not everyone has. Value is the ability to do so. As the amount of data grows, the amount of useful information that it contains will spread out.

In the past, when the amount of the data was relatively minimal, it was very simple for existing technologies to handle and analyze the data. Big data is distinct from other types of data in terms of its volume, velocity, and value; thus, the technologies that are now available are unable to process it [4]. Smart grids are also known as "gentle grids." Big data is an important part of smart grids because it makes it easier to collect, process, and understand the huge amounts of data that smart grid systems create. This makes big data a vital element of smart grids. Table 4.1 represents the list of properties that big data exhibits in smart grids.

4.6 EVOLUTION CLOUD COMPUTING

Over the last ten years, both big data and cloud computing have grown a lot. The two technologies work together to drive innovation and open up new use cases.

Figure 4.2 shows the development of computing on the cloud:

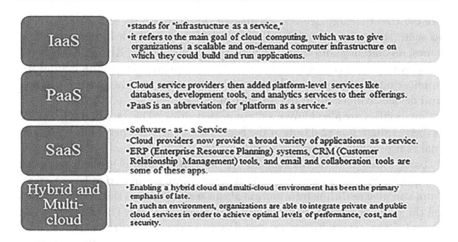

Figure 4.2 Different types of cloud services.

In Figure we see that the provision of the infrastructure and tools required to handle, store, and analyze this data has become more important as the quantity, complexity, and significance of big data have increased. Cloud computing has played an essential part in this provision.

Cloud computing has been a very useful tool in the delivery of this offering [5]. The cloud has also made it possible for companies to use big data analytics on a pay-as-you-go basis, which has increased the number of enterprises that are able to access these capabilities. A virtuous cycle of innovation and acceptance has resulted as a consequence of the increased need for big data analytics, which in turn has pushed innovation in the cloud.

4.7 EDGE COMPUTING IN SMART CITIES USING BIG DATA

Edge computing is a type of distributed computing architecture in which data is processed at or near its source instead of being sent to a central data center or the cloud. The term "edge computing" refers to computation that takes place at the network edge, which is the barrier between a local network and the Internet as a whole.

The introduction of edge computing creates new obstacles, despite the fact that it is an enticing solution to compensate for latency-related concerns that are strict [6].

Instead of using a central server in the cloud, edge computing processes and analyzes data right on the edge devices themselves or on servers that are close to the edge devices. Because of this strategy, there is less of a need to send data across extensive distances, which may result in faster reaction times, less latency, and more efficient use of bandwidth. Also, it enables the processing and analysis of data in real time, which is especially helpful for applications that need to make snap decisions, such as industrial automation and devices connected to the internet of things.

Smart cities are also known as "connected cities." The data that is gathered is then evaluated in real time at the edge, which provides helpful insights and makes it possible for decisions to be made quickly.

Using video analytics to keep an eye on traffic patterns is one use of edge computing that may be seen in smart cities. Cameras placed at key intersections can give real-time information about traffic, such as the number of cars on the road, the average speed, and the length of a trip. These cameras can record video data, which is then evaluated at the edge of the network. This information may then be put to use to improve the flow of traffic and lessen the impact of congestion.

Using air quality sensors to track pollution levels in real time is another example of this. The data that these sensors collect is then looked at at the edge. This lets authorities find areas with high pollution levels right away and take steps to fix them.

Edge computing is also utilized in smart cities to manage the amount of energy that is consumed and ensure that it is used most effectively [7]. Smart grids that have edge computing capabilities can collect and analyze data from internet of things devices like smart meters and solar panels. This enables real-time monitoring of energy usage as well as optimization of energy use.

In conclusion, edge computing is quickly becoming a technology that smart cities can't do without when it comes to processing and analyzing large amounts of data. Its capability to deliver real-time data, in addition to its ability to minimize network latency, makes it a perfect choice for controlling and improving urban infrastructure.

4.8 CLOUD COMPUTING FOR SMART GRID AND BIG DATA

In the past few years, cloud computing has become more popular, pushing out other popular ways to store data, like virtualization, utility computing, cluster computing, and grid computing. The "cloud services" that are used to process and store data on distant servers are at the core of the cloud computing concept. This model was developed by Amazon Web Services.

Cloud computing can meet the need for processing power that smart grid applications have. Even though most people think that cloud computing works well for smart grids, there are still some problems with it. Virtualization is an essential component of cloud computing and serves as its underlying technology.

With the deployment of distributed architecture, future smart grids are anticipated to feature power management that is dependable, efficient, secured, and cost-effective [8].

Because of the versatility, agility, and effectiveness that cloud infrastructure provides, it is becoming an increasingly significant component of smart grid and big data technologies. The following are some examples of how cloud computing is being used for purposes involving smart grids and large amounts of data:

Data Storage: Smart grids create a lot of data, and cloud computing offers a scalable and inexpensive way to store this data. Smart grid operators may quickly store and manage massive amounts of data by using cloud storage services, while also benefiting from aspects such as automatic backup and disaster recovery. This is made possible by the cloud's scalability and accessibility.

Data Analytics: Cloud computing offers an excellent platform for big data analytics by delivering the processing power and scalability required to analyze massive and complex datasets. Data analytics cloud computing provides an ideal platform for big data analytics by offering these features. When smart grid operators use analytics platforms that are hosted in the cloud, they can quickly and easily learn from the data that smart grid devices and systems create. These insights give them the power to optimize performance, cut costs, and increase reliability.

Demand Response: It allows utilities to balance supply and demand by changing how much energy is used based on market conditions, are using cloud computing more and more to help them. Demand response programmes are increasingly supported by cloud computing, which improves their effectiveness and capacities. Utility companies may rapidly and effectively manage demand response by using cloud-based systems, which gives the ability to dynamically change energy use based on data that is collected in real time.

Customer Engagement: As part of the smart grid project, cloud-based technologies are also being used to help consumers get involved and talk to each other more. Utilities may assist consumers in better understanding their energy use patterns by giving them access to real-time energy usage data and analytics. This lets customers make better decisions about how much energy they use and possibly lower their energy costs.

Cloud computing will become an increasingly important tool for smart grid and big data applications because it has the throughput, flexibility, and cost savings needed to handle and analyze huge amounts of data while also allowing new scenarios and improving customer interaction. In general, this statement is true. As new technologies like smart grids and big data analytics improve over time, it is expected that cloud computing will play an ever more important role in supporting them. Intelligent processing techniques use cutting-edge algorithms, AI, machine learning, and other computer methods to find insights and useful information in large datasets.

4.9 DATA SOURCES IN SMART GRIDS

The smart grid is a rich source of data because it includes information about how electricity is made, sent, distributed, and used. It is an intelligent energy and information system. Along with market, weather, and regional economic data, these data also include information about electricity from distribution stations, distribution switch stations, and electricity meters. Non-electrical information includes market data, meteorological data, and regional economic data. This information needs to be collected and analyzed so that power plants can be scheduled, subsystems can run, important power equipment can be kept in good shape, and marketers can understand how customers behave. Up to this point, we've talked about three types of data sources: measurement data, business data, and outside data. The vast majority of the operational characteristics of installed sensors and smart meters are used to keep an eye on the vast majority of the energy system's working parts and circumstances of the system. The functioning of the elect the weather and social events like festivals can have an effect on how the electricity system works and how it is planned, but smart meters can't measure these things. Businesses are mostly made up of marketing strategies and the actions of competitors. As shown in the picture later, the data producers like market providers who provide products and services to the smart grid market, which includes software and hardware services. The operation providers manage the operations of smart grid including transmission, distribution, and other grid operations. Service providers provide a vast variety of services to smart grid operations including maintenance, data analytics, and cybersecurity. These service companies collaborate on the design, installation, and operation of smart grid networks, which have the potential to increase energy efficiency, dependability, and sustainability.

In Figure 4.3, we see that these service providers then assist in the operation of smart grid technologies, which make use of contemporary forms of digital communication and technology to control and improve the efficiency of the flow of electric power. In order to improve the reliability, efficacy, and safety of the electrical system, smart grids use a broad variety of different technologies.

Some important technologies and features of smart grid [9]:

Advance Metering Infrastructure (AMI): This technology makes it possible for utilities and customers to communicate in real time with one

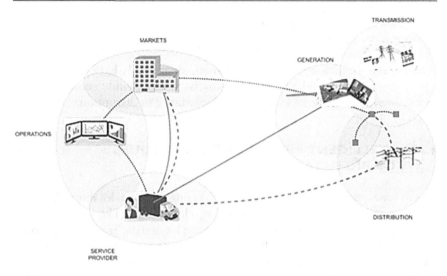

Figure 4.3 Different service providers.

another. AMI meters are able to analyze patterns of power consumption and communicate this information back to the utilities, which enables the utilities to more efficiently monitor and manage the electrical system.

Distributed Energy Resources (DERs): DERs are defined as decentralized energy sources that are situated in close proximity to the point of consumption. Some examples of DERs are solar panels, wind turbines, and energy storage devices. These resources may be included into the electricity distribution network via smart grids, which can boost both the network's efficiency and its dependability.

Energy Storage: By storing extra power during moments of low demand and distributing it during times of high demand, energy storage devices may assist in maintaining a stable supply of electricity across the grid. This may contribute to a reduction in the need for costly peaking power plants.

Microgrids: Microgrids are little electricity networks that are completely self-sufficient and able to function independently of the larger main grid. During power outages, they may be used to supply backup power, and in distant regions where there is no connection to the main grid, they can be utilized to supply electricity.

Automated Distribution System: In order to monitor and regulate the flow of power via the grid, smart grids make use of technologically sophisticated sensors and control systems. This makes it possible for utilities to immediately identify power failures and other concerns and react accordingly.

When these technologies are implemented, smart grids have the potential to cut down on wasted energy and associated costs while simultaneously increasing the power grid's stability and resistance to disruption.

4.10 INTELLIGENT PROCESSING TECHNIQUES FOR BIG DATA

Due to how quickly digital technology is changing, there is a lot more electronic data being made all the time. Because of this, a lot of things, like social networking sites, cellphones, sensors, and so on, create a lot of data. Traditional processing techniques struggle to handle massive amounts of data. In order to solve large data challenges, appropriate data analysis methods must be developed.

The term "big data analytics techniques" refers to the many different approaches and software programs that are used to handle and examine massive amounts of data. These methods are essential for getting useful insights and information from huge datasets, which would be hard to do with traditional methods of data analysis. Some of the most common ways to analyze large amounts of "big data" are machine learning, data mining, predictive modeling, and natural language processing. Data mining is the process of looking for patterns and insights in large datasets. Machine learning methods let computers learn from data and make predictions based on what they have learned. Both predictive modeling methods and natural language processing look at how people speak and write to figure out what they mean and how they feel. The goal of predictive modeling techniques is to predict what will happen in the future based on what has happened in the past. Companies and organizations that want to improve their position in the market by taking advantage of what big data can do need to use these strategies.

Processing big data requires the use of intelligent processing methods. The term "big data" is used to describe collections of data that are so big and complicated that they make it hard to analyze, process, and manage them in the usual ways. Intelligent processing techniques use AI, machine learning, and other cutting-edge computing methods to find insights and useful information in large datasets [10].

Figure 4.4 gives a few examples of clever data processing methods for large amounts of data:

- A branch of artificial intelligence called "machine learning" lets computers "learn" from datasets without being told what to do. It may be used to spot trends, make educated guesses, and improve the reliability of findings.

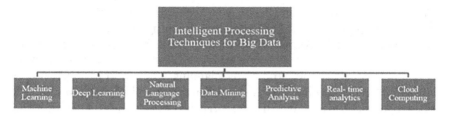

Figure 4.4 Different ways of data processing.

- Deep learning, a branch of machine learning, is based on the idea that neural networks may be used to model how the human brain functions. Natural language processing and advanced pattern recognition both rely on it.
- Natural Language Processing (NLP) is a type of artificial intelligence that translates between human and machine language. This method is used to process and analyze a lot of text, audio, and video data.
- Data mining, or "data mining," is a process that uses statistical and computational methods to find useful information in large datasets. It helps people get useful knowledge from large amounts of data.
- "Predictive analytics" is the process of using modern statistical and machine learning tools to look at past data and predict what will happen in the future. It's a tool for seeing into the future, finding danger spots, and making the best decisions possible.
- The term "real-time analytics" refers to the practice of analyzing data as it is being created in order to make decisions in the moment. Financial trading, social media monitoring, and cybersecurity are just a few of the fields that are put to use to track and react to real-time events.
- Cloud computing, or just "the cloud," is a type of computer technology that lets users access a network of remote servers whenever they want. By storing and processing data remotely, cloud computing gets rid of the need to buy and install expensive hardware and software.

When dealing with a lot of data, these smart processing methods can help companies learn a lot and make better decisions, which can be very helpful. Yet efficient implementation calls for specialized technical knowledge and substantial computing resources.

4.11 CONCLUSION

Eventually, this book chapter sums up the state of the art in big data analytics for smart grid interoperability. It is a good example of how smart grids have progressed to the point where they can effectively regulate electricity production and delivery. Monitoring, coordinating, and controlling smart grid equipment using AI and ML is made possible by big data analytics. In this chapter, we look at how smart grids may help us save money and time via things like automation and better planning. The report also delves into how cloud computing might be used in smart grids and big data. In sum, this chapter stresses the need for efficient large data processing techniques in the creation of smart grids.

REFERENCES

[1] D. K. Panda, and S. Das, "Smart grid architecture model for control, optimization and data analytics of future power networks with more renewable energy," *The Journal of Cleaner Production*, vol. 301, p. 126877, 2021, doi: 10.1016/j.jclepro.2021.126877.

[2] M. Gottschalk, M. Uslar, and C. Delfs, "The smart grid architecture model – SGAM," in *The Use Case and Smart Grid Architecture Model Approach: The IEC 62559-2 Use Case Template and the SGAM applied in various domains*, M. Gottschalk, M. Uslar, and C. Delfs, Eds., (in SpringerBriefs in Energy). Cham: Springer International Publishing, pp. 41–61, 2017, doi: 10.1007/978-3-319-49229-2_3.

[3] Y. Zhang, T. Huang, and E. F. Bompard, "Big data analytics in smart grids: A review," *Energy Information*, vol. 1, no. 1, p. 8, 2018, doi: 10.1186/s42162-018-0007-5.

[4] B. P. Bhattarai, et al., "Big data analytics in smart grids: State-of-the-art, challenges, opportunities, and future directions," *IET Smart Grid*, vol. 2, no. 2, pp. 141–154, 2019, doi: 10.1049/iet-stg.2018.0261.

[5] A. A. Munshi, and Y. A.-R. I. Mohamed, "Big data framework for analytics in smart grids," *Electric Power Systems Research*, vol. 151, pp. 369–380, 2017, doi: 10.1016/j.epsr.2017.06.006.

[6] Ishwarappa, and J. Anuradha, "A brief introduction on big data 5Vs characteristics and hadoop technology," *Procedia Computer Science*, vol. 48, pp. 319–324, 2015, doi: 10.1016/j.procs.2015.04.188.

[7] Z. Lv, D. Chen, R. Lou, and Q. Wang, "Intelligent edge computing based on machine learning for smart city," *Future Generation Computer Systems*, vol. 115, pp. 90–99, 2021, doi: 10.1016/j.future.2020.08.037.

[8] L. U. Khan, I. Yaqoob, N. H. Tran, S. M. A. Kazmi, T. N. Dang, and C. S. Hong, "Edge-computing-enabled smart cities: A comprehensive survey," *IEEE Internet of Things Journal*, vol. 7, no. 10, pp. 10200–10232, 2020, doi: 10.1109/JIOT.2020.2987070.

[9] Y. Liu, C. Yang, L. Jiang, S. Xie, and Y. Zhang, "Intelligent edge computing for IoT-based energy management in smart cities," *IEEE Network*, vol. 33, no. 2, pp. 111–117, 2019, doi: 10.1109/MNET.2019.1800254.

[10] J. Popeang, "Cloud computing and smart grids," *Database Systems Journal, Academy of Economic Studies – Bucharest, Romania*, vol. 3, no. 3, pp. 57–66, 2012.

Chapter 5

Advanced Machine Learning Methods for Big Data Analytics Used in Smart Grid

R. K. Viral and Divya Asija

5.1 DATA GENERATION IN SMART GRID

The depletion of conventional fossil fuels in the power grid and the need for decarbonization compel the power system to cut down its carbon emissions. With a high penetration of renewable energy sources, smart grid and super grid are viable options to speed up the progress of electrification of rural and urban areas [1]. Even though the use of renewable energy sources is being stimulated by the growing awareness of sustainable energy development, the intermittent nature of wind and photovoltaic energy poses significant difficulties for the secure and stable operation of a low inertia power system [2]. Under these conditions, several forecasting strategies based on data analytics techniques for renewable energy sources have shown to be an excellent option for regulating and dispatching resources [3].

The term "Smart Grid" (SG) refers to the integration of data communication technologies with the enhancement of the robust system's capability, reliability, and security [4]. With the assistance of the smart grid, service providers and consumers may communicate and exchange power, creating a two-way flow of both energy and information [5]. Plans for upgrading the smart grid have recently been recognized by various nations [6]. Electricity customers, energy producers, and regulators all benefit from smart grids in different ways. Electrical services become more robust, accountable, scalable, and cost-effective because of SG. A sensible grid is mostly employed in a few places, despite its many benefits [7]. The implementation of sensible grids across larger regions is hindered by several obstacles, including those related to operating, storage, processing, and management. Large-scale real-time data processing is mandatory for processing huge data available in smart grid.

A smart grid's built-in communication system produces an enormous volume of data. Different sources of data in SG are shown in Figure 5.1. Big Data Analytics (BDA) is developed to handle huge volumes of data for simplifying the process at the next level. The field of smart grid data analytics

DOI: 10.1201/9781032665399-5

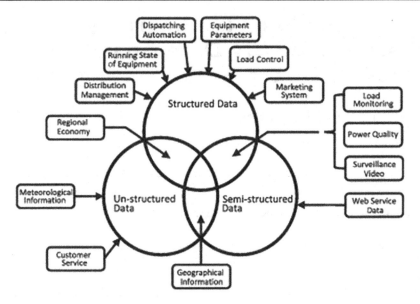

Figure 5.1 Conventional and smart grid data sources [3].

has witnessed a notable advancement owing to big data analytics [6]. The major goal of BDA in the smart grid is to utilize analytics techniques to optimize the generation, transmission, distribution, and storage of power system data.

Data analytics plays a vital role in today's modern industrial systems. Due to huge demand and adoption of smart meters and sensors in electrical applications, it is mandatory to include an information layer in existing information and communication technologies involved with traditional transmission and distribution network. It is mainly employed to extract, store, and analyze data [8]. The data acquired through SG assists in estimating demand and supply, equipment conditions, customer behavior, power optimization, and other tasks [7, 9]. For the security of the power system, data analytics undertaken through Advanced Metering Infrastructure (AMI) is more important for fault detection and predictive maintenance [9]. AMI data is divided into three basic classes: measurement data, business data, and external data [10]. BDA procedures are used in the processing of the AMI data. Consequently, this assessment using BDA supports several key decisions and assists in understanding the grid's present state [11, 12]. Machine learning, pattern recognition, artificial intelligence, and statistical analysis are different BDA techniques employed to deal with accumulated data in the smart grid.

With the proper execution of BDA techniques in SG, consumers can regulate their energy consumption intelligently after they are informed about energy efficiency and its advantages. Both consumers and energy suppliers gain from this demand-side control. The energy suppliers are also able to better understand consumer profiles, demands, and behavior results with the aid of the data gathered by smart meters. The decision-making process for load control during peak hours, outage management (such as managing blackouts), and quality of power management is aided by this information. Customers can also turn on/off certain appliances as needed because of the load management capability of smart meters [13].

Figure 5.2 depicts the smart grid analytics components along with related areas contemplated for identification and implementation of data analytics techniques. It is being segregated in to six foremost vital areas for employment and identification of data units as mentioned as follows:

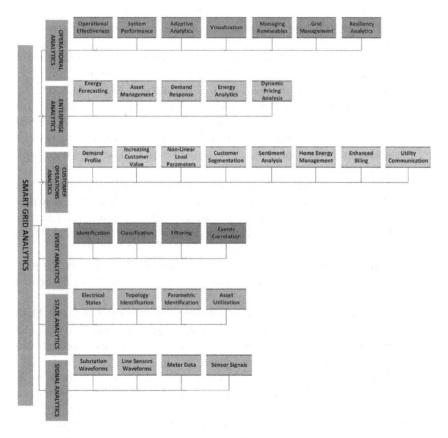

Figure 5.2 Smart grid analytics components with associated areas of identification for implementation of data analytics techniques [14].

    i.   Operational Analytics
   ii.   Enterprise Analytics
  iii.   Customer Operations Analytics
  iv.   Event Analytics
   v.   State Analytics
  vi.   Signal Analytics

5.2 BIG DATA ATTRIBUTES

Big data constitutes certain important attributes which help in discerning the acquired data into different datasets as per its category. Figure 5.2 shows major Vs of big data which play an important role in context of data retrieval as per the specific category. Its significance as per the data traits is explained as follows.

Big data characteristics:

    i.   5 Vs of Big Data and Additional V as Variability (Data Dynamicity)

- *Veracity:* The Veracity of Big Data, also known as Validity, is the guarantee of the quality or credibility of the collected data. The data in the actual world is so dynamic that it is difficult to discern what is correct and what is incorrect. The degree of trustiness or disarrangement of data results into veracity, and the greater the level of trustiness, the lesser the disarrangement and vice versa.
- *Value:* In the context of big data, value refers to the amount of data that is positively influencing a company's bottom line. It is critical to assess the cost of resources and time involved in big data accumulation, as well as the value delivered at the completion of the data processing process.
- *Velocity:* Velocity describes the rapid pace at which this data is produced, as well as the accelerating rate at which relational databases can process, store, and analyze this data.
- *Volume:* Volume in big data represents the amount of data. Data can be from multiple sources like social media platforms, business organizations, universities, banks and financial institutes, etc. in structured and unstructured form.
- *Variety:* Variety refers to several types of data. Big data tools handle a variety of data kinds acquired from multiple sources of information.
- Additional element or fragment of big data: Data Dynamicity *(Variability)* and Linkage.

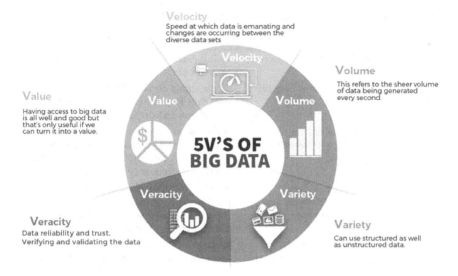

Figure 5.3 Major Vs of big data [15].

   ii. New Data Models
- Data linking, provenance, and referral integrity.
- Data Lifecycle and Variability

  iii. New Analytics
- Real-time/streaming analytics, interactive, and machine learning analytics

  iv. New Infrastructure and Tools
- High performance computing, storage, network
- Heterogeneous multi-provider services integration
- New Data-centric (multi-stakeholder) service models
- New Data-centric security models for trusted infrastructure and data processing and storage

   v. Source and Target
- High velocity/speed data capture from a variety of sensors and data sources
- Data delivery to different visualization and actionable systems and consumers
- Full digitized input and output, (ubiquitous) sensor networks, full digital control

In a process to show the real outcome of all the components of big data characteristics, we can summarize it as the tool or technology which processes

Table 5.1 Big Data Elements in Agreement with Smart Grid

Elements	5 Vs Concept	Agreement with Smart Grid
Veracity	Reliability and quality of data	Reliable data is crucial for safeguarding system operation and stability.
Value	Extracting useful benefits and insights	Applications derive value from smart grid data, for example, predicting future generation and demand.
Velocity	Frequency of data generation, transfer, or collection	If data were gathered every 15 minutes, a million smart meters could generate 35.04 billion data entries annually, or 2920 Tb [7]. The frequency of data gathering is vital for real-time monitoring and analysis.
Volume	Number of records and required storage	High volumes of data from smart meters, advanced sensor technology, and communication system.
Variety	Diversity of sources, formats, multidimensional fields	Existence of structured (e.g., relational data) and semi-structured (e.g., web service data).

large volume, increased velocity, dispersed variety datasets to extract reliable and relevant information from the crisp and refined data for decision-making, enhanced insight, and processes control. All of these necessitates novel data structures which support all data states and levels throughout the entire data life cycle as well as new infrastructure services and tools that enable obtaining (and evaluating data) from a wide range of sources (which includes sensor networks) as well as providing data in diverse forms to various information bearer, data clients, and devices [16]. Table 5.1 presents the different big data elements in agreement with smart grid. It is meant to show the direct association of the Vs of big data with the smart grid, considering its relationship and direct impact on the system.

Major data contributors in smart grid system:
Figure 5.4 depicts the key contributing elements of data in smart grid system.

Data is being collected from various contributors, but the important task is handling of collected data, whether it is for smart grid system or any business unit. With the help of advanced data analysis, we can derive useful insights from the collected data. These insights, in turn, enrich the decision-making process.

Figure 5.5 shows the architecture of the core components of smart grid big data, including data acquisition, data storage, data processing, data acquisition, and data analysis components [18].

Figure 5.6 represents 3 Es in the energy sector, namely energy, exchange, and empathy which are the backbone of the distribution companies.

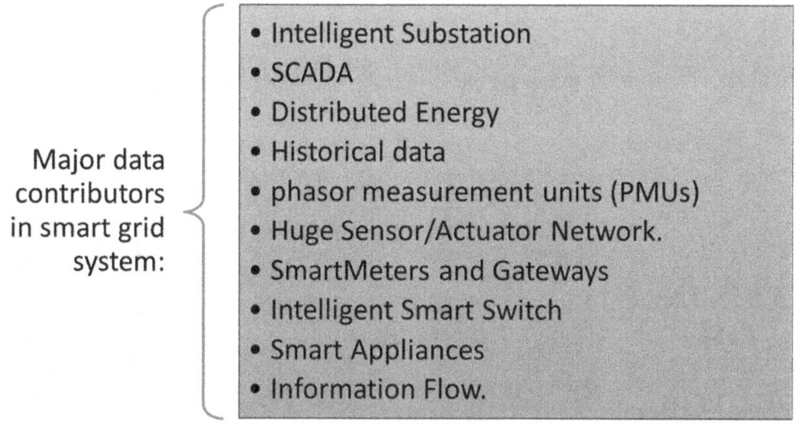

Major data contributors in smart grid system:
• Intelligent Substation
• SCADA
• Distributed Energy
• Historical data
• phasor measurement units (PMUs)
• Huge Sensor/Actuator Network.
• SmartMeters and Gateways
• Intelligent Smart Switch
• Smart Appliances
• Information Flow.

Figure 5.4 Major data contributors in smart grid system [17].

Data Analytics
•Tableau
•Mahout
•SAMOA
Data Querying
•HIVE
•IMPALA
Distributed Data Processing
•MapReduce
•YARN
Distributed Data Storage
•HDFS
Data Acquisition
•Flume

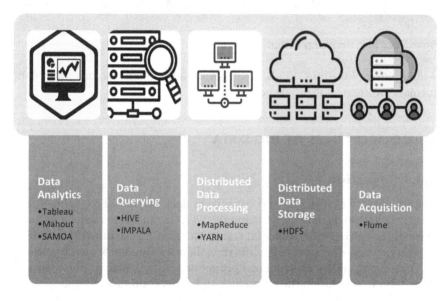

Figure 5.5 Hierarchical architecture of core components of smart grid big data.

Additional characteristics known as the three Es have been shown to be particularly significant in the power energy sector, including energy (that can be avoided), exchange (data exchange between energy players to add value to large data), and empathy (improve consumer pleasure) [19, 20]. Today's information concerning energy comes from a variety of sources, spanning a

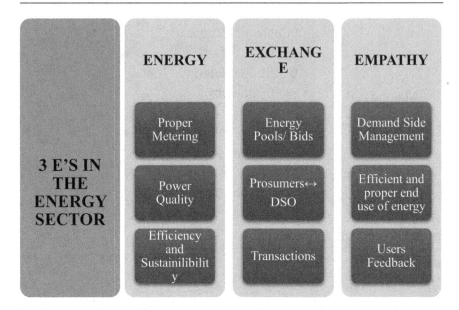

Figure 5.6 3 Es in the energy sector.

wide range of locations, kinds, and uses. In addition, numerous mesh data formats are created at rapid speeds.

5.3 COMPONENTS OF BIG DATA

5.3.1 Ingestion

The technique of collecting and organizing data is referred to as ingestion. Data preparation is done by utilizing the ETL (extract, transform, and load) procedure. During this step, data sources must be identified, determining whether to collect data in batches or in the stream and process it by cleansing, massaging, and organizing in a proper manner. The data is obtained and then optimized by using the extraction and conversion procedures.

5.3.2 Storage

You would need to save the information after you had obtained it. The load procedure, the last action in the ETL, is performed here. Depending on your needs, you could store the information in a data lake or a data warehouse. Because of this, it's critical to comprehend your organization's objectives while carrying out any big data execution.

5.3.3 Analysis

You would analyze the data to produce insightful findings for your organization at this stage of your big data approach. Big data analytics come in four categories: prescriptive, predictive, descriptive, and diagnostic. In this stage, data is analyzed using artificial intelligence and machine learning techniques.

5.3.4 Consumption

The big data process ends with this stage. You must communicate your ideas with others after you finish analyzing the data. In this situation, you would need to use data narratives and data visualization to successfully communicate your findings to non-technical audiences like stakeholders and project managers.

Applications for network big data provide new opportunities for intelligent energy management and span a variety of operational tasks. Datasets that are created and communicated are utilized for applications such as monitoring, optimization, forecasting, and planning.

5.4 SELECTION, VISUALIZATION, CORRELATION, FORECASTING, CLASSIFICATION, AND CLUSTERING OF DATA

Data Selection: The process of choosing the proper data source, data type, and tools to gather the data is known as data selection. Before beginning to gather data, data selection is done. The main goal of data selection is to choose the right data sources, instruments, and types to enable researchers to answer research questions effectively. This judgment is frequently discipline-specific and is largely determined by the nature of the inquiry, current literature, and accessibility to relevant data sources.

Data Visualization: The graphic depiction of data and information is known as data visualization. Data visualization tools offer an easy approach to observe and comprehend trends, outliers, and patterns in data by utilizing visual components like charts, graphs, and maps. Additionally, it offers a fantastic way for customers or business owners to clearly present data to non-technical audiences.

Data Correlation: A data correlation occurs when two measurements have a strong relationship and follow one another in a straight line. There are two possible outcomes for a correlation. A positive correlation results in a rise in value; on the other hand, a negative value results in a declining value. Data exhibits strong correlation when the variables exhibit the least amount of variation and the line connecting every dot on the chart exhibits virtually no difference.

Data Forecasting: It is a method of anticipating the future using the outcomes of the past data. In order to anticipate future events, a thorough examination of past and present patterns or events is required. It makes use of statistical methods and tools. As a result, statistical analysis is another name for it. In other terms, we may argue that it serves as a planning tool that aids businesses in preparing for potential future uncertainties. It commences with management offering their expertise and knowledge.

Data Classification: The procedure of categorizing data into groups that make it simple to obtain, sort, and store for later use is known as data classification. A well-designed data classification system renders it simple to locate and retrieve crucial data. For risk management, legal discovery and compliance with regulations can be very significant.

Data Clustering: A well-known machine learning-based data mining approach called clustering separates collections of abstract objects into classes of related items. Clustering assists in dividing data into several subgroups. These clusters are made up of data objects with a high degree of inter- and low degree of intra-similarity.

The following classifications can be used to group clustering techniques:

i.   The Partition Technique
ii.   The Hierarchy Technique
iii. The Density-Based Approach
iv.   Grid-Based Approach
v.   Model-Based Approach
vi.   Constraint-Based Approach

5.5 ADVANCEMENT IN DATA MINING METHODS

Data mining is not a new technology; it has been around since the 1930s, according to Hacker Bits. However, it became widely recognized in the 1990s, as businesses sought to extract significant value from the enormous amounts of data produced by society. Thanks to the development of modern computers and sophisticated data mining techniques, companies can now analyze large datasets and reveal valuable insights that were previously concealed. Such insights are crucial in predicting business outcomes, risk management, and leveraging new opportunities [21]. Data mining has undergone numerous advancements in recent years, resulting in more accurate and efficient analysis. The development in data mining methods is illustrated in Figure 5.7 [22].

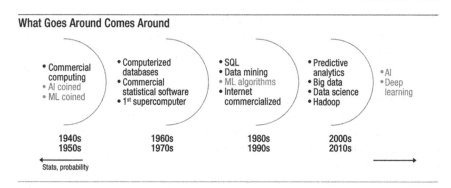

Figure 5.7 The development in data mining methods [22].

Some notable advancements [22]:

i. *Deep Learning:* This technique utilizes artificial neural networks with multiple layers to achieve advanced machine learning capabilities. It has uses in things like recommendation systems, audio and image recognition, and natural processing of language.

ii. *Association Rule Mining:* With the help of this method, correlations between various dataset pieces are found. Analysis of market baskets can benefit from it, where it can identify frequently purchased products.

iii. *Decision Trees:* These are visual representations of decision-making processes that are useful in identifying patterns and relationships within a dataset. They are particularly effective for classification problems.

iv. *Ensemble Learning:* This technique utilizes multiple machine learning algorithms to improve prediction accuracy. It has been successful in fraud detection, credit scoring, and customer churn prediction.

v. *Clustering:* This technique groups similar data points together and is useful in customer segmentation, Anomaly Detection, and image segmentation.

vi. *Time Series Analysis:* This technique analyzes time-based data and has applications in financial forecasting, weather forecasting, and stock market analysis.

vii. *Text Mining:* Text mining involves analyzing unstructured data like emails, social media posts, and customer reviews. It is helpful in text categorization, topic modeling, and sentiment analysis.

These advancements in data mining have enabled more extensive insights to be extracted from complex datasets, resulting in better business decisions and results.

The research work on "Advanced Analytics: Moving Towards Machine Learning, Natural Language Processing, and Artificial Intelligence" by SAS demonstrates that these technologies have been around for a while. Despite their long existence, businesses have only recently started exploring these advanced analytics technologies. These technologies offer significant benefits, and among them are raising operational effectiveness, comprehending behavior, and acquiring an edge in the market [23]. When used on enormous datasets, conventional data mining techniques like association mining, clustering, and classification are ineffective and unable to produce scalable and reliable results. It is hard for conventional approaches to analyze data stacks properly due to the sheer number, pace, and variety of data streams. In order to increase processing capacity while using minimal resources, researchers have created novel optimization techniques and analytical frameworks.

5.6 AI AND MACHINE LEARNING FOR BIG DATA ANALYTICS

In order to get meaningful insights and useful knowledge from huge datasets, Big Data Analytics is increasingly using artificial intelligence (AI) and machine learning (ML). Businesses are looking for ways to analyze their data efficiently and get a competitive edge as a result of the exponential rise of data. Many Big Data Analytics tasks, including data preparation, visualization, exploration, modeling, and predictive analytics, are being performed using AI and ML. These tools enable data-driven decision-making by seeing patterns, trends, and anomalies in data that may be hard for people to notice. The capacity of AI and ML to analyze enormous volumes of data swiftly and accurately is a key benefit of Big Data Analytics. Businesses may use this to analyze data in real time and base choices on the most recent information. Additionally, many data analysis tasks can be automated by AI and ML, saving time and resources compared to manual analysis [24]. The capacity of AI and ML to scale and manage complicated datasets is another benefit of Big Data Analytics. Businesses want technologies that can handle the breadth and complexity of their data as data volumes continue to rise. Large datasets may be used to train AI and ML systems, which thus grow more precise and effective over time [25]. To sum up, AI and ML are crucial technologies for Big Data Analytics. They let companies swiftly and correctly extract insightful information from their data, which is essential for data-driven decision-making. The application of AI and ML in Big Data Analytics will be even more important as data continues to rise [26].

The use of artificial intelligence to develop inductive models that have been learned with little data input is known as machine learning. It is a subfield of computing science. It has been especially established to expand computational knowledge and pattern recognition systems.

The training set and samples, which are the parameters of the database, are defined by the patterns in the input data, which the learning algorithm uses to analyze and identify relationships between them. Three major sorts of methodologies make up the learning categories in machine learning systems: supervised, unsupervised, and Reinforcement Learning [24]. The most popular machine learning algorithms and data processing techniques are listed in Table 5.1 [24–26].

Two of the most popular models in machine learning systems are support vector machines (SVMs) and artificial neural networks (ANNs). The enhanced initialization techniques, robust learning models, and multilayered architecture of ANNs—often referred to as deep learning—were all particularly developed to analyze bigger datasets [26].

In addition to the previously described algorithms, a wide range of sophisticated technologies are accessible to enable effective data analytics. The majority of these technologies are employed in business settings and are based on Standard Query Language (SQL) architecture. Additionally, businesses prefer dedicated data servers to cut down on the expense of processing and storing data. Big Data Analytics frequently use corporate-level machine learning technologies like R and Weka to deploy machine learning algorithms

Table 5.2 The Most Popular Machine Learning Algorithms [24–26].

Type of Algorithm	Method of Data Processing
Naive bayes	Classification
K-nearest neighbor	Classification
Support vector machine (SVM)	Classification
Linear regression	Classification/regression
Support vector regression	Classification/regression
Classification and regression trees	Classification/regression
Random forest	Classification/regression
Bagging	Classification/regression
Artificial neural network (ANN)	Clustering/classification/regression
Feed forward neural network	Clustering/classification/regression
K-means	Clustering
Density based spatial clustering	Clustering

and models. Healthcare, smart cities, traffic management, the financial sector, security, banking, and many more industries are just a few of the areas where big data benefits businesses. However, to guarantee secure data processing, it is crucial to take security and privacy considerations into account [27, 28].

5.7 ADVANCED MACHINE LEARNING FOR DATA ANALYTICS

Advanced machine learning methods are becoming more popular in data analytics because they can extract more accurate and meaningful insights from complex datasets. These methods can handle vast amounts of data and find links and patterns that can be hard for people to see. One of the most sophisticated machine learning methods, called deep learning, involves processing input through numerous layers of linked nodes. Tasks like speech recognition, picture recognition, and natural language processing benefit most from its effectiveness. Reinforcement Learning is another advanced technique used in applications such as gaming, robotics, and autonomous vehicles. It involves training agents to make decisions in an environment by maximizing a reward signal [29].

Generative Adversarial Networks (GANs) is another technique that involves two neural networks working in opposition to each other to generate new data. GANs have been used in applications such as image generation and natural language generation. Another method is called "transfer learning," which includes applying models that have already been trained on a similar task to new tasks that have little or no data. It is commonly utilised in applications like computer vision and natural language processing. Although these cutting-edge machine learning approaches offer a potent set of tools for data analytics, they necessitate a large investment in computer power and knowledge, which can be difficult for smaller firms. As data continues to grow in complexity, the use of advanced machine learning techniques in data analytics will become increasingly important for businesses to stay competitive [30].

Improving a machine learning model typically involves several methods such as adding more features, eliminating redundant ones through feature selection, optimizing hyper-parameters, and ensembling multiple models. Although these techniques can be effective, there exist various other approaches to enhance the model's performance such as pseudo-labeling, outliers' removal by model predictions, data augmentation, and explaining the model predictions [31].

5.8 DATA SCIENCE, CLOUD, AND EDGE COMPUTING

In the context of the smart grid, Big Data Analytics incorporate crucial components including data science, cloud computing, and edge computing. Smart grids are cutting-edge energy systems that employ digital technology to control the production, distribution, and use of energy better effectively [26].

Data science is essential for gaining insights from the vast and complex information in the field of the smart grid. To analyze the data produced by smart grids, data scientists use statistical analysis, machine learning algorithms, and visualization approaches. Additionally, they create predictive models that help grid operators predict demand and take preventative action to minimize disruptions [32].

With the use of cloud computing, massive amounts of data produced by smart grids can be processed and stored. Scalable, adaptable, and economical methods for storing and processing data are provided by cloud platforms like Microsoft Azure and Amazon Web Services (AWS). This makes it possible to perform real-time data analysis, which is essential for the smart grid industry's need for prompt decision-making. Data processing and analysis may now be done closer to the data source thanks to a new technology called edge computing. This method is particularly helpful in the smart grid sector, where real-time analysis is crucial and data is generated in distant areas. Edge computer lowers latency, lessens network congestion, and boosts system performance by moving computer resources closer to the data source.

Big data analytics in the context of the smart grid hence requires the use of data science, cloud computing, and edge computing. It enables real-time analysis, prompt decision-making, and the extraction of insights from enormous and complicated databases, resulting in a more effective and sustainable energy system [25].

5.9 APPLICATION IN SMART GRID

In order to increase the effectiveness, dependability, and safety of energy generation, transmission, and distribution, sophisticated power networks known as "smart grids" have been developed. Machine Learning (ML) is a crucial technology used in Smart Grids to analyze massive volumes of data and extract insightful knowledge to improve grid management and operations. Advanced ML techniques are applied in this context to tackle problems including load forecasting, fault detection and diagnostics, energy consumption optimization, and demand response. Some examples of cutting-edge ML techniques used to Smart Grid data analytics are provided as follows [25, 27, 30–33]:

   i. *Deep Learning:* A part of machine learning is called "Deep Learning" that draws out high-level characteristics from data by use of multi-layered neural networks. Applications in the Smart Grid for load forecasting, fault detection, and diagnostics employ convolutional neural networks and recurrent neural networks are two examples of deep learning approaches.

ii. *Reinforcement Learning:* A type of machine learning called Reinforcement Learning (RL) uses agents to interact with their surroundings and learn from feedback presented as rewards or penalties. Energy usage, demand response, and control techniques are optimised in Smart Grid applications using RL algorithms.

iii. *Probabilistic Graphical Models (PGM):* PGMs, also known as probabilistic graphic models, are a class of models that depict probabilistic connections between variables in a graph. Applications for the Smart Grid employ PGMs for fault detection, diagnosis, and forecasting, such as Bayesian Networks (BNs) and Markov Random Fields (MRFs).

iv. *Ensemble Learning:* Ensemble Learning is a method for combining many ML models to increase prediction accuracy and lower model variation. In Smart Grid applications for load forecasting, demand response, and fault diagnostics, Ensemble Learning techniques like Random Forests and Boosting are employed.

v. *Clustering and Anomaly Detection:* These unsupervised learning methods are employed to find patterns and abnormalities in data. These techniques are applied to load profiling, defect detection, and cybersecurity in Smart Grid applications.

The optimization of grid operations and administration, the reduction of energy costs, and the improvement of grid reliability and security are all made possible by sophisticated ML algorithms, which are crucial in the analysis of Smart Grid data.

5.10 CONCLUSION

In conclusion, there are many prospects for improving the functionality and efficiency of electricity grids now that Big Data Analytics and sophisticated machine learning techniques have been integrated into smart grids. These technologies have revolutionized the energy sector by making it possible to analyze massive amounts of grid-generated data and gain insights into a variety of grid-related topics, including load forecasting, energy consumption optimization, fault detection and diagnosis, and demand response. The approaches adopted, including Deep Learning, Reinforcement Learning, Probabilistic Graphical Models, Ensemble Learning, Clustering, and Anomaly Detection, have shown to be quite successful in overcoming the difficulties associated with Smart Grid data analytics. Big Data Analytics and cutting-edge ML techniques will continue to be crucial as the energy sector develops in order to increase grid dependability, security, and cost-effectiveness, ultimately paving the way for a more robust and sustainable energy future.

REFERENCES

[1]   I. Worighi, A. Maach, A. Hafid, O. Hegazy and J. Van Mierlo. 2019. Integrating renewable energy in smart grid system: Architecture, virtualization, and analysis. *Sustainable Energy, Grids and Networks* 18: 100226. https://doi.org/10.1016/j.segan.2019.100226.

[2]   S. Souabi, A. Chakir and M. Tabaa. 2023. Data-driven prediction models of photovoltaic energy for smart grid applications. *Energy Reports* 9(Suppl 9): 90–105 (ISSN 2352–4847). https://doi.org/10.1016/j. egyr.2023.05.237.

[3]   Y. Zhang, T. Huang and E. F. Bompard. 2018. Big data analytics in smart grids: A review. *Energy Information* 1: 8. https://doi.org/10.1186/s42162-018-0007-5.

[4]   Z. Fan et al. 2013. Smart grid communications: Overview of research challenges, solutions, and standardization activities. *IEEE Communications Surveys & Tutorials* 15(1): 21–38. https://doi: 10.1109/SURV.2011

[5]   M. Ghofrani, A. Steeble, C. Barrett and I. Daneshnia. 2018. Survey of big data role in smart grids: definitions, applications, challenges, and solutions. *The Open Electrical & Electronic Engineering Journal* 12(1): 86–97.

[6]   C. Miller, M. Martin, D. Pinney and G. Walker. 2014. *Achieving a Resilient and Agile Grid*. National Rural Electric Cooperative Association (NRECA), Arlington, VA, USA.

[7]   B. P. Bhattarai, S. Paudyal, Y. Luo, M. Mohanpurkar, K. Cheung, R. Tonkoski, R. Hovsapian, K. S. Myers, R. Zhang, P. Zhao, M. Manic and S. Zhang. 2019. Big data analytics in smart grids: state-of-theart, challenges, opportunities, and future directions. *IET Smart Grid* 2(2).

[8]   B. Dhupia and S. Sanober. 2020. A review: Big data analytics in smart grid management. *International Journal of Advanced Science and Technology* 29(6s): 171–179. http://sersc.org/journals/index.php/IJAST/article/view/8743.

[9]   C. Tu, X. He, Z. Shuai and F. Jiang. 2017. Big data issues in smart grid – A review. *Renewable and Sustainable Energy Reviews* 79: 1099–1107.

[10]   Z. Teng, Y. Zhang and D. Zhang. 2014. Application technology of big data in smart distribution grid and its prospect analysis. *Power System Technology* 38.

[11]   C. Fan, F. Xiao, Z. Li and J. Wang. 2018. Unsupervised data analytics in mining big building operational data for energy efficiency enhancement: A review. *Energy and Buildings* 159: 296–308.

[12]   Y. Cheng, K. Chen, H. Sun, Y. Zhang and F. Tao. 2018. Data and knowledge mining with big data towards smart production. *Journal of Industrial Information Integration* 9: 1–13.

[13] K. Ahuja and A. Khosla. 2019. Data analytics criteria of IoT enabled smart energy meters (SEMs) in smart cities. *International Journal of Energy Sector Management* 13(2): 402–423.

[14] A. Amr, Y. A.-R.I. Munshi. 2017. Mohamed, Big data framework for analytics in smart grids. *Electric Power Systems Research* 151: 369–380 (ISSN 0378-7796). https://doi.org/10.1016/j.epsr.2017.06.006.

[15] www.techentice.com/the-data-veracity-big-data/ (accessed April 23, 2023)

[16] D. B. Rawat and C. Bajracharya. 2015. Cyber security for smart grid systems: Status challenges and perspectives. *SoutheastCon* 2015: 1–6.

[17] S. Sagiroglu, R. Terzi, Y. Canbay and I. Colak. 2016. Big data issues in smart grid systems. In *2016 IEEE International Conference on Renewable Energy Research and Applications (ICRERA)*, Birmingham, UK, pp. 1007–1012. https://doi.org/10.1109/ICRERA.2016.7884486.

[18] L. Nige, X. Min, C. Wantian and G. Peng. 2015. Researches on data processing and data preventing technologies in the environment of big data in power system. In *2015 5th International Conference on Electric Utility Deregulation and Restructuring and Power Technologies (DRPT)*, Changsha, China, pp. 2491–2494. doi: 10.1109/DRPT.2015.7432672.

[19] T. Popovic, M. Kezunovic and B. Krstajic. 2015. Smart grid data analytics for digital protective relay event recordings. *Information Systems Frontiers* 17: 591–600. https://doi.org/10.1007/s10796-013-9434-9.

[20] N. Yu, S. Shah, R. Johnson, R. Sherick, M. Hong and K. Loparo. 2015. Big data analytics in power distribution systems. In *2015 IEEE Power & Energy Society Innovative Smart Grid Technologies Conference (ISGT)*, Washington, DC, USA, pp. 1–5. https://doi.org/10.1109/ISGT.2015.7131868.

[21] https://bootcamp.pe.gatech.edu/blog/10-key-data-mining-techniques-and-how-businesses-use-them/ (accessed April 28, 2023).

[22] www.imaginarycloud.com/blog/data-mining-techniques/ (accessed April 28, 2023).

[23] TDWI Best Practices SAS Report. 2017. *Advanced Analytics: Moving Toward AI, Machine Learning, and Natural Language Processing.* www.sas.com/en/whitepapers/tdwi-advanced-analytics-ai-ml-nlp-109090.html (accessed April 28, 2023).

[24] A. Stetco, F. Dinmohammad, X. Zhao, V. Robu, D. Flynn, M. Barnes, J. Keane and G. Nenadic. 2019. Machine learning methods for wind turbine condition monitoring: A review. *Renewable Energy* 133: 620–635. https://doi.org/10.1016/j.renene.2018.10.047.

[25] I. Portugal, P. Alencar and D. Cowan. 2018. The use of machine learning algorithms in recommender systems: A systematic review. *Expert Systems with Applications* 97: 205–227. https://doi.org/10.1016/j.eswa.2017.12.020.

[26] M. S. Mahdavinejad, M. Rezvan, M. Barekatain, P. Adibi, P. Barnaghi and A. P. Sheth. 2018. Machine learning for internet of things data analysis: A survey. *Digital Communications and Networks* 4: 161–175. https://doi.org/10.1016/j.dcan.2017.10.002.

[27] N. Dey, A. E. Hassanien, C. Bhatt, A. S. Ashour and S. C. Satapathy (Eds.). 2018. *Internet of Things and Big Data Analytics Toward Next-Generation*

Intelligence, Springer International Publishing, Cham. https://doi. org/10.1007/978-3-319-60435-0.

[28] C. Tu, X. He, Z. Shuai and F. Jiang. 2017. Big data issues in smart grid— A review. *Renewable and Sustainable Energy* 79: 1099–1107. https://doi. org/10.1016/j.rser.2017.05.134.

[29] S. S. Band, et al. 2022. When smart cities get smarter via machine learning: An in-depth literature reviv. *IEEE Access* 10: 60985–61015. https://doi. org/10.1109/ACCESS.2022.3181718.

[30] F. Ünal, A. Almalaq, S. Ekici and Glauner P. 2021. Big data-driven detection of false data injection attacks in smart meters. *IEEE Access* 9: 144313–144326. https://doi.org/10.1109/ACCESS.2021.3122009.

[31] https://towardsdatascience.com/4-advanced-machine-learning-techniques-71d485e9fcab (accessed April 28, 2023).

[32] L. Gu, W. Zhang, Z. Wang, D. Zeng and H. Jin. 2023. Service management and energy scheduling toward low-carbon edge computing. *IEEE Transactions on Sustainable Computing*, 8(1): 109–119. https://doi.org/10.1109/ TSUSC.2022.3210564.

[33] O. A. Omitaomu and N. Haoran. 2021. Artificial intelligence techniques in smart grid: A survey. *Smart Cities* 4(2): 548–568. https://doi.org/10.3390/ smartcities4020029.

Chapter 6

Perspective of Cybersecurity and Ethical Hacking with Vulnerability Assessment and Exploitation Tools

Devyanshi Bansal, Madhulika Bhatia, Aniruddh Atrey, and Arun Kumar Yadav

6.1 INTRODUCTION

Cybersecurity is the set of practices used to protect computers, computer services, android/iOS devices, various electronic systems, communications and computer networks, and data from malicious attacks and threats. An example of cybersecurity is the 2007 cyberattack on the United Nations website, which displayed a message protesting US and Israel policies in the Middle East. The hacker group called themselves cyber protest, and they also hacked the websites of Harvard University, the UN environment program, and industrial giants like Toyota and Nestle.

The timeline of hacking security started in 1962 with the first role attack when MIT, for Massachusetts Institute of Technology, set the password for computers for sustaining time limits and student privacy. In 1969, Stanford Research Institute students tried to transmit the world login to another internet appliance over the ARPAnet. In 1970, Nokia and Motorola were world hacking victims when Kevin Mitnick broke into 21 of the world's most highly protected networks using social engineering methods. In 1972, the message "I am the creeper, catch me if you can" was the first computer virus in history founded by Bob Thomas. Reaper, the first antivirus developed against creepers, arrived shortly after. The cyberattack in threats comes in all types and sizes and has caused the world economy more than one trillion dollars, almost one percent of the global GDP, where a company with individual credentials, their bank account details, and other confidential information are at risk.

6.2 WHY DO WE NEED CYBERSECURITY?

Cybersecurity protects people, companies, and governments against illegal access, theft, and harm to their digital data and systems. Cybersecurity is important for these reasons:

DOI: 10.1201/9781032665399-6

- Cybersecurity: Cybersecurity prevents hackers, malware, phishing, and ransomware. These assaults may steal data, financial information, and harm digital systems.
- Privacy protection: Cybersecurity safeguards sensitive data and prevents illegal access.
- Compliance with regulations: Finance, healthcare, and government need cybersecurity safeguards to secure sensitive data.
- Business continuity: Cybersecurity measures protect digital systems and data, ensuring business continuity and preventing interruptions.
- Reputation management: Cybersecurity breaches may damage a company's reputation and lose customers.
- National security: Cyberattacks may damage key infrastructure, government systems, and military assets.

Cybersecurity protects data, systems, privacy, compliance, business continuity, reputation, and national security.

In cybersecurity there are basically three types of hackers—white hat hackers, black hat hackers, and the last one, grey hat hackers.

6.2.1 White Hat Hackers

White hat hackers, also known as ethical hackers, are cybersecurity professionals who use their expertise to find vulnerabilities and weaknesses in computer systems, networks, and software applications, in order to help organizations identify and fix security flaws before they can be exploited by malicious hackers.

Unlike black hat hackers, who engage in illegal activities for personal gain or to cause harm, white hat hackers work within the boundaries of the law and use their skills to protect systems from cyberattacks. They may be hired by companies, governments, or other organizations to conduct penetration testing, vulnerability assessments, or other security assessments, with the goal of identifying and addressing potential security issues.

White hat hackers may also participate in bug bounty programs, where companies offer rewards to individuals who discover and report security vulnerabilities in their systems. By identifying and reporting these vulnerabilities, white hat hackers help improve the overall security of computer systems and protect users from cyberattacks.

6.2.2 Black Hat Hackers

Black hat hackers are individuals or groups who engage in unauthorized or malicious activities with the goal of exploiting security vulnerabilities in computer systems, networks, and software applications for personal gain or to cause harm. Unlike white hat hackers who work within the law and ethical boundaries, black hat hackers use their technical skills to commit cybercrimes, steal sensitive information, or cause disruption to computer systems.

Black hat hackers often use techniques such as phishing, malware attacks, and social engineering to gain unauthorized access to computer systems or steal sensitive data. They may also engage in activities such as distributed denial-of-service (DDoS) attacks, which involve flooding a targeted system with traffic to overwhelm and disrupt its normal operation.

Black hat hackers are a serious threat to individuals, businesses, and governments, and their activities can have far-reaching consequences. Their actions can result in financial losses, damage to reputations, and even physical harm in some cases. It is important for individuals and organizations to take proactive measures to protect their computer systems and networks from cyberattacks by implementing strong security measures and regularly updating their software to address vulnerabilities.

6.2.3 Grey Hat Hackers

Grey hat hackers are individuals who use their hacking skills to identify vulnerabilities in computer systems, networks, and software but do not always obtain explicit permission to do so. They fall somewhere in between white hat hackers, who are ethical hackers who have explicit permission to test systems, and black hat hackers, who use their skills for illegal activities.

Grey hat hackers may expose security flaws to companies or organizations in an attempt to help them improve their security, but they may also publicly disclose vulnerabilities without permission, which can create security risks for the organization.

While some grey hat hackers may have good intentions, their actions can still be considered illegal and can lead to serious consequences, including criminal charges and imprisonment. It is important for individuals to use their hacking skills ethically and with the appropriate permissions to avoid such consequences.

6.3 CYBERSECURITY AND ETHICAL HACKING

Cybersecurity is a combination of different tools and skills that provide the best security environment for users. Ethical hacking is a part of cybersecurity, which is responsible for detecting a system's vulnerabilities and resolving them before any malicious or black-headed criminal penetrates it. Risk register files are used to maintain all risks, and their solutions prevent any future security breach. Cybersecurity experts are accredited as hackers and can help organizations find out and apply measures that can prevent their data from theft or fraud [1–3].

6.4 COMPARISON

A comparison of ethical hacking and cybersecurity is provided in Table 6.1, because it is essential to understand the distinctions that exist between the two in all respects.

Table 6.1 Ethical Hacking vs Cybersecurity

Aspect	Ethical Hacking	Cybersecurity
Goal	To identify and exploit weaknesses and vulnerabilities in computer systems and networks in order to improve their security	To protect computer systems and networks from unauthorized access, theft, damage, or other malicious activities
Approach	Attacker's perspective	Defender's perspective
Focus	Finding vulnerabilities and weaknesses in computer systems and networks	Protecting computer systems and networks from threats and attacks
Authorization	Requires permission from the owner of the system/network being tested	Doesn't require permission as it is a preventative measure
Methodologies	Penetration testing, social engineering, vulnerability assessments, etc.	Risk assessment, security policies, firewalls, intrusion detection/ prevention, etc.
Skills and Knowledge	In-depth knowledge of computer systems, programming languages, networking protocols, and security tools	Knowledge of security frameworks, risk management, security policies, compliance regulations, and security tools
Responsibility	To find and report vulnerabilities to the system owner and suggest solutions to improve security	To maintain and improve security measures and policies to prevent unauthorized access and data breaches
Outcome	Improves security by identifying vulnerabilities and recommending solutions to mitigate them	Protects the system/network from threats and attacks, reducing the risk of data breaches and financial losses

Note that while there are differences between ethical hacking and cybersecurity, they are both important aspects of maintaining the security of computer systems and networks. Ethical hacking helps identify vulnerabilities that need to be addressed, while cybersecurity implements measures to prevent unauthorized access and maintain the security of computer systems and networks.

6.5 HISTORY OF CYBERSECURITY

Table 6.2 tells us about the complete history of cybersecurity.

6.6 PROBLEMS ARISING DURING COVID-19

The COVID-19 pandemic has brought significant changes to the way people work, communicate, and interact with each other. Unfortunately, it has also created new opportunities for cybercriminals to exploit vulnerabilities and launch cyberattacks. Some of the challenges faced in cybersecurity during COVID-19:

- Increased phishing attacks: Cybercriminals have been taking advantage of the pandemic by sending out phishing emails that appear to

Table 6.2 History Stating the Beginning of Cybersecurity Requirement

Year	Description
1970s	The first computer viruses appear, primarily affecting mainframe computers.
1988	The Morris Worm, one of the first computer worms, infects thousands of computers across the internet.
1990s	The rise of the internet leads to an increase in cyberattacks, including hacking, phishing, and malware distribution.
2002	The National Cyber Security Division is established within the US Department of Homeland Security.
2007	Estonia experiences a large-scale cyberattack, leading to the creation of the Tallinn Manual, a set of guidelines for international law in cyber warfare.
2010	Stuxnet, a sophisticated computer worm, is discovered and believed to be the first example of a state-sponsored cyberattack.
2013	Edward Snowden leaks classified documents revealing widespread surveillance by the US government.
2016	The Mirai botnet, composed of compromised Internet of Things devices, launches a massive DDoS attack on DNS provider Dyn, causing widespread internet disruption.
2017	The WannaCry ransomware attack infects hundreds of thousands of computers worldwide.
2018	The EU's General Data Protection Regulation (GDPR) goes into effect, imposing strict data protection rules on companies operating in the EU.
2020	The COVID-19 pandemic leads to a surge in cyberattacks targeting remote workers and healthcare organizations.
2021	The SolarWinds supply chain attack is discovered, affecting numerous US government agencies and private companies.

come from reputable sources, such as healthcare organizations or government agencies. These emails often contain links or attachments that, when clicked, can infect computers with malware or steal personal information.

- Remote workforce security: With more people working from home, there is an increased risk of cyberattacks. Employees may be using personal devices that are not secure or accessing sensitive data through unsecured networks, making it easier for cybercriminals to gain access to sensitive information.
- VPN and remote access vulnerabilities: Many organizations have had to quickly set up remote access systems to enable their employees to work from home. However, these systems can be vulnerable to cyberattacks if they are not properly secured.
- Malware and ransomware attacks: Cybercriminals have been taking advantage of the pandemic to launch malware and ransomware attacks. Malware can infect computers and steal sensitive information, while ransomware can encrypt files and demand payment in exchange for the decryption key.
- Lack of cybersecurity awareness: With so many people working from home, there is a risk that employees may not be as aware of cybersecurity best practices as they would be in an office setting. This can make them more vulnerable to cyberattacks.

To address these challenges, it is important for organizations to prioritize cybersecurity and ensure that their employees are trained in cybersecurity best practices. This may include providing employees with secure devices, implementing secure remote access systems, and regularly updating security software to protect against new threats.

6.7 CYBERSECURITY VULNERABILITY ASSESSMENT

Cybersecurity is a critical aspect of modern computing, and vulnerability assessment is an essential component of a comprehensive cybersecurity strategy. Vulnerability assessment involves identifying weaknesses or vulnerabilities in computer systems, applications, or networks that could be exploited by attackers.

The process of vulnerability assessment typically involves the following steps:

Identification: This involves identifying all the systems, applications, and networks that need to be assessed for vulnerabilities. This step may involve conducting a comprehensive inventory of all the hardware and software in the organization.

Scanning: Once the systems, applications, and networks have been identified, the next step is to scan them for vulnerabilities. This step may involve using automated vulnerability scanning tools or manual testing techniques.

Evaluation: Once vulnerabilities have been identified, the next step is to evaluate the severity of each vulnerability. This step may involve assigning a risk rating to each vulnerability based on its likelihood of being exploited and the potential impact if it were to be exploited.

Remediation: Once the vulnerabilities have been identified and evaluated, the next step is to develop a plan for remediation. This may involve patching software, changing configuration settings, or implementing new security controls.

Monitoring: Finally, it is essential to monitor the systems, applications, and networks for new vulnerabilities continually. This may involve ongoing scanning or testing, as well as staying up to date with the latest security threats and best practices.

Overall, vulnerability assessment is a crucial component of a comprehensive cybersecurity strategy, as it helps organizations identify and remediate vulnerabilities before they can be exploited by attackers.

6.8 VULNERABILITY ASSESSMENT TOOLS

Vulnerability assessment tools are used to identify vulnerabilities or weaknesses in computer systems, networks, and applications that can be exploited by attackers to gain unauthorized access or compromise the system's integrity. There are various types of vulnerability assessment tools available, and these are some of the most used ones [4–6]:

6.8.1 Burp Suite

Burp Suite is a popular web application security testing tool developed by Port-Swigger. It is widely used by security professionals and penetration testers to identify and exploit vulnerabilities in web applications.

Burp Suite has a few powerful features, including a proxy server, scanner, spider, repeater, sequencer, decoder, comparer, and intruder. The proxy server allows the user to intercept and modify requests and responses between the client and server, while the scanner can automatically identify security vulnerabilities in the web application. The spider is used to crawl the website and discover its structure, and the repeater can be used to repeat a request with different parameters.

The sequencer analyzes the randomness of session tokens and other data, while the decoder can be used to decode and encode various data formats.

The comparer allows the user to compare two responses to see if they are different, while the intruder is used to automate attacks against the web application.

Steps for Burp Suite professional work:

Step 1: Open Burp Suite professional.
Step 2: Go to the Burp Suite Pro dashboard and click on "New Scan". This opens a scan launcher. You can select the scan type from the top.
Step 3: Click on crawl and audit, which is the default option.
Step 4: After that, you need to enter the URL or multiple URLs to scan.
Step 5: Then select scan using HTTP and HTTPS protocol.
Step 6: At last, click OK.

It will start scanning the website and will identify the vulnerabilities of the website. I have used this tool like this, but it can be optimized as per the need.

6.9 NIKTO

Nikto is a web vulnerability scanner or a website web server security scanner. It's fantastic for detecting vulnerabilities on the server. Nikto is generally used by professional penetration testers and web security analysis for professional projects because it particularly finds out and detects server misconfigurations, as most of the time system administrators for the people who actually set up website hosting really don't know what they are doing, and this comes in the form of leaving subdomains wide open for people to just find out and, furthermore, exploit. However, the Nikto tool makes it simple to find haphazard server setup errors, such as incorrect port settings for handling GET and POST comments.

There is an increase in the web application on the internet today because all businesses are now working on an online platform, and internet and online platforms are really required nowadays. It raises security concerns, because in some cases, security is haphazardly considered during development because there are lots of developers, lots of languages, and lots of platforms available for different functionalities. As a result, we often end up having vulnerable web apps where attackers might exploit users' personal information because there are lots of things which we can get from the user's side like bank information, phone numbers, emails, personal data, and company service data, etc. So if the website is vulnerable, that data can get directly into the hands of the hacker [7, 8].

Nikto is a web application scanner that penetration testers, malicious hackers, and web application developers use to identify vulnerabilities for a security issue on web applications.

Nikto was originally written, developed, and maintained by sullo, CIRT, Inc. It is currently under the maintenance of David Lodge, though other contributors have also been involved in this project as well.

Nikto working mechanism:

Here, I have already installed Kali Linux on my laptop.
So I did not install anything separately as Nikto is available in Kali Linux.

Step 1: I had to login to Kali Linux.
Step 2: Then go to Applications.
Step 3: Then select "Vulnerability Analysis", and select Nikto.

After that, it will open a window or terminal for performing the scan for the web server.

Syntax for proceeding with the scan:

nikto -n $ webserver url
This syntax will start the scan and will help us in doing the vulnerability assessment of the website.
So the vulnerability assessment is successfully performed using these three tools, and it is found that these three tools are very effective in website vulnerability assessment.

6.9.1 OWASP Zed Attack Proxy (ZAP)

OWASP (Open Web Application Security Project) is an open-source project that focuses on improving the security of software applications. One of the tools that OWASP provides is the Zed Attack Proxy (ZAP), which is a widely used web application security testing tool.

ZAP is designed to help developers and security testers find vulnerabilities in web applications. It can be used to intercept and modify HTTP/HTTPS requests and responses, perform automated scanning for common vulnerabilities such as SQL injection and cross-site scripting (XSS), and report the results of the scans.

ZAP is highly configurable and can be used for a variety of different testing scenarios, from quick automated scans to in-depth manual testing. It also has a powerful scripting engine that allows users to customize and extend its functionality.

Overall, ZAP is a valuable tool for anyone involved in web application development or security testing. Its open-source nature means that it is constantly being updated and improved by a large community of developers and security professionals.

OWASP ZAP working mechanism:

Step 1: Open the Owasp ZAP tool and click on the Quick Start tab.

Step 2: Select the Automated Scan option.

Step 3: You will see a text box where you need to enter the URL of the website in which you want to find the vulnerabilities.

Step 4: After entering the URL, simply click on "Attack". After that it will identify and list the vulnerabilities with the necessary countermeasures.

Step 5: Figure 6.1. shows the results of OSWASP ZAP.

6.9.2 Metasploit

The Metasploit framework is a flexible tool that may be used for system vulnerabilities inside a network, penetration testing, and exploit research. Metasploit Framework is an open-source tool, and it's written in Ruby language, which means if you know the Ruby language and you know how to write codes in Ruby, then you can contribute to the Metasploit framework. The Metasploit framework contains more than 1200 exploits, 330 +

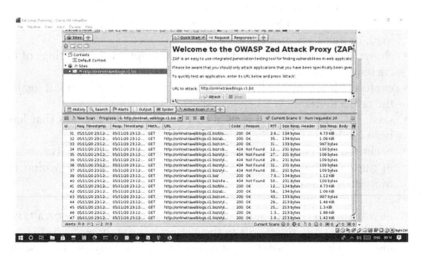

Figure 6.1 Result of OWASP ZAP.

payload, and 30 + encoders. In Metasploit architecture, Metasploit contains many modules such as encoders, exploits, payload, nops, and Aux. It also contains libraries such as Erx and MSF Core and interfaces such as console, GUI, web, and some plug-ins.

Metasploit is an exploitation framework; it's a group of tools and utilities to make exploit development, system administration, and hacking stuff easier.

Metasploit real-life scenario means how penetration testers use Metasploit in real time in order to exploit or penetrate into the systems. In order to use Metasploit, there are three steps. The first step is to find open ports services and their version numbers running on the remote version. So once we find open ports and services running on them, we'll try to find the version of number of services, and once we got the version number, then we'll try to find exploit in Metasploit framework database, correspond to that version number which we found, and if that exploit is present in the Metasploit framework database, then we will use that exploit in order to penetrate that system. Every penetration tester and security analyst follows this method to achieve success.

Metasploit interfaces are of three types: web interface, GUI interface (also known as Armitage), and command line interface (msfconsole); and it is a cross platform tool, so it can be used on Windows, Mac, and Linux.

Different commands of Metasploit [9, 10]:

- search: This command is used to search for specific exploits, payloads, or auxiliary modules in the Metasploit framework.
- use: This command is used to select a specific exploit, payload, or auxiliary module that you want to use.
- set: This command is used to set options for the selected exploit, payload, or auxiliary module.
- show: This command is used to display the options and settings of the currently selected exploit, payload, or auxiliary module.
- exploit: This command is used to launch the selected exploit against the target system.
- sessions: This command is used to view the active sessions that have been established with the target system.
- background: This command is used to run a currently active session in the background, allowing you to perform other tasks within the Metasploit console.
- exit: This command is used to exit the Metasploit console.
- db_nmap: This command is used to perform a Nmap scan on a target system and store the results in the Metasploit database.
- msgrpc: This command is used to start the Metasploit RPC server, which allows you to connect to the Metasploit console remotely.

6.9.3 SQL Map

SQL Map Tool is an open-source login testing tool that can be accessed from BackTrack 5 distro or Sourceforge. This tool is used to detect and apply SQL injection errors. It can perform many functions. The top ten OWASP errors of 2010 prioritize SQL injection errors, and SQL injection can lead to a variety of problems, including data loss or corruption and complete system capture. Hql Map handles stored fingerprints, data downloads, access to subtitle files, and off-band command creation. SQL map software can be used on all OS applications, such as Windows, Mac, and Linux, and on Android phones with termux.

Step 1: Using SQLMAP to test a website for SQL Injection vulnerability:
Step 2: List information about the existing databases.
Step 3: List information about tables available on this database.
Step 4: List information about columns in a specific table.
Step 5: Dump the data from the columns.

Figure 6.2 shows all the commands of SQLMAP. Similarly, we can access information in a particular column by using the following command, in which -C can be used to specify the name of most of the comma-separated columns, and the dump query returns data.

sqlmap -u http://testphp.vulnweb.com/listproducts.php?cat=1
-D acuart -T artists -C aname --dump

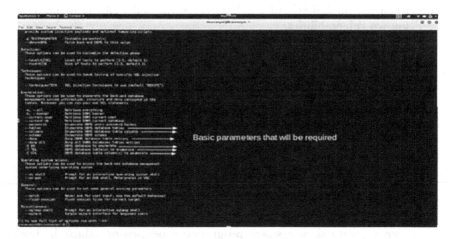

Figure 6.2 SQLMAP.

From the image earlier, we can see that we have accessed the data on the website. Similarly, on such endangered websites, we may be able to perform a "search of the site" in order to provide information.

6.9.4 Microgrid cybersecurity

Microgrid cybersecurity is the protection of microgrid systems against cyber threats that can lead to disruption of operations, data theft, or compromise of critical infrastructure. Microgrids are decentralized energy systems that can operate independently or in conjunction with the main power grid, providing backup power during power outages or as a primary power source in remote areas. The integration of communication technologies, control systems, and smart devices in microgrids makes them vulnerable to cyber-attacks. Cybersecurity measures are essential to ensure the reliability and resilience of microgrid systems.

Some best practices for microgrid cybersecurity:

- Conducting regular risk assessments to identify vulnerabilities and potential threats.
- Implementing secure communication protocols and encryption methods to protect data and information.
- Applying access controls to limit user privileges and prevent unauthorized access to critical systems.
- Installing firewalls, intrusion detection systems, and antivirus software to detect and prevent cyberattacks.
- Providing training and awareness programs to employees and users to enhance their understanding of cyber threats and how to prevent them.
- Regularly updating and patching software and systems to address known vulnerabilities.
- Designing microgrid systems with cybersecurity in mind from the outset.
- Creating a response plan for cyber incidents to minimize their impact and facilitate recovery.

Overall, microgrid cybersecurity is crucial to ensure the reliability, resilience, and security of microgrid systems. Implementing appropriate cybersecurity measures is essential to protect against cyber threats and ensure the smooth operation of microgrids.

6.10 CONCLUSION

Therefore, a good risk assessment program can be used to reduce the burden of compliance effort. This also helps companies reduce their risk levels, exercise due diligence, provide intelligence data, and generate reports that can be used as a technical matrix. We will be adding another layer to our deep defence and adding peace of mind to the company's management team by building a comprehensive risk assessment system. Identifying those critical weaknesses in a business entity and performing mitigation actions prior to the use of DDoS risks is actually at the core of risk management. Comprehensive risk management rules mandate the development of a strong risk monitoring system, guaranteeing the safety of your company and any personal data kept on your servers and establishing a safe computing environment.

REFERENCES

[1] www.geeksforgeeks.org/use-sqlmap-test-website-sql-injection-vulnera-bility/
[2] www.golinuxcloud.com/metasploit-tutorial/
[3] https://blog.avast.com/history-of-cybersecurity-avast
[4] www.kaspersky.co.in/resource-center/definitions/what-is-cyber-security
[5] https://m.economictimes.com/news/defence/cybercrimes-in-india-during-pandemic-have-gone-up-by-500-per-cent-cds-gen-bipin-rawat/videoshow/87667441.cms
[6] www.business-standard.com/article/technology/india-becomes-favourite-destination-for-cyber-criminals-amid-covid-19–121040501218_1.html
[7] www.coursera.org/articles/cybersecurity-analyst-job-guide
[8] https://www.simplilearn.com/tutorials/cyber-security-tutorial/what-is-cyber-security
[9] https://cybermagazine.com/cyber-security/history-cybersecurity
[10] https://resources.github.com/appsec/

Chapter 7

Communication and Measurement Technologies for Smart Grid

Vishal Kumar Gaur and Subho Paul

7.1 INTRODUCTION: COMMUNICATION AND MEASUREMENT TECHNOLOGIES

Smart grid is a modern interconnected electrical system that improves reliability, efficiency, and sustainability by utilizing power generation, transmission and distribution systems, energy storage systems (ESS), demand response programs, electric vehicles (EVs), distributed energy resources, microgrids, and communication and control systems. The main objective of smart grid is to decrease energy waste and improve the quality and reliability that greatly relies on utilization of measuring and communication technologies. Real-time monitoring, control, and integration of distributed energy sources in smart grid are possible due to communication technologies. Wired and wireless communication networks, such as cellular networks, Wi-Fi, and Ethernet, are examples of these technologies. In contrast, measurement technologies include sensors, meters, and monitoring systems that are used to monitor the smart grid's operation, including the flow of power and the condition of the equipment.

Together, communication and measurement technologies enable the smart grid in making intelligent decisions regarding electricity generation, transmission, and distribution and keeping the system performance optimized. In addition to this, customers can also be provided with more control over their energy consumption as well as enable them to take part in demand response programs.

7.2 SMART GRID COMMUNICATION TECHNOLOGY

Communication technology can be referred to as tools or techniques to transmit information between distant locations. In the scenario of smart grid, demand of transmitting tele-control data, voice and data communication, monitoring signals, and remote surveillance makes the communication system a crucial component.

DOI: 10.1201/9781032665399-7

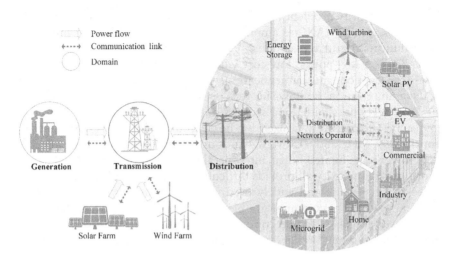

Figure 7.1 Structural framework of smart grid system.

However, wired and wireless communication technologies are available for deployment in the smart grid, but each has its own limitations, such as limited bandwidth, distance, data loss, or success in underground installations. Hence, the choice of technology is an important task which also depends on cost, reliability, security, interoperability, geographic location, and availability.

7.2.1 Wired Communication Technologies

The two popular types of wireline communication are Power Line Communication (PLC) and Optical Fiber (OF). These are preferred due to their good reliability and minimal interference. PLC is mainly utilized for grid monitoring and control because it permits two-way communication over existing power lines and also cost-effective. OF is widely implemented and perfect for smart grid applications due to its fast speed and low latency. Optical fiber ground wire (OPGW) is a recent development and serves the two purposes of power transmission and communication. Although it is reliable and cost-effective, installation of OPGW can be expensive.

7.2.2 Wireless Communication Technologies

Due to its simplicity of implementation and low installation cost, wireless communication is a preferred alternative for smart grid. However, it has some disadvantages, including attenuation, interference, a restricted range, and major security problems. ZigBee, Wi-Fi, Cellular/Mobile Networks (4G and LTE), and WiMAX are among the wireless communication protocols utilized in smart grid applications.

ZigBee is a low-power, low-cost wireless communication protocol with robust encryption and authentication, making it suited for secure smart grid communication. It allows for the creation of low-cost, low-power wireless mesh networks with good security and energy efficiency. The 2.4 GHz frequency is extensively utilized for home automation and smart lighting, but the 868 MHz and 915 MHz bands are mostly used in Europe and the US. However, its limited range, interoperability constraints, restricted bandwidth, and complexity all provide difficulties for smart grid applications.

Wi-Fi is a mature and widely used wireless technology that uses radio frequency waves to communicate between devices inside a LAN/HAN. It is preferred for HAN architecture and is based on the IEEE 802.11 standard. It has a limited range, however, and cannot handle NAN or WAN applications.

Cellular/Mobile Networks (4G and LTE) are commonly employed in smart grid communication due to their reliable infrastructure and ability to provide economical and secure WAN services. Fourth-generation (4G) and LTE technologies deliver faster data speeds in NAN and WAN networks, making them perfect for implementing SG applications quickly. However, they have inherent limitations, such as network congestion during crises and may not guarantee service under abnormal situations.

WiMAX (IEEE 802.16) is a wireless communication technology that enables high-speed, reliable, and secure data transmission in smart grid applications. Because of its high bandwidth, scalability, and security, it can transfer data across long distances with high throughput and low latency, making it perfect for smart grid applications. It provides real-time monitoring of power consumption, optimization of power utilization, and increased grid efficiency and reliability.

7.3 SMART GRID COMMUNICATION NETWORK INFRASTRUCTURE

Communication networks are the underlying infrastructure that enables modern communication technologies. These networks, which can be either wired or wireless, facilitate the exchange of information across long distances between devices. In the context of a smart grid, communication networks play a critical role in connecting different components and enabling real-time data exchange. This is particularly important for the sensing and management of data from a vast array of sensors and meters used to detect the grid's status and control its operations.

The communication network architecture is composed of several layers that work in unison to facilitate the seamless transfer of data between different components. These layers are categorized based on their geographical coverage and communication characteristics.

7.3.1 Classification of Network Architecture Layers Based on Communication Characteristics

The communication network architecture layers can be classified based on communication characteristics, as shown in Figure 7.2. It includes component layer, communication layer, information layer, function layer, and business layer [1].

The component layer forms the foundation of the smart grid, consisting of the hardware and software components that enable the grid to operate. The communication layer connects the different components of the grid and can be divided into the physical layer, network layer, and application layer. The information layer collects, stores, and analyzes data from various sources, facilitating accurate and timely data exchange between the grid components.

The function layer manages and controls the grid infrastructure, including sensing, communication, automation, and control systems, linking the physical layer and the business layer. Finally, the business layer enables the delivery of energy services to customers and utilities, incorporating economic and regulatory aspects of the grid.

7.3.2 Classification of Network Architecture Layers Based on Geographical Coverage

The smart grid communication system connects a large number of electrical devices and manages complicated device communications. It should be

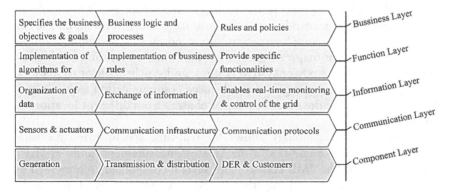

Figure 7.2 Classification of communication network layers based on communication characteristics.

designed using a hierarchical architecture approach with interconnected individual subnetworks that take responsibility for separate geographical regions. The communication network architecture layers can be classified based on geographical coverage, including LAN (Local Area Network), HAN (Home Area Network), NAN (Neighbourhood Area Network), MAN (Metropolitan Area Network), WAN (Wide Area Network), and FAN (Field Area Network). Each network has different characteristics and advantages for smart grid applications. LAN is ideal for the efficient collection and dissemination of data from multiple sources confined in a building or small geographical area. HAN is specifically designed for home automation, allowing for the control of smart devices and energy management. NAN is used to connect devices within a larger geographic area than LAN and HAN, and it enables the transfer of data from multiple locations to a central control center, allowing for better energy utilization and management.

MAN connects multiple LANs and/or NANs in a metropolitan area and provides an efficient way to share digital resources between multiple connected networks. FAN is a communications network used in the smart grid for collecting data from field devices and distributing commands to those devices. It typically consists of a variety of sensors and controllers which collect data from the field and pass it on to the data center. WAN spans a large geographical area and is used for long-distance communication between different parts of the smart grid. Each network may be vulnerable to cyberattacks and has different management and maintenance requirements.

7.4 SMART GRID MEASUREMENT TECHNOLOGIES

7.4.1 Synchrophasor Technology

The modern power system is a complex network that is made up of five parts—generation, transmission, sub-transmission, distribution, and loads. Due to the system's complexity, continuous monitoring and protection are necessary to prevent major contingencies. Real-time monitoring has become crucial in preventing power system failures, and synchrophasor technology, made possible by a smart grid and advanced communication technology, is used to synchronize the measurement of phasors from different locations in the power system.

Synchrophasor technology allows for real-time synchronized measurement of electrical quantities using phasor measurement units (PMUs). Figure 7.3 shows the PMU consisting of several components represented by different blocks that work together to measure, process, and transmit the phasor data. Voltage and current sensors in the PMU carry out the measurement of voltage and current signals in the power grid. The current and

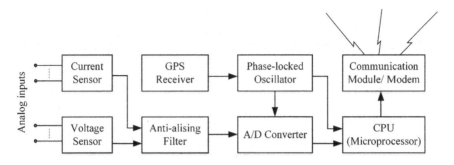

Figure 7.3 Block diagram of typical PMU.

voltage sensors convert the three-phase current and voltage to the appropriate level for Analog-to-Digital Converter (ADC). Before the ADC, they also process through anti-aliasing filter that eliminates the harmonics and interferences. The ADC is considered as a critical component of the PMU because it enables the processing of signals by the Digital Signal Processor (DSP). In addition, the PMU also includes a GPS receiver to provide a 1 pulse per second (PPS) output signal, which is used to synchronize with Universal Time (UT). The DSP performs signal processing on the digital signals to obtain phasor measurements of the voltage and current signals. A mathematical algorithm estimates the voltage and current phasors based on the processed digital signals. The phasor measurements are time-stamped with universal time synchronized by GPS. Communication interface is the final component of the PMU, which is used to transmit the measured phasors to control center for further analysis and control.

Real-time monitoring, assessment, and control applications such as state estimation [2], control of frequency fluctuation [3], torque angle control of rotor [4] etc. requires synchrophasor measurements from various locations of grid network. Typically, data is measured by PMUs at local substations in power system and sent to the phasor data concentrator (PDC), located in a control center, through a communication network. Figure 7.4 shows the synchrophasor measurement of voltage or current phasor using PMU at two distant locations, A and B.

At location A, the PMU measures the voltage or current phasor at a specific time and sends it to the PDC (phasor data concentrator) or control center. The time stamping is a critical aspect of synchrophasor measurement, as it ensures that the data from multiple PMUs can be synchronized and compared accurately. The time stamping is typically done using GPS. GPS generates a synchronized reference time signal to all PMUs in the network

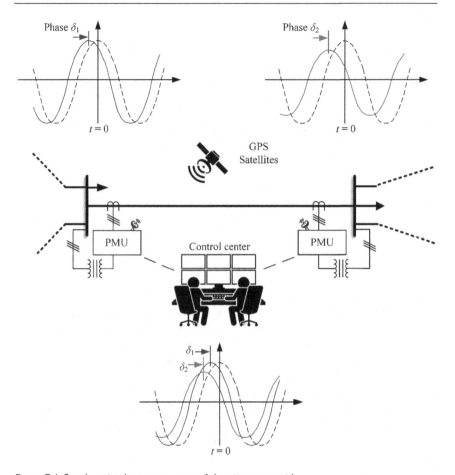

Figure 7.4 Synchronized measurement of data in smart grid.

for monitoring and control of power systems. The voltage or current phasor measurements are then time-stamped with the help of a synchronized reference time signal generated by a GPS clock.

The PMU at location B also simultaneously measures the voltage or current phasor and sends it with a time stamp to the PDC or control center. The PDC or control center receives the PMU data from both locations and the corresponding time stamps. Hence, based on the corresponding time stamps, the PDC or control center can align the voltage or current phasor measurement data from both or multiple locations. This allows for detecting any phase angle differences or frequency deviations between the two locations. If any discrepancies are detected, the PDC or control center can take corrective actions to maintain the system stability and prevent power outages. Overall, synchrophasor measurements using PMUs at distant locations are critical for monitoring and maintaining the stability of power systems. By providing accurate and synchronized phasor data, PMUs and PDCs enable grid operators to detect and respond to any deviations in system performance, thereby ensuring reliable and efficient power delivery to consumers.

7.4.2 Wide Area Measurement System (WAMS)

WAMS uses synchrophasor technology to provide synchronized measurements of the power system by deploying multiple PMUs at various locations to cover a vast geographical area [5], as shown in Figure 7.5. It allows for a better analysis of system behavior and performance. The WAMS utilizes the synchrophasor technology to monitor and control the power system. It transmits the measurements to the PDC for further analysis and control

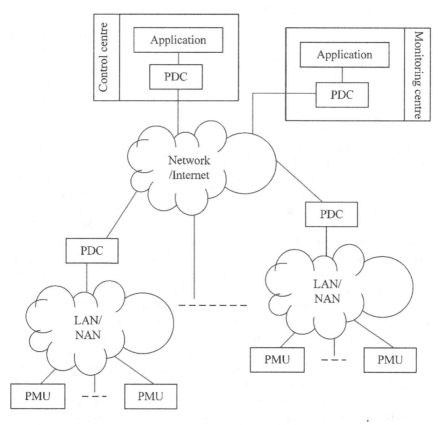

Figure 7.5 WAMS for monitoring and control of smart grid.

actions. The measurements' high sampling rate and synchronization enable the detection and analysis of system disturbances and oscillations that could cause instability or blackouts. The feature of time stamping is a crucial concept and actually provides a common time reference for all measurements taken across the system. This enables identification of any time delays or phase shifts that could impact the stability of the power system.

The PDC serves as the central hub for collecting and analyzing the synchrophasor measurements from the PMUs. The PDC processes the data in real time, identifying any system abnormalities or disturbances, and sends control signals to the system operator to take appropriate corrective actions. The use of synchrophasor measurement technology with PMUs and a WAMS enables the power system to operate more efficiently, with greater stability and reliability, ultimately improving the overall performance and resilience of the system.

7.4.3 Smart Metering System

The recent developments in smart grid technology have resulted in increased research and evolution of smart metering systems that improved the power network infrastructure and communication. This progress is driven by latest progresses in information and communication technologies (ICTs), measurement requirements, and sensor technologies. Communication and measurement requirements are essential in smart grid improvements and power network advancements. Smart metering systems consist of Automated Meter Reading (AMR), Advanced Metering Infrastructure (AMI), and Automatic Meter Management (AMM) applications [6].

Smart meters offer numerous benefits and management opportunities for both utilities and customers. Watt-hour meters, which are the basis of smart meters, rely on voltage and current measurements via sensor networks. A block diagram of a single-phase smart meter is presented in Figure 7.6. The first section of a smart meter is the grid interface, which houses the current and voltage sensors. These sensors measure the current and voltage magnitudes and convert them into conditioned signals. Signal conditioning devices then generate output signals that are compatible with the ADC port of any microprocessor. Most modern smart meters are equipped with phase and frequency detection capabilities. The microprocessor acquires the conditioned signal/data through its ADC ports and stores the processed data in an internal database. The microprocessor also manages communication interfaces through its serial and parallel communication interfaces to transmit data/signal to remote monitoring and operation centers. This allows for accurate measurement and real-time monitoring of energy consumption. Smart meter data is typically transmitted via various wireless networks. These real-time data enable utilities to monitor usage and detect anomalies, leading to

Local load side

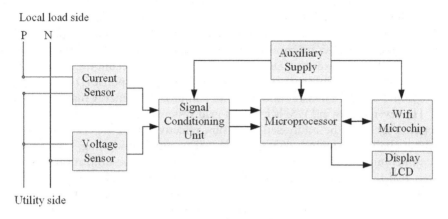

Utility side

Figure 7.6 Block diagram of a typical smart meter.

increased efficiency and corrective measures. Two-way communication and power transmission allow for remote monitoring, measurement, control, and decision-making. For this purpose, interval measurements are required once every hour or once every 15 minutes, or even at a rate of once every five minutes, depending on the application of the data. In addition to wireless communication capabilities, smart meter microprocessors are typically equipped with infrared, RFID communication interfaces, Ethernet, CAN bus, RS232, and RS485. As a result, they can be integrated into HAN, NAN, and WAN networks with ease.

7.4.4 Wireless Sensor Network

A wireless sensor network (WSN) is a collection of small wireless devices known as nodes, which are equipped with sensors, communication capabilities, and processing capabilities. WSNs are commonly utilized in smart grid systems to gather energy consumption data from remote locations, such as buildings and electrical grids. The collected data can enhance operational efficiency, reduce energy consumption, and provide real-time performance data on renewable energy sources like solar and wind power. Various protocols are available for WSNs in smart grid applications, including IEC 61850, Zigbee, Wi-Fi, and Bluetooth, among others. These protocols enable WSNs to communicate with one another, exchange information, and manage electricity and other energy consumption in the smart grid.

WSN technology offers several benefits for smart grid systems, including its ability to operate reliably in harsh environments, thanks to its rugged and durable design, weatherproof casings, long battery life, and self-repair capabilities. Additionally, WSNs are highly adaptable and can be customized to meet specific energy management needs, allowing energy providers to optimize energy consumption and production based on real-time conditions. WSNs can also integrate with other smart grid technologies, such as advanced metering infrastructure (AMI) and demand response (DR) systems, providing a comprehensive and integrated approach to energy management.

However, deploying WSNs in smart grid systems can present several challenges that must be addressed to ensure effective and efficient operation. These challenges include heterogeneity, distributed processing, low bandwidth communication, large-scale coordination, effective utilization of sensors, real-time computation, and reliability and latency requirements. Careful consideration of device characteristics and network architecture is crucial to achieve seamless interoperability. Decentralized algorithms are necessary to manage data processing on different nodes in the WSN. Efficient communication protocols and network architecture are required to ensure data is transferred reliably and efficiently, despite low bandwidth communication. Large-scale coordination of sensors is necessary to produce the required results, and effective utilization of sensors requires a thoughtful deployment strategy. Real-time computation requires efficient algorithms and processing capabilities that can handle the large amounts of data generated and processed quickly. Lastly, robust network architecture and communication protocols are necessary to ensure that data is transferred reliably and efficiently to meet reliability and latency requirements.

7.4.5 Internet of Things

Readers who are new to the world of Wireless Sensor Networks (WSNs) and the Internet of Things (IoT) may have difficulty understanding the differences between the two technologies when applied in smart grid applications [7]. WSNs are networks of interconnected devices that use sensors to monitor environmental or physical conditions, while IoT is a broader concept that encompasses interconnecting various devices beyond sensors via the internet. IoT devices are usually more powerful than WSN devices and can communicate with each other and cloud services, allowing for more complex functionality, such as actuators that control physical systems based on data inputs. In smart grid applications, WSNs are often used for monitoring and data collection, while IoT devices can be utilized for control and energy system optimization. Various communication protocols can be used to enable IoT-based communication in the smart grid, such as MQTT (Message Queuing Telemetry Transport), CoAP (Constrained Application Protocol), AMQP (Advanced Message Queuing Protocol), igBee, and LoRaWAN. These protocols offer a range of solutions for IoT-based smart grid communication, depending on the specific requirements of the application. By selecting the appropriate protocol, IoT-based smart grid can be designed to operate efficiently and reliably, enabling effective communication between devices and systems.

7.5 OPTIMAL INTEGRATION OF RENEWABLE GENERATIONS, STORAGES, AND EVS IN SMART GRID

The structural framework of smart grid, as shown in Figure 7.1, shows that the installation of distributed energy sources, especially renewable energy (RE) based, ESSs, and EVs are encouraged in smart grid, unlike the traditional grid, to alleviate the overreliance on scarce fossil fuel reserve and meeting the growing energy demand due to urbanization and massive population growth. EVs are also paving their way in the automobile sectors by replacing the traditional combustion engines with batteries. Both RE and EV reduce the carbon footprint of the globe but also bring severe economic and technical challenges in smart grid like the following:

1. It is strenuous to forecast the exact fluctuation of RE generation and EV charging power. Therefore, higher level of integration leads to significant frequency and voltage transients.
2. It is difficult to determine the optimal capacity and location of renewable energy sources and EV charging stations in a network.

To address these issues, new research are emerging for optimally planning the power system architectures. Compared with traditional power grids, smart grids allow a more optimal dispatch strategy to outperform the conventional power system management methods [8].

7.5.1 Optimal Planning Framework

The term optimal planning signifies the process to find out the most beneficial scheme from all equipment specifications (like capacity, quantity, location etc.) and design parameters by utilizing any optimization tool while considering all the operating constraints of the network resources, environmental concerns, and security issues related to the network. An optimally planned power system architecture can provide maximum support in all the three working modes, that is, blue sky (the grid is in normalcy), gray sky (the grid is experiencing voltage and frequency instabilities or fluctuations), and black sky (one or more outage conditions). The overall time frame for different power system investigations is depicted in Figure 7.7. In this section, we will mainly focus on the long-term planning strategies developed for installation of RE resources, ESSs, and EV charging stations. This planning theme primarily aims to determine the most economic and safe capacities and location of the earlier-mentioned resources for the network. Optimal planning is a multi-time period and multidimensional task which covers all aspects related to source, network, storage, and loads. Long-term forecast of spatial and temporal variations of renewable power generations, load demands, and assessment of available space for equipment installation are the prior needs of optimal planning. Generally, the optimization model of power system planning includes both continuous (like capacity) and integer (like bus location) variable sets $x_{n,t}^{C}$ and $x_{n,t}^{D}$ respectively.

$$\text{minimize} \sum_{n \in N} \sum_{t \in T} O\left(x_{n,t}^{C}, x_{n,t}^{D}\right) \tag{7.1}$$

$$\text{Subject to, } LB_{n,t}^{C} \leq x_{n,t}^{C} \leq UB_{n,t}^{C}, LB_{n,t}^{D} \leq x_{n,t}^{D} \leq UB_{n,t}^{D}, \forall n \in N \tag{7.2}$$

$$EOC\left(x_{n,t}^{C}, x_{n,t}^{D}\right) \leq 0, \forall t \in T \tag{7.3}$$

$$PFE\left(x_{n,t}^{C}, x_{n,t}^{D}\right) = 0, \forall t \in T \tag{7.4}$$

$$PFI\left(x_{n,t}^{C}, x_{n,t}^{D}\right) \leq 0, \forall t \in T \tag{7.5}$$

Here objective function $O\left(x_{n,t}^{C}, x_{n,t}^{D}\right)$ represents the total monetary cost required for successful installation of total 'N' number of equipment. This cost includes capital investment for purchasing the equipment, installation cost, maintenance cost, and operational cost for the entire planning period, which is subdivided into T number of equal time intervals. Constraint (7.2) reflects the boundary values for the decision variables like maximum capacity to be installed, service life, maximum possible investment amount, etc. The operational constraints of the equipment, that is, $EOC\left(x_{n,t}^{C}, x_{n,t}^{D}\right)$, are included in 7.3, like limits on total number of charging/discharging cycles per day for ESSs, maximum number of PV panels, and wind farms hosting capacity of the network, etc. The set of power flow equality conditions, $PFE\left(x_{n,t}^{C}, x_{n,t}^{D}\right)$, like active and reactive power balance equations, are accumulated as constraint (7.4). Finally, $PFI\left(x_{n,t}^{C}, x_{n,t}^{D}\right)$ signifies the inequality security concerns like voltage boundary limits, line flow limits, etc.

i. **Overview on optimized integration of renewable energy sources, ESSs, and EVs:**

The study regarding optimized integration of RE sources, ESSs, and EVs includes choosing technology, capacity estimation, and proper location identification considering four major aspects, viz. input data, objective function, design constraints, and effective optimization algorithm for solution.

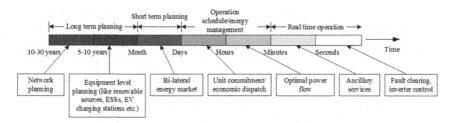

Figure 7.7 Time frame for different power system investigations.

Input data: Majorly, three types of input data are needed for optimal planning of solar system, wind system, ESSs, and EV charging stations, viz. financial data, technical data, and periodic data. Financial data are highly dependent on the country for which the planning process is conducted. It includes installation cost, maintenance cost, annual interest/discount rate on the total investment, purchase cost, and annual escalation/inflation rate. In addition to that, presently, governments of different countries are declaring incentives for installing renewable energy resources, behind-the-meter storage units, and driving EVs. Technical data involves the capacity and details of the network where the equipment will be installed, specifications of the different technologies (like efficiency, life span etc.) corresponding to the PV panels, wind generators, ESSs, and EV chargers. The network data is important for the power system planners as that will tell whether the existing network is capable of holding the new equipment and running in a secure manner or not. Network data includes network strength, capacity of the existing energy sources, maximum energy demand, capacity of the power lines, overall network losses, candidate locations where the new resource can be installed, and the specification of the new equipment, etc. Third most important data is the periodic data corresponding to climate (viz. temperature, wind speed, rainfall, etc.), solar irradiation, daily and seasonal variation of energy demand for the entire planning period are required. A certain planning framework's operating expenses and profitability are both heavily impacted by the power pricing programmes in a given area. Presently, time of use and real-time price are mostly followed to develop planning frameworks. Apart from these three major data types, geographic data (like elevation, altitudes, presence of river or any water body) for building PSH facilities, and the details regarding EV traffic along the routes, EV owner density at a particular location, and behavior of the EV owners (like driving time, pattern) are also necessary for installing charging stations.

Objective function: The most crucial parameter in an optimal planning portfolio is the objective function. The objective functions can either be financial or technical or social types. Financial objective functions aim either to minimize total capital investment, or to maximize the annual profit, or to minimize the payback period, that is, the total time period required to recover the amount of capital investment. Technical objective functions primarily target to operate the power system network (both transmission and distribution) in safe and reliable manners. These objectives include Loss minimization, minimization of total bus voltage deviation, maximization of renewable energy usage or minimization of renewable energy curtailment, maximizing the life of the installed equipment, reducing contingency events, reduction in line congestion, maximum utilization of the capacity of the lines, etc. Social objectives aim to provide environmental or customer benefits, viz. maximization of customer satisfaction (or reliability maximization) or minimization of load curtailment and emission reduction.

Depending upon the number of objectives chosen for planning, the problem can be of single-objective (SO) or multi-objective (MO) types. SO planning problems aim to optimize any one particular consideration mentioned earlier, whereas in MO, several contradictory objectives are considered simultaneously. In case of MO optimal planning problem non-dominated solutions in Pareto fronts are obtained, and the solutions depend on the individual weights assigned to each objective.

Design constraints: Design constraints are defined as some conditions imposed on the planning framework which must be satisfied for secure, efficient, and reliable operation of the existing resources, the network itself, and the newly introduced equipment. The most crucial constraints are active and reactive power balance constraints which equals total generation with the total demand. Other specific constraints are financial constraints, social and geographical constraints, PV and wind generation constraints, ESS and EV constraints, and network constraints.

Effective solution algorithms: The overall planning problem takes form of a mixed integer non-convex programming. It is impossible to consider all the earlier-mentioned aspects in a single optimization problem, so depending upon the planning concerns, the solution algorithm is adopted in the exiting literatures. These solution algorithms are based on either classical optimization technique like mixed integer linear programming, mixed integer quadratic programming etc., or heuristic search techniques (genetic algorithm, particle swarm optimization, Tabu Search etc.). Otherwise, the original non-convex problems are solved by using any paid solver present in specific software (GAMS, HOMER, etc.).

7.6 REAL-TIME PRICE (RTP) ALGORITHMS

In wholesale energy market, electricity price varies substantially depending upon the market clearing scenarios. This price fluctuation happens because of changing power grid state, dynamic load demand, and fluctuation in fuel price. To cope with volatile market clearing energy price, utilities are now incorporating real-time pricing structure for their consumers. In case of RTP, the retail electricity cost varies dynamically at each time step. This variation may be hourly or half hourly or quarterly depending upon the energy market clearing time. This is the most ideal pricing scheme for smart grid to reflect the time varying behaviour of the energy consumption pattern and to check the response of the consumers against electricity price. RTP electricity price is set to comparatively higher values when the power system is under stressed condition (or during higher energy demand hours) and lower values during off-peak hours. Therefore, RTP encourages the consumers to lower their consumption during peak hours in order to relieve stress on the grid. The RTP values are announced by the utilities to its customers generally one day or at least one hour ahead so customers can take possible actions to leverage maximum benefits like electricity bill savings, peak load curtailment, maximum utilization of renewable energies, network efficiency enhancement, etc.

7.6.1 Scopes of Different RTP Algorithms

At present, real-time prices are adopted widely to design different power grid management algorithms. Peak load reduction and energy cost minimization are the immediate benefits of such algorithms. However, the range of the obtained advantages is highly influenced by the consumer type, climate conditions, range of the price variation, etc. Though due to price volatility RTP structures may not be proved potential for short-term goals, those are proven to provide long-term electricity bill savings to the customers [9]. Generally, RTPs are the retail energy price; hence, they are used by the DNOs or the end consumers. The major application of RTP is to design optimal power flow (OPF) algorithms, and then the basic OPF portfolio is modified into some special application scopes (like volt-VAR optimization (VVO), peer-to-peer (P2P) energy transaction, transmission system operator and distribution system operator (TSO-DSO) interaction, demand side management (DSM), etc.).

i. **Optimal power flow:** Optimal power flow, abbreviated as OPF, algorithms aim to determine the best and most stable operating scenarios for the network resources for meeting the energy demand by minimizing a particular objective function under safe network conditions. OPF algorithms incorporating RTP take cost minimization as the objective function. Therefore, the solutions of any OPF algorithm have the highest impact on the operation of any power system network and ensures lowest cost, voltage stability, least probability for occurring any contingency events, reliable operation, and low carbon emission.

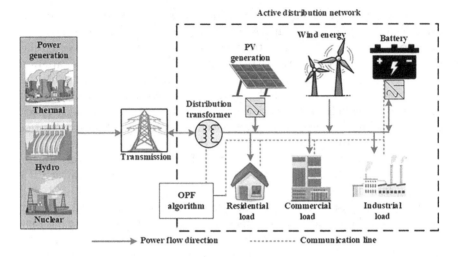

Figure 7.8 Framework of an active distribution network.

Traditionally, due to the passive nature of the distribution networks, the OPF analysis was just limited to consuming power from main grid for catering the energy demand considering only the voltage and line power flow limits. However, due to penetration of distributed energy resources, the conventional passive distribution networks are transforming into active ones. Therefore, the OPF formulation has been changed significantly to operate these local power resources optimally to achieve the lowest-cost situation. The framework of typical active distribution network is shown in Figure 7.8. The local PV generation, wind generation, and battery help to meet the total power demand along with the power purchased from the upper grid. The OPF algorithm controls the dispatch of the battery and power consumed from the upper grid depending upon the values of the real-time energy price. At peak price, it is supposed to send discharge command to the battery, and at off-peak price hours, the charging commands are conveyed. A well-maintained communication infrastructure is needed for data transfer between the OPF algorithm and the controllable resources in the network. Therefore, keeping the energy cost minimization as the objective function, the multi-time period OPF is as follows.

$$\text{Minimize } f(\mathbf{X}, \mathbf{Y}, \mathbf{Z}) = \sum_{t \in T} \left[u_t c_{t,p} P_{t,p} - (1 - u_t) c_{t,s} P_{t,s} \right] \Delta t \qquad (7.6)$$

$$\text{Subject to } g(\mathbf{X}, \mathbf{Y}, \mathbf{Z}) = 0, \forall t \qquad (7.7)$$

$$h(\mathbf{X}, \mathbf{Y}, \mathbf{Z}) \le 0, \forall t \qquad (7.8)$$

$$V_{\min} \le V_{n,t} \le V_{\max}, -\frac{\pi}{2} \le \phi_{n,t} \le \frac{\pi}{2} \qquad (7.9)$$

$$S_{t,\text{line}} \leq S_{\max} \tag{7.10}$$

Where, X, Y, and Z are the set of controllable variables, dependent uncontrollable variables and input parameters. T is the total number of time period. $P_{t,p}$ denotes amount of power purchased from the upper grid at RTP $c_{t,p}$. $P_{t,s}$ is the amount of surplus renewable generation sold back to the grid at selling price $c_{t,s}$. Obviously, $c_{t,s} < c_{t,p}$. u_t is a binary variable which is used to avoid simultaneous power purchase and sell (if $u_t = 1$ then purchase and if $u_t = 0$ then sell). Here,

X = active power purchase (sell) from (to) the upper grid, reactive power $(Q_{t,p})$ drawn from the upper grid, binary status of the power purchase/sell, active $(P_{t,b}$, if $P_{t,b} > 0$ then charging, if $P_{t,b} < 0$ then discharging) and reactive power $(Q_{t,b})$ dispatch from the battery (reactive power support can be obtained from the battery inverter), reactive power support from the solar inverters $(Q_{t,pv})$ and wind generators $(Q_{t,w})$.

Y = bus voltage magnitudes $(V_{n,t}, \forall n \in N)$ and angles $(\phi_{n,t}, \forall n \in N)$, power flow through the distribution lines $(S_{t,\text{line}})$. N is the total number of buses/nodes in the distribution network.

Z = forecasted solar power generation $(P_{t,pv})$, wind energy $(P_{t,w})$, cumulative, active, and reactive power demand $(P_{t,L}, Q_{t,L})$, and the RTP values received from the upper grid.

Now $g(X,Y,Z)$ represents the power flow equality constraints corresponding to active and reactive power balances. Inequality constraints $h(X,Y,Z)$ are minimum/maximum limits for battery active and reactive power dispatch, battery energy levels, reactive power support from solar inverters, and wind generators. Inequalities (7.9 and 7.10) represent the bus voltage and line flow limits. Now the active and reactive power balance equations are

$$u_t P_{t,p} + P_{t,pv} + P_{t,w} - (1-u_t)P_{t,s} - P_{t,b} - P_{t,L} = \sum_{m \in M} P_{mn,t} \tag{7.11}$$

$$Q_{t,p} + Q_{t,pv} + Q_{t,w} + Q_{t,b} - Q_{t,L} = \sum_{m \in M} Q_{mn,t} \tag{7.12}$$

In 7.11 and 7.12, M denotes the set of neighboring buses of the bus 'n', and $P_{mn,t}, Q_{mn,t}$ are the active and reactive power flow between bus n and its neighbors. Non-convex AC power flow equations are written as follows (G and B represent line conductance and susceptance values respectively).

$$P_{mn,t} = G_{mn}V_{m,t}^2 - G_{mn}V_{n,t}V_{m,t}\cos\left(\phi_{m,t} - \phi_{n,t}\right) - B_{mn}V_{n,t}V_{m,t}\sin\left(\phi_{m,t} - \phi_{n,t}\right) \tag{7.13}$$

$$Q_{mn,t} = -B_{mn}V_{m,t}^2 + B_{mn}V_{n,t}V_{m,t}\cos\left(\phi_{m,t} - \phi_{n,t}\right) - G_{mn}V_{n,t}V_{m,t}\sin\left(\phi_{m,t} - \phi_{n,t}\right) \tag{7.14}$$

Generally, the obtained solution from any OPF problem can be classified into two broad categories, viz. deterministic and stochastic/probabilistic solutions. OPF solutions which are obtained by considering the forecasted values as 100% accurate data are known as deterministic solutions. In contrast with the deterministic OPF, stochastic OPF determines the optimal solutions by considering the uncertainties, and those uncertainties are modelled as probabilistic distribution functions. Generally, uncertainties associated with solar energy generation, wind energy generation, and load variation are approximated as Beta, Weibull, and Normal distribution. Multiple discrete scenarios are generated from these continuous probability distributions using different scenario generation techniques like Monte Carlo Simulation, point estimations, etc. After generating the scenarios, stochastic OPF is solved for each scenario, and the optimal solutions are derived as the expected value.

ii. **Special application of RTP:** OPF with RTP has wide range of applications in smart grid era. Few are discussed as follows.

Volt-VAR Optimization: Achieving most energy efficient operation is one of the primary aims of any DNO. This can be attained by minimizing the network loss or indirectly the distribution line currents. Now to reduce line currents, the load demand needs to be decreased. However, load curtailment causes large dissatisfaction among the consumers. So, utilities lower the bus voltage magnitudes to reduce the power consumption of voltage dependent loads. This process is named as conservation voltage reduction (CVR). However, to keep the voltage magnitudes within the safe boundary limits (i.e. 0.95 pu to 1.05 pu), the voltage regulators (VRs) are operated. VR comprises of multiple tap positions to increase and decrease bus voltage magnitudes from its nominal values. Network loss can also be reduced by decreasing the reactive power flow in the lines. So, capacitor banks (CBs) are placed at the load points to supply reactive power demand locally. As, both voltage magnitudes and reactive power or VAR are optimally controlled in this, hence it is named as volt-VAR optimization (VVO). Schematic of a VVO operation is portrayed in Figure 7.9.

Peer-to-Peer Energy Transaction: Penetration of local energy generation is changing the energy production and consumption scenarios rapidly and making the passive energy consumers to energy prosumers. Net metering service deployed in different countries is promoting this idea by allowing the consumers to sell their surplus amount of energy to the main grid [10]. The main difference between consumer and prosumer is that consumers only consume energy but the prosumers do both energy production and consumption. Therefore, the prosumer can experience both

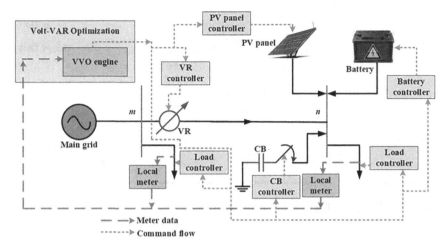

Figure 7.9 Volt-VAR optimization framework

energy surplus and deficit conditions. During energy surplus condition the prosumer either can store that much energy in the battery or can sell it to the upper grid or to its neighboring consumers. Similarly, a consumer can buy energy either from the upper grid or from its neighbors under energy-deficit conditions. This direct energy transaction between one prosumer and a consumer is known as peer to peer (P2P) energy transaction. A typical model for P2P energy transaction is shown in Figure 7.10. The entire negotiation process is controlled by an energy sharing aggregator. P2P algorithm is mostly followed in low voltage power systems where consumers are directly involved in energy selling. This mutual cooperation among different communities lowers the burden on the main grid and by P2P transactions local communities try to achieve net zero energy scenario.

TSO-DSO Interaction: The large penetration of distributed energy resources into distribution networks in smart grid era has made the distribution networks capable of selling energy to the transmission grids. Therefore, a chance of reverse power flow, over voltage, and transmission line congestion may occur. Therefore, active coordination between the transmission system operator (TSO) and distribution system operator (DSO) needs to be established to ensure the proper integration of the distributed energy resources (DERs). Mainly, TSO-DSO integration is modelled in an open energy market environment to ensure the optimal and effective operation of the DERs in a distribution network by catering all the security and contingency constraints imposed by TSO.

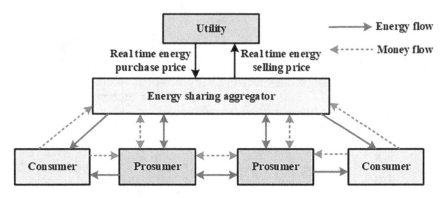

Figure 7.10 Energy trading model in P2P transaction

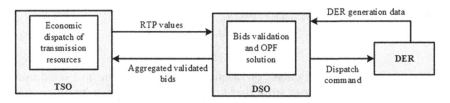

Figure 7.11 TSO-DSO interaction model.

In this open market model, DSOs submit their energy bid at each time step to the TSO, and in response to that, TSO determines the time-varying dynamic real-time energy price for the DSO. A typical TSO-DSO interaction model is depicted in Figure 7.11. Overall, interaction model is segregated into three layers, where at the lower layer, DERs submit their generation data to the DSO. Then DSO solves its local OPF, keeping profit maximization as the objective, and determines the aggregated energy bidding. DSO submits the bidding value to the TSO. After that, TSO solves the economic dispatch problem with all the transmission network resources and determines the RTP values, which are conveyed back to the DSO. Considering the RTP values, DSO revises its bidding and sends the modified bidding to TSO. This process continues till both TSO and DSO reach the point where they cannot update their decisions anymore. Then DSO sends dispatch command to the DERs. In the solution process, TSO solves a DC OPF, while the DSO solves the previously described AC OPF with the RTP values.

Demand Side Management: The volatility in renewable power generation causes power imbalance issues, and that calls for excess power

consumption from the conventional fossil fuel–based generations. However, another way of nullifying this power imbalance is to modify the load pattern. Demand side management (DSM) is the process of modifying the energy utilization pattern of the consumers in order to minimize the energy usage during peak hours and to maximize the utilization of the renewable energies. Generally, peak load demand occurs at evening hours (6:00 PM to 9:00 PM), whereas maximum solar and wind energy generations happen during afternoon (11:00 AM to 3:00 PM) and late night (11:00 PM to 3:00 AM) hours. Therefore, maximum utilization of renewable energy can only be possible if some amount of loads is shifted from the evening hours to the maximum renewable generation hours. Again, at peak load hours, the RTP values are comparatively higher than the off-peak hours, therefore load reduction during peak hours and catering that amount of load with free renewable generated power provides the lowest possible electricity bill to the consumers. DSM makes it possible by six different strategies, viz. peak curtailment, valley filling, load shifting, strategic conservation, strategic load growth, and flexible load. DSM strategies mainly targets the flexible loads, whose operation can be delayed and will not cause large dissatisfaction to the user, and schedule them according to the time-varying dynamic energy price values. DSM can be of two types, viz. direct load control (DLC) and mutual load management (MLM). In the case of DLC, consumers concede the load scheduling decisions to the utility; whereas in the case of MLM, the utility sends the price signal to the consumers and motivates them to alter the energy consumption.

7.6.2 Difficulties to Implement RTP Algorithms

Despite of having many advantages of RTP schemes, it is still not preferable by most of the utilities and consumers across the globe due to the following issues:

1. The RTP implementation needs well-constructed communication infrastructure between utility and its consumers to send the RTP signals. Therefore, huge capital investment is required along with continuous maintenance.
2. Smart metering services are highly needed for RTP deployment. Any malfunctioning of the smart meter or the communication channels cause erroneous RTP calculation and huge monetary loss to both the parties.
3. Maximum gain from RTP can only be obtained if the consumers must be equipped with smart appliances and automated control system at their premise. However, smart appliances are very costly and therefore not affordable for low-income consumers.

4. The lack of awareness among the customers regarding the details of RTP programs and its benefits impede them to participate in such programs.

7.7 DYNAMIC ENERGY MANAGEMENT SYSTEM (DEMS)

In smart grid, an uncertain or volatile RE generation source will try to meet demand. Under this scenario, the generation and consumption can only be balanced efficiently by developing smart energy management frameworks. The optimal decisions of these strategies keep on changing depending upon the time-varying operating scenarios; hence, those are called dynamic energy management systems. DEMS aims to balance the supply demand portfolios in the most economical way by maintaining the network safety, reliability, and customer satisfaction constraints. As per Department of Energy (DOE), USA, in smart grid era, an efficient and advanced EMS should have the capability to do load management, to regulate active and reactive power demand of voltage-dependent loads by changing the bus voltage magnitude (by employing CVR), and to restore the system quickly after fault occurrence [11]. Fault clearing is a fast response process, and a fault needs to be cleared within 20 mins, thus it cannot be included into the optimization algorithms of EMS. Therefore, considering the scope of EMS in smart grid to design optimization methods, a taxonomy chart is shown in Figure 7.12.

7.7.1 Energy Management Framework

DEMS considers different RE resources, ESSs, EV charging stations, main grid, critical and flexible customers, along with the energy management

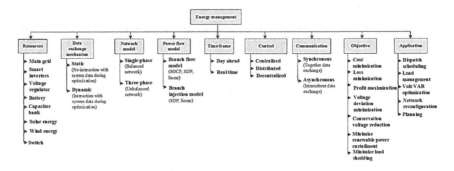

Figure 7.12 Taxonomy of energy management.

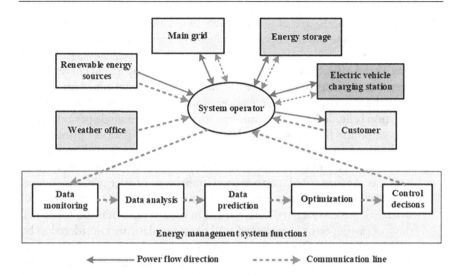

Figure 7.13 Typical energy management framework.

system function present at the system operator premise shown in Figure 7.13. In this methodology, supply-demand balance is established by taking into account climate data from weather office and energy price data from main grid through the advanced communication and control infrastructure.

Apart from this data from other parties, system operator accumulates the load data from the consumers, data on operating conditions from energy storage, and EV charging station and sends them to EMS functions for further processing. EMS function performs data monitoring, data analysis, data prediction, and optimization sequentially to generate the optimal real-time dispatch control decisions which is further sent back to the corresponding resources through the system operator. EMS is present in small-scale residential microgrids [12], multistory apartment buildings, distribution networks, and bulk transmission grids to decide optimal source-storage-load dispatch schedules for cost-effective network planning, optimal power flow determination, and meeting critical load demand during outage events under blue sky (i.e. normal), gray sky (i.e. voltage and frequency instability), and black sky (i.e. outage or fault) operating conditions. EMS performs optimization algorithms with a certain objective function such as energy cost minimization, reducing greenhouse gas emission, voltage profile improvement, reliability enhancement by reducing the probability of occurring outage events and durations, maximization of system efficiency by reducing losses and improving the life span of the system resources, privacy and security preservation, etc. Depending upon the decision time frame of the EMS, the energy management methods are classified into two categories, viz. day ahead offline and real-time online energy management methodologies.

i. **Day ahead offline energy management:** In case of day ahead energy management, the dispatch schedule for the next day is determined by considering the forecasted renewable generation and energy price. The objective function is modelled to minimize the total sum of the single period objective value for the subsequent day. This is a multi-period optimization problem where all the decision variables corresponding to all time intervals are solved simultaneously, and then those are saved for utilization at next day. As forecasted data are used in this type of energy management, the derived solutions are categorized into four types, viz. deterministic, stochastic, risk associated, and robust. In case of deterministic solutions, the forecasting error is neglected, and the input data are considered to be perfectly accurate. Stochastic and risk-constrained programming express the uncertain input parameters as probability distribution functions and generate pertinent scenarios from the distribution functions. Both solve the optimization process for each scenario, and the optimal decisions are decided by calculating probabilistic expected values of a particular variable for all the scenarios. In addition to that, risk-associated studies consider the amount of risk due to the uncertain scenarios in the optimization problem as value at risk (VaR) or conditional value at risk (CVaR). In case of robust optimization, the volatile parameter is modelled under box uncertainty by defining possible boundary limits for the uncertain parameters. Robust optimization takes form of min-max-min optimization and provides overly cautious decisions.

ii. **Real-time online energy management:** Day ahead EMS are simple and proven as most optimal as it can consider long-term beneficial aspects. However, the solutions become awful if the actual real-time scenarios differ much from the forecasted one. Further, expressing an uncertain parameter perfectly by a probability distribution is a strenuous job. Hence, presently real-time energy management frameworks are developed. Real-time frameworks consider online present data of the input parameters and generate optimal decisions. These techniques are mostly single period short-sighted deterministic type, that is, the optimal decisions for each time interval are derived separately by neglecting the long-term advantageous attributes.

7.7.2 Control Strategy

As mentioned before, the DEMS considers data from different resources. Those data are collected at the resource locations using sensors, and, following the optimal control decisions, the actuators placed at those resources operate them. Therefore, success of EMS hinges upon the selection of a proper control strategy and the communication infrastructure between the controller and the resources under it. Generally, three popular control actions are followed, as shown in Figure 7.14, viz. centralized control, decentralized or local control, and distributed control. Local agents (LAs) in Figure 7.14 signify the local sensors and the actuators. Let, DEMS optimization problem for a power system (say a distribution network) is given by 7.15.

$$\underset{x}{\text{Min}} \ f(x), \ \text{subject to}, \ g(x) = c, h(x) \leq b \tag{7.15}$$

Here x is the set of decision variables for the entire network. Equality constraint represents the AC power flow constraint, and inequality depicts different limiting constraints.

In the case of centralized control, all the LAs present at the entire network communicate with a central controller (CC). The CC is generally present at the main substation where the distribution network is connected with the upper grid or the transmission network, whereas decentralized control is framed by segregating the entire network into multiple areas. Let, for the earlier problem, the distribution network is parted into 'n' number of areas with x_n number of decision variables. In this case, there is no CC; rather, each

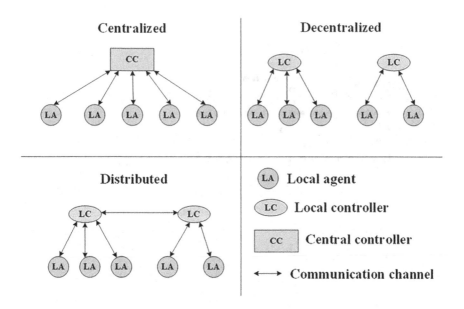

Figure 7.14 Different energy management control strategies.

area will have a dedicated local controller (LC). Las of an area communicate only with the LC corresponding to that area, and each LC is responsible for performing EMS separately only for the area underneath it, without sharing any information with its neighboring LCs; that is, there is no communication between the LCs.

Distributed control works similarly as decentralized control, but unlike decentralized control, the LCs also communicate with their neighboring LCs and share data to achieve an optimal condition for the entire network through consensus. Similar to decentralized control, there is no CC, and the LAs of an area communicate only with the LC corresponding to their area. The distributed energy management for three areas is depicted in Figure 7.15. It is seen from Figure 7.15 (a) that a distribution network is segregated into three areas. Each area has local variables x_1, x_2, and x_3 and global variables corresponding to the boundary buses y_1, y_2, and y_3 (as shown in Figure 7.15 (b) and (c)). Global variables of one area are shared with the neighboring areas to attain consensus.

This global information are bus voltage or power flow between two areas. Now in the distributed control, the global variables of one area are duplicated in its neighboring areas with the help of dummy buses (see Figure 7.15(d)). For example, global variable corresponding to area 1, that is, y_1, will be duplicated to area 2 as y_{1c}. At starting, each area will initialize or assume the value of the global variables of its adjacent areas and solve the

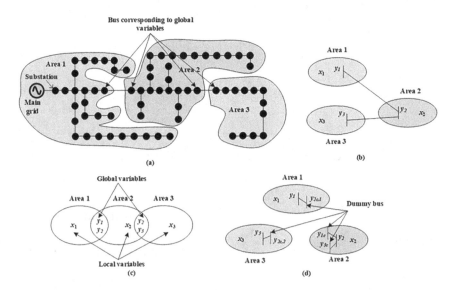

Figure 7.15 Distributed energy management with three areas.

decentralized optimization problem locally along with an extra constraint named as coordination or coupling constraint. Coupling constraint aims to make the values of the duplicate and actual variables same. After solving the local optimization, solutions regarding global variables are shared, and this process continues till the consensus is attained.

$$\left.\begin{array}{l} \underset{x_1,y_1}{\text{Min }} f(x_1,y_1) \\ \text{subject to, } g(x_1,y_1) = c_1, \\ h(x_1,y_1) \le b_1 \\ y_2 - y_{2c,1} = 0 \end{array}\right\} \text{Area 1} \quad \left.\begin{array}{l} \underset{x_2,y_2}{\text{Min }} f(x_2,y_2) \\ \text{subject to, } g(x_2,y_2) = c_2, \\ h(x_2,y_2) \le b_2 \\ y_3 - y_{3c} = 0, y_1 - y_{1c} = 0 \end{array}\right\} \text{Area 2}$$

$$\left.\begin{array}{l} \underset{x_3,y_3}{\text{Min }} f(x_3,y_3) \\ \text{subject to, } g(x_3,y_3) = c_3, \\ h(x_3,y_3) \le b_3 \\ y_2 - y_{2c,2} = 0 \end{array}\right\} \text{Area 3} \tag{7.16}$$

It is noted that the success of distributed control lies on the performance of the communication channel. Mal-operation of communication infrastructure can produce an erroneous solution. Some popular distributed control algorithms are alternating direction method of multipliers (ADMM), auxiliary problem principle (APP), and analytical target cascading (ATC). Distributed control may produce nearly most optimal solutions as it is considering the entire network objective through consensus. Further, as LCs solve their own optimization in parallel, it is suitable for bulk network as well. Again, if any area is affected by cyber threats, then the hacker will have access only to its neighboring local controllers but not the entire network. Therefore, distributed control is somehow resilient to cyber threats.

7.8 CONCLUSION

This chapter provides a comprehensive overview of the communication as well as measurement technologies used in smart grids. In our modern world where energy demand is rapidly growing, and sustainable and reliable energy sources are integrating, the importance of this topic cannot be overstated. Synchrophasor technology highlighted in the chapter is a key technology that enables high-speed data acquisition and analysis. Further, it enables grid operators to quickly respond to any change in conditions and maintain the stable grid operation. Furthermore, the chapter discussed the different layers of communication architecture necessary for data transmission in smart grids. In addition, the integration of renewable energy sources, EVs, and ESS in smart grids are discussed to achieve a more sustainable and reliable energy system. The concept of smart cities and its role in the efficient management of energy demand and supply has been covered. Finally, the chapter examines optimal real-time pricing algorithms and dynamic energy management systems that ensure reliable and efficient power supply. Incorporating these advanced algorithms and systems enable grid operators to more effectively manage energy demand and supply in real time, reducing the risk of blackouts and improving the overall efficiency of the grid. In conclusion, this chapter is an essential resource for researchers and professionals to provide valuable insights into the latest advancements for smart grids.

REFERENCES

[1] Liu, Y., Zhou, Y. and Xu, L. 2013. Communication networks in smart grid: Issues and challenges. *Electric Power Systems Research*, no. 107; 1–10. doi: 10.1016/j.epsr.2013.08.013.

[2] Xia, N. H. B. Gooi, S. X. Chen et al. 2015. Redundancy based PMU placement in state estimation. *Sustainable Energy, Grids and Networks*, no. 2; 23–31. doi: 10.1016/j.segan.2014.10.003.

[3] Kamwa, I., Pradhan, A. K. and Joos, G. 2011. Adaptive phasor and frequency-tracking schemes for wide-area protection and control. *IEEE Transactions on Power Delivery*, no. 26; 744–753. doi: 10.1109/TPWRD.2010.2071075.

[4] Yan, J., Liu, C. C. and Vaidya, U. 2011. PMU-based monitoring of rotor angle dynamics. *IEEE Transactions on Power Systems*, no. 26; 2125–2133.

[5] Singh, A. K. and Agarwal, P. 2016. State-of-the-Art Phasor Measurement Unit (PMU) and Wide-Area Monitoring Systems (WAMS) applications in electric power systems. *Electric Power Components and Systems*, no. 44; 1813–1825. doi: 10.1080/15325008.2016.1190026.

[6] Zhang, Y., Zhang, J., Chen, J. and Lin, W. 2015. A survey of wireless sensor network applications in smart grid. *International Journal of Distributed Sensor Networks*, no. 11; 1–14.

[7] Singh, S. N., Singh, A. and Singh, B. 2018. Wireless sensor networks and internet of things for smart grid: A review. *The IEEE Internet of Things Journal*, no. 5; 3572–3583.

[8] Yang, Z., Yang, F., Min, H., Tian, H., Hu, W. and Liu, J. 2023. Review on optimal planning of new power systems with distributed generations and electric vehicles. *Energy Reports*, no. 9; 501–509.

[9] Savolainen, M. K. and Svento, R. 2012. Real-time pricing in the Nordic power markets. *Energy Economics*, no. 34; 1131–1142.

[10] Soto, E. A., Bosman, L. B., Wollega, E. and Leon-Salas, W. D. 2021. Peer-to-peer energy trading: A review of the literature. *Applied Energy*, no. 283; 116268.

[11]   Experience, V. O. 2015. Insights into advanced distribution management systems. In *The United States Department of Energy*, Washington, DC, USA.

[12]   Paul, S. and Padhy, N. P. 2019. A multi-objective genetic algorithm approach for synergetic source-storage-load dispatch in a residential microgrid. In *20th International Conference on Intelligent System Application to Power Systems (ISAP)*, New Delhi, India.

Chapter 8

Big Data for Smart Grid
A Case Study

Taha A. Taha, Mohd Khair Hassan, Hussein I. Zaynal, and Noor Izzri Abdul Wahab

8.1 INTRODUCTION

This section gives the context necessary to comprehend the tests and work undertaken for this research. The regular electric power grid model and the smart grid model are both described initially. Afterwards, a few cyber threats and their respective detection and mitigation methods are discussed. The chapter finishes with a summary of the preceding material and a review of its content.

8.2 CONVENTIONAL/TRADITIONAL ELECTRIC POWER GRID

Most engineered systems in the modern world are known as power grids. These grid systems are interconnected systems comprised of power generation plants, distribution via transmission lines, substations, and users [1].

The primary purpose of the electrical power grid is to transmit electricity from the location where it is produced to the end users, including households and commercial establishments [2]. This whole phenomenon is achieved by several steps in the traditional power grid systems, as illustrated in Figure 8.1, and stated as follows.

8.2.1 Generation

Electricity consumed by the users is basically generated at the power plant generators. These generators run on crude oil and other resources to produce electricity [1]. A power plant may have one or more than one generator which are electro-mechanical and steered by natural gas, coal, and fuel and are usually installed far away from populated areas [3]. The electrical power generation is mainly obtained using the spinning turbine; hence, the majority of the algorithms emphasize managing the power output, voltage, and frequency of the generator [1]. Furthermore, additional protective systems

 DOI: 10.1201/9781032665399-8

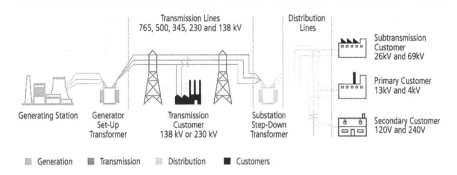

Figure 8.1 Elements of conventional grid [2].

must also be implemented by the generation system in order to prevent the system from having any physical issues.

8.2.2 Transmission

After the generation of electricity at power plants by different resources, the generated voltages are stepped up to high voltages in order to transfer over the transmission lines [1]. This amount of electric power is then transferred to substations for further distribution via the transmission lines as the power-generated plants are constructed distantly from the crowded areas of the city [3].

8.2.3 Distribution

Over the transmission lines, the electric power is transferred towards the substations where the electric power is reduced to low voltages to transfer it to consumers via distribution lines [1]. The part of the grid station is known as the distribution phase.

8.2.4 Consumption

After the distribution phase, the voltages are much higher to be used by users; therefore, these voltages are further stepped down to the required service voltages using transformers [3]. The following are the complete components used in a conventional grid station.

8.2.5 Problems Associated with Traditional Power Grids

It is worth noting that power transferred and distributed over the transmission lines and distribution lines in the conventional power grids are all in the unidirectional network. That means power is transferred one way only, and there are no consumer outlets [4]. Moreover, it also noted that in the traditional electricity supply mechanisms, the transmission lines and distribution networks were installed many years ago. These are huge investments and require a lot of maintenance in order to maintain power flow. Further, the conventional grid system generates electricity using fossil fuels only. This makes electricity more expensive to consumers [5]. Besides, the conventional power grids have a few challenges, too, as follows:

i.   Traditional power grids are installed around the communities. It is challenging to power up the rural areas as it will cost more transmission and distribution lines.

ii.   Conventional power grids are installed, keeping the historical electricity demand rather than the current demand [2].

iii. Existing power grid infrastructure faces the challenge of more power consumption during peak hours in companies, homes, and businesses.

iv.   In traditional power grids, load balancing presents a challenge. Load balancing refers to the need to consume electricity immediately as it is generated. In case the demand surpasses the supply, then the grid will shut down, and no user will get electricity on that particular grid. In another scenario, if the supply exceeds the demand, then the energy gets wasted. This excess amount of energy can be stored in electric storage devices. However, in conventional power grids, the electricity storage mechanism is more expensive [2].

v.   In the power grids, it has always been a one-way communication setup. Energy and communication take place from generation to destination. This means that the traditional power grid faces difficulties in diagnosing the electric failure in the grid and is incapable of adjusting the demand for energy. It is challenging to reroute the electricity transmission in these grids. Moreover, transmission and distribution lines get overheated as well.

vi.   Maintaining electric power in conventional grids is usually manual. Technicians and supervisors log the details in the logbook.

vii. Frequent power outages are more common due to weather conditions such as rainy, natural disasters, and other environmental conditions. These power outages in these traditional power grids are more common than grid failure, and they increase the risk of harm and loss [1].

To tackle these challenges, traditional power grids are being upgraded with various technologies to become more intelligent and efficient. The smart grid is a promising solution to the issues highlighted earlier. The succeeding section will delve into the constituents of a smart grid and how they relate to one another in examining the factors, incentives, and resolutions for a more adaptable electrical grid [6].

8.3 SMART GRID

A smart grid is essentially an interconnection of power generation, distribution, aspects for communications, automation, control, new technology, computers, and management systems that are all working together to improve the grid's dependability, efficiency, security, and environmental friendliness [5].

8.3.1 Conventional Power Grids

The smart grid gets the term modernized grid, which means that the smart grid is the enhancement of the conventional grids [6]. A conceptual model of a smart grid is depicted in Figure 8.2. Additionally, a comparison between the smart and traditional grid is depicted in Figure 8.3. The smart grid adds the following enhancement to the current/conventional power grids.

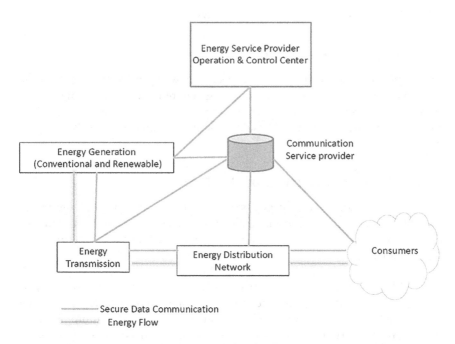

Figure 8.2 Conceptual model of smart grid [7].

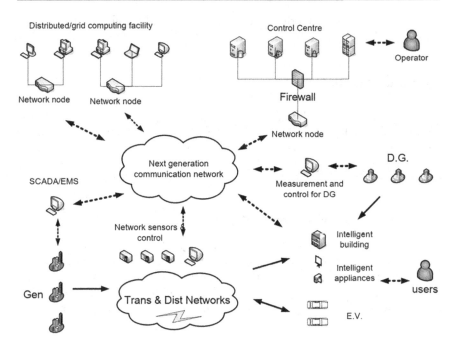

Figure 8.3 Comparison of smart and traditional power grids [6].

8.3.2 Production of Power

In the conventional power grids, the electricity was produced by fossil fuels, whereas in the smart grid, electricity is generated using renewable energy sources like wind and tidal power, among others [6]. The reserves of fossil fuels are running out now, and the electricity generated by those was much more expensive.

8.3.3 The Infrastructure of the Grid

The infrastructure of current grid stations must be enhanced to the upper level to transport more amount of electricity from the generation plants to the service areas [6]. Therefore, the modern smart grid infrastructure have following features:

i. More transmission and distribution lines are needed to build with sensors and actuators in order to reroute the electrical energy, diagnose the failure in transmission lines, and get rid of power failure [8–10].

ii. The modern infrastructure of the smart grid consists of a lot of communication devices, the IoT, actuators, sensors, controls, and automation. The conventional grid transmission lines, distribution, and generation plant must be equipped with the latest smart transmission and distribution lines along with sensors and actuators and smart meters. The generation plant needs to be modified with other renewable energy resources [11, 12].

iii. The smart grid infrastructure must be able to transfer electric power and information in a two-way direction from source to destination and from destination to source in a decentralized architecture.

8.3.4 Demand Response

In modernized grid architecture, the demand for electricity is continuously monitored [1]. The smart grid infrastructure will incorporate sophisticated information monitoring, metering, and management equipment for this function. This will enable consumers to monitor their energy consumption, view billing information, and identify which appliances are consuming the most power.

8.3.5 The Framework of Smart Grid

As stated earlier, the present electrical infrastructure relies on the conventional grid, and completely switching to the smart grid model is a highly troublesome task [5]. Numerous concept-based frameworks have been proposed by various standardization bodies; however, the most widely used and adapted smart grid model is the one given by the National Institute of Standards and Technology (NIST). The NIST's model states that there are seven primary parts of a smart grid which are interconnected with the help of a secure network, as portrayed in Figure 8.4. The seven parts are generation, distribution, transmission, customers, markets, operations, and service providers [4].

8.3.6 The Subsystem of Smart Grid

A smart grid entails a complete system which comprises multiple subsystems. Among them, the significant subsystems are Operations and Advanced Metering Infrastructure [13]. Both subsystems are explained in the sub-subsections.

8.3.6.1 Operations

In this subsystem of the smart grid, various technologies are included such as Wide Area Management System (WAMS) and SCADA. The WAMS is based on the PMU which provides both control and optimization with the help of measuring phase angle and magnitude, while SCADA is a combination of

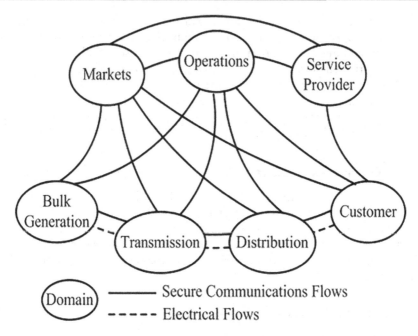

Figure 8.4 Smart grid's conceptual model given by NIST [13].

hardware and software parts utilized for supervision, optimization, and controlling of generation as well as transmission [14]. Comparatively, SCADA is slower than WAMS, thus making it preferable for smaller areas, whereas the WAMS is implemented where wider geographic areas are involved.

8.3.6.2 AMI

The Advanced Metering Infrastructure (AMI) consists of a set of technologies that cooperatively allow data transmission between the operators and the consumers [14]. The set of technologies includes certain communication technologies and smart meters as well. Such a facility aids both the supplier and the consumer in real-time management of energy usage [14]. For example, the consumer is capable of adjusting his usage, while the supplier may easily acquire the power consumption records. A smart grid's AMI consists of multiple communication networks based on the required coverage area as shown in Figure 8.5, for instance, HAN, BAN, FAN, and WAN [14].

8.4 TYPES OF CYBERATTACKS IN SMART GRID

A huge amount of work has been involved in analyzing various types of cyberattacks or cyber threats as these are the most studied and discussed in

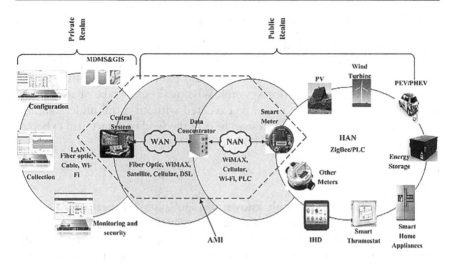

Figure 8.5 AMI's communication network based on the coverage area [15].

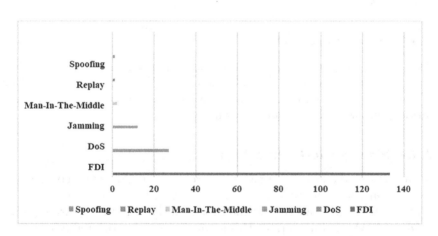

Figure 8.6 The number of articles that have studied different cyberattacks [18].

smart grids [16]. Smart grids nowadays are more vulnerable to cyber threats [17]. These cyber threats can destroy the total power system mechanism. Mainly, cyber threats are divided into two main categories, active and passive, based on their effects on the system [18]. Spying, eavesdropping, and traffic analysis are key aspects of passive cyber threat, while an active attack on denial of service (DoS) and FDI [19]. Each type of attack has been repeatedly studied by multiple researchers, among which a few are discussed here and highlighted in the graph in Figure 8.6.

8.4.1 False Data Injection Attack

A false data injection attack (FDIA) involves the insertion of erroneous information into the power meters or system. This type of attack involves manipulating the network measurements and parameters and can often go undetected by current detection systems. What makes this type of attack particularly concerning is that it can be executed without a full understanding of the power system network. Researchers in the field of smart grid cybersecurity have extensively studied FDIA [20].

8.4.2 DoS Attack

A Denial-of-Service, commonly known as a DoS, attack is performed to disrupt or shut down a network while making it inaccessible to the consumers. This is achieved with the help of flooding certain parts of the network with specific data packets, requiring it to respond with a huge amount of data. This, in turn, overloads the network, causing it to ultimately black out [21]. The prime targets of such attacks in smart grids are the systems that integrate IoT devices [22].

8.4.3 Jamming Attack

As the name suggests, this sort of attack affects the transmission of data by jamming certain specific signals in the network [23]. The performance of the affected network is significantly decreased due to disruption in data transmission and unreliable communication.

8.4.4 Man-in-the-Middle Attack

In this attack, the attacker assumes the role of a middleman between the network and the intended recipient [24]. Address Resolution Protocol (ARP) is utilized to execute this attack, where the attacker maps their address to the hardware's MAC address [25]. This grants the attacker the ability to intercept the communication channel and access all the data that was initially intended for the recipient.

8.4.5 Replay Attack

The replay attack is sort of a smart attack as initially it understands the pattern of the network and later replays the data in the network while remaining undetected. This allows the attack to induce incorrect information such as reduced or increased energy prices [25]. The systems integrated with IoT devices are more vulnerable to replay attacks.

8.4.6 Spoofing Attack

The term spoofing means tricking; thus, similar use is intended in this sort of attack as it tricks the network into allowing it to access by either using a modified IP address or using ARP similar to a Man-in-the-Middle attack or even by using GPS signals by broadcasting wrong information from/to the satellites [26].

The conventional grids are being converted into smart grids in the modern era, and such cyberattacks mentioned in Figure 8.4 mostly affect the smart grids. In these smart grids, multiple devices are interconnected such as communication devices, energy routers, advanced smart meters, and Internet of Things (IoT) which are more prone to cyberattacks. In this research work [27], the author carried out the main work on cyber-physical security of the WAMPAC system using the game-theoretic technique. In this game formulaic approach, the most likely scenario of attack was considered, and it also provides the security measurement based on the classification and characteristics of cyber threat type [28]. Table 8.1 shows the extensive thematic taxonomy of cybersecurity attacks on smart grids, and Table 8.2 represents smart grid attacks that occur worldwide.

Table 8.1 Extensive Thematic Taxonomy of Cybersecurity Attacks on Smart Grids

Attack Type	Activities Involved
False Data Injection Attack	• Congestion of transmission lines • Illegal economic benefits • Compromising power system state estimation • Damages the load forecasting • Generation scheduling disturbance
Denial-of-Service attack (DOS)	• Attack sends fake request • Resource exhaustion • Exploitation of vulnerabilities • Large degree of disruption
Man-in-the-Middle attack	• Sniffs communication • Supervises control and data acquisition • Records and reads exchange messages
Dynamic load alerting attack	• Damages the stability of power systems • Runs the trajectory under damaged roads
Static load alerting attack	• Changes the amount of load
Replay Attack	• Deliberately jams a system • Steals information on a wireless network
Load redistribution attack	• Tampers with the measurements units • Cascading failures

Table 8.2 Smart Grid Attacks that Occur Worldwide [29]

Time	Location	Attack Target(s)	Impact and Consequence
2010	Iran	Disrupt the nuclear centrifuges	Approximately 20% of Iran's nuclear centrifuges were destroyed as a result of the worm, which specifically targeted industrial control systems, infecting over 200,000 computers and damaging 1,000 pieces of equipment.
2011	California	Impacted approximately 2.7 million clients	This issue caused a significant reduction in frequency, tripping, and a blackout as a consequence of a large disparity between power demand and supply.
2014	Korea	Goal	A total of 5,986 phishing emails which carried harmful malware were distributed to 3,571 personnel responsible for operating nuclear plants.
2015	Ukraine	Electricity transformer stations	Around 1.4 million people experienced power outages in their residences, impeding their ability to reach their electricity providers by phone.
2016	Israel	The electricity grid at a national level	The Israeli government was compelled to shut down a considerable number of computers in its power plants.
2017	Ukraine	The nuclear power plant located in Chernobyl	Numerous power plants at the national level were compromised, leading to abnormal operations.
2018	France	Ingerop, a company based in France	Cybercriminals grabbed around 65 GB of vital information. These documents comprised designs for nuclear power plants and personal and personal data, posing a grave security risk.
2019	United States (U.S.)	U.S. power grid	The event did not result in a power outage, and the machine failed in less than five minutes.
2019	South Africa (Johannesburg)	City Power company	The hack prohibited consumers from purchasing power, recharging their devices, processing bills, and accessing the City Power website.
2020	Portugal	Energias de Portugal	The individual responsible asserted that they had acquired ten terabytes of private data, comprising invoices, contracts, transactions, sensitive materials regarding customers and partners, as well as other classified information [30].

Time	Location	Attack Target(s)	Impact and Consequence
2020	Europe	Enel Group, an Italian multinational energy corporation	The internal IT network experienced a brief disruption, resulting in a temporary halt in customer service operations.
2020	Brazil	Light S.A, a power company based in Brazil.	The assailant requested a payment of $14 million as a ransom, and only their private key could decipher the encrypted file.
2020	Palestine	K-Electric (power supplier)	An unknown amount of data was stolen, and electricity bills and internet services were temporarily suspended.
2021	Texas	–	The "Big Freeze" winter storm that occurred in February exposed vulnerabilities in the Texas energy market.
2022	Ukrainian	Energy company	Industroyer2 is designed to connect directly to electrical utility equipment and issue commands to the substation devices responsible for regulating the flow of power.

8.4.7 Detection and Mitigation of Cyberattacks

There are various techniques available to detect and mitigate various cyber-attacks in electrical power systems. In this context, another survey related to cyberattacks was performed [31]. Various mechanisms of security and defense were proposed against the cyberattacks named 7D model cybersecurity, as shown in Figure 8.7.

i. Discovery
ii. Denial
iii. Detection
iv. Disruption
v. Destruction
vi. Degradation
vii. Destroy

8.4.7.1 Discovery

Locating and identifying sensitive data for the purpose of protection is involved in the discovery process in cybersecurity. It also carries the authority to audit sensitive information in general applications of cybersecurity

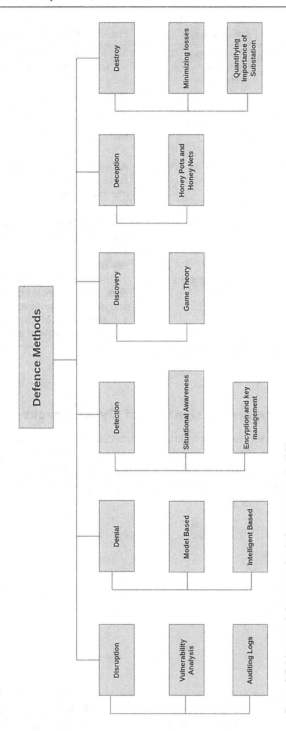

Figure 8.7 Various defence methods for smart grids [33].

to ensure protection. It provides help to the system as it contains the context security within the system. As a consequence, the information within the system is secured. In smart grid security, the discovery contains information related to vulnerabilities inside the system. Various methodologies have been proposed to detect and analyse the vulnerability in smart grids. These graphs reveal the significance of nodes in the system and relationships among them [32].

8.4.7.2 Detection

Typically, cyberattacks in the smart grid are detected by analyzing data and measurements from various layers of communication, protocols, network devices, and infrastructure. Advanced metering measurements and state estimation techniques are utilized to detect cyberattacks in the power system. Model-based algorithms are also employed to identify any threats or cyberattacks that may be present.[31]. Moreover, statistical variation in cyberattack vectors is revealed through distributed algorithms [28]. Modus protocol vulnerability to flooding attacks was demonstrated in this research paper [6, 34] worked on a real-time cyber-physical test bed embedded with a power simulator system and communication. In another work, the authors developed a novel RBAC to secure authorization of the system.

8.4.7.3 Denial

Preventing or mitigating cyberattacks and threats is a crucial security method employed in the smart grid. The main objective of these methods is to safeguard the smart grid from potential cyberattacks or threats and implement measures to secure the communication of the system [35]. These methods are known as encryption methods, and mostly the encryption methods used are symmetric and asymmetric keys [36]. A one-time password key is also proposed in this research paper [13] to develop mutual communication between servers and devices of the smart grid. Through the use of an innovative key management protocol, mutual authentication among smart meters HAN and smart grid is also explored [37].

8.4.7.4 Disruption

Disrupting cyber threats is a crucial aspect of securing any system when it becomes infected with such threats. In the smart grid system, game-theory approaches are used to disrupt these threats. Many surveys have been conducted in this area, and one research paper proposed countermeasures that are disruptive in nature to mitigate the impacts of cyber threats based on non-compromised component knowledge [38].

8.4.7.5 Degradation

Deceiving the attacker is a crucial aspect of smart grid security that aims to disrupt the impact of cyberattacks by redirecting the attack. This is achieved by altering the direction of the attack in the smart grid system, which ultimately helps in securing the system. Although limited work has been done in this area of security, one article proposed a concept for a honeypot game that can be used to defend against Denial-of-Service attacks in the smart grid [39].

8.4.7.6 Destruction

Destruction of cyberattack is the final part of the smart grid security system. For that purpose, the techniques used are defining security metrics. Other techniques were proposed in the paper [40] that is a distinctive modeling techniques with the capability to modify network topology. Kill Chain's course of action matrix (7D Model) is represented in Table 8.3.

8.4.8 Related Works

This research work proposes an effective solution to cyberattacks, especially False Data Detection Cyber Attacks (FDDCA) in smart grids using Feed Forward Network (FFN) algorithm. Another research work related to cyber-physical test beds is presented in [41] for the smart grids. Authors over-viewed interconnected smart grid cyber-physical security test bed systems which include the set of communication, physical, and control system that

Table 8.3 Kill Chain Course of Action Matrix (7D Model)

	Detect	Discover	Disrupt	Deny	Deceive	Degrade	Destroy
Reconnaissance	Web analytics	Hunting		Traffic filtering	Fake posting		
Weaponization							
Delivery	NID, User education	Hunting		Email AV scanning	Filter out-of-office messages	Email queuing	
Exploitation	Hids	Hunting	DEP	Patch			
Installation							
Command and control	NIDS	Hunting	NIPS	HTTP whitelist		HTTP throttling	
Action on objectives	Proxy detection	Hunting	NIPS	Firewall ACL	Honeypot	HTTP throttling	

incorporates the cyber-physical environment. Particularly they test the power cyber test bed including applications, architecture, and RTDS, virtualization, and ISEAGE Emulators. Different cyberattacks were evaluated using this test bed in order to explore cyber-physical impacts. Furthermore, researchers have demonstrated available and integrated attacks using isolated parameters such as rotor stability angle, these attacks were evaluated. Similar work was addressed in [15], in which authors presented the model to reconstruct the damaged states of cyber-physical power systems (CPPS) cyberattacks. Initially, they estimated the small signal model of CPPS reduced to a non-linear continuous-time system under cyberattack disturbance. Based on the observer results, the authors developed the defense strategy using economic optimum and demonstrated their work on IEEE 9 bus systems [42].

Adam Hahn (2013) from Iowa State University presented a comprehensive framework for enhancing the cybersecurity of the smart grid, which included three component-based mechanisms. The first mechanism was the Quantitative Exposure Analysis Model, which detected cyber threats related to communication and computation of critical information. To support this model, an Attack Exposure Metric utility was developed to determine the impact of new cyber vulnerabilities and analyze the effectiveness of smart grid protection measures. The second mechanism was the Model-based Hierarchical Intrusion Detection for the Smart Grid (MHINDS), which identified attacks on grid stations. Finally, the Power Cyber Testbed was designed to provide accurate cybersecurity to power systems using a layered approach of communication, control, and power systems layers, along with simulation and emulation techniques. The Real-time Digital Simulator (RTDS) was used for developing the Power Cybersecurity Testbed for real-time evaluation, and DIgSILENT Power Factory Software was used for non-real-time evaluation [43].

Many surveys were carried out on the dynamics of the attacks of cyber threats on the power grids. Conversion of conventional grid to smart grid involves the information and communication technologies, communication protocols, routers, cyber-physical systems, and smart meters. As a consequence, these grids are more vulnerable to cyberattacks. Cyberattacks on smart grids are different from attacks on traditional cyber environments; to attack the cyber system of a smart grid, an attacker must know the cyber elements and their negative impact on the power system [44].

A thorough analysis was carried out to investigate the weaknesses in the fundamental cyber infrastructure and the different sets of energy applications used to facilitate the various aspects of the smart grid [45]. The smart grid is made up of various communication devices, each with varying levels of importance and security requirements, as outlined in Table 8.5. These communication devices play a critical role in the functioning of the smart grid. However, they are also vulnerable to various types of cyberattacks such

Table 8.4 Evaluating the Reviews on Blockchain's Potential Energy-Sector Uses

Author and Year	Area of Focus	Grid Balancing	Intermittency and Uncertainty	Issues Identified Power Quality	Integration of EVs
[47]	Energy Management Systems	X	Method of uncertainty quantification Uncertainty management techniques	Systems for power quality management Loss reduction and dependability	EV behaviors EV nonlinear loads
[48]	Smart Grids	Decentralization in order to balance unpredictable supply and demand	The time-varying characteristics of RES	Frequency and voltage control	Dynamic distribution integration in the power grid
[49]	Distribution and Transmission Systems	Incorporating balancing markets	TSO must have greater flexibility to accommodate DER uncertainties DSO must engage in active grid management	Power quality is controlled by DSO DSO must procure flexibility to provide congestion management services	X
[50]	Impacts of Renewable Energy Resources	Balancing markets Balancing procurement methods	The need for adaptability in the face of unpredictability	Capacity management systems	X
[51]	Deregulated Electricity Market	X	Methods for analyzing dependability and possible hazard markets for surplus capability	Difficulties in enforcing quality control measures by system operators	X

Table 8.5 Smart Grid Communications

Domain	Networks	Application	Protocols
Transmission/ Generation	SCADA	• Telemetry and control data • EMS functions	• IEC 61850 • DNP3 • Modbus
	Substation	• Protective relaying • Special protection schemes	• IEC 61850
	WAMS	• Processing and publishing PMU information	• IEC 61850–90–5 • C37–118
	Inter-Control Center	• Generation scheduling • Transmit grid status	• ICCP
Distribution	SCADA	• Distribution Automation • Distributed energy resources • Fault detection	• IEC 61850 • Modbus • DNP3
	Substation	• Protective relaying	• IEC 61850
AMI	Home Area Network	• Consumption monitoring • Pricing information	• ZigBee
	Field Area Network	• Usage data • Update energy pricing • Meter maintenance	• ANSI C12.22 • ZigBee

as Spoofing, Denial-of-Service (DoS), misconfigurations, and Man-in-the-Middle attacks. It is essential to safeguard against these potential cyberattacks to ensure the secure and reliable operation of the smart grid [46].

In addition to communication, the system and devices associated with the smart grid are the decentralization of the smart grid, while providing benefits in balancing supply and demand also exposes it to increased vulnerability to cyberattacks. Wing and Manadhata (2011) conducted a study on evaluating the attack surface of the system. They defined the attack surface as a combination of entry points, exit points, and data channels that attackers can exploit and used this information to quantify the security of the system. The authors utilized software environments to demonstrate the impact of excess attack surface on decreased security levels.

The SCADA cybersecurity model has been developed using attack tree mechanisms [52]. Models of attack trees like Morda show how risk to a system may be estimated by considering the attacker's goals, tactics, and the effect on the mission. Developing reliable trees is challenging work, especially when little is known about the attacker's skills and ambitions [53].

Dacier [54] conducted a security modeling study by using a privileges graph that examines different privileges states in the computer system to identify any violated states. The study was further developed by including transiting nodes in the privilege graphs, which can be exploited by attackers as they escalate their privilege level. Additionally, Dacier and Deswarte [55] explored the correlation between safety and route features such as length and frequency. By creating privilege graphs and evaluating attack pathways through known vulnerabilities, attack graphs offer a new approach to modeling security issues.

In order to ensure sufficient protection of critical resources, a comprehensive assessment of potential attack capabilities is required. Wang and colleagues (2017) employed attack graphs to compute security metrics that considered the quantity and length of possible attack paths. Idika and Bhargava (2018) further advanced the path-based analysis using a comparative approach. Although the attack graph method offers an overview of a system's defenses, the difficulty in identifying and resolving vulnerabilities limits the model's precision and its suitability for complex systems with unknown weaknesses.

Another author [1] reviewed possible attackers and cyberattacks on the network components of the smart grid and proposed the following solutions:

i. To ensure secure access to the network, a robust authentication mechanism should be implemented for identification purposes. Additionally, the organization should have an explicit access permission policy to govern network access.

ii. It is essential to install malware protection systems on both embedded and general-purpose systems. Since embedded systems typically rely on manufacturer-supplied software, manufacturers should be instructed to install protection measures such as keys.

iii. To safeguard the smart grid network from both external and internal attacks, a Network Intrusion Protection System (IPS) and Network Intrusion Defense System (IDS) should be utilized. Vulnerability assessments should be performed annually or monthly to keep updated on the system's security and to check cyberattacks on the power systems.

iv. Sometimes users' actions possess network vulnerability to the systems; therefore, training programs, seminars, and workshops should be arranged to train network users about network tools, systems, and their applications. Moreover, they should be trained properly to protect the network system from any malware.

v. Devices on both ends of the smart grid system must be aware of their sources and destinations to communicate with. They rely on the communication protocol, and this is designed through the transport layer and internet protocol security.

vi. Virtual private networks (VPN) should be supported by network devices in order to develop secure connections within network communication.

vii. Devices must use Public Key Infrastructure (KPI) to secure communication.

8.5 BLOCKCHAIN OVERVIEW

Blockchain is a distributed ledger that records all network transactions and is held by every node in the network, as shown in Figure 8.8. Each block in the chain is linked to the previous one using cryptographic techniques, which makes it secure and resistant to malicious activities. Before a block is added to the blockchain, the transactions are verified and consensus is reached by the nodes, which results in a transparent and reliable system. The blocks in the chain are linked through cryptographic hash functions, and any modification to a block would require the subsequent blocks to be changed as well. The older the block, the harder it becomes for an attacker to modify it, and each network node has a copy of the blockchain, making it easy to detect any wrongdoing. The block header contains a time stamp, the hash of the

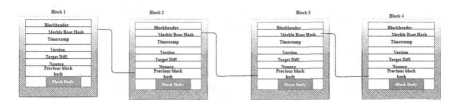

Figure 8.8 Blockchain structure [56].

Table 8.6 History of Blockchain [57]

Year	Blockchain History
1982	Proposed blockchain-like protocol
1991	Described a cryptographically secure chain of block
1993	Incorporated Merkle trees
1998	Designed bit gold
2008	Permissionless (public) blockchain Distributed ledger: Bitcoin term of blockchain Ethereum
2013	Permissionless (public) blockchain Bitcoin term of blockchain Ethereum
2015	Permissioned (public) blockchain Distributed ledger plus smart contract Hyperledger
2020–2022	Ethereum 2.0

previous block, and the Merkle root hash of all transactions included in the block. The version indicates the format and type of data in the block.

The Merkle tree is created through the hashing of pairs of data, resulting in a unique hash known as the Merkle root. The Merkle root acts as a cryptographic identifier for all the transactions in a block, allowing users to verify the presence of a specific transaction in the block securely. To meet the blockchain's consensus requirements, mining nodes utilize a nonce, a randomly chosen integer, to alter the block's hash value [56]. The block body of a blockchain contains two essential parts that record transaction information, such as its value, time, and location, and information about the parties involved in the transaction. These blocks are linked together to form a chain storing the most recent network transactions, which is shared among all network nodes [56].

8.5.1 Blockchain Applications in Smart Grid

Recently, there have been various cyberattacks on smart grids, including Denial-of-Service (DoS) and Data Injection Attacks (DIA), which can cause significant issues such as large-scale power failures and blackouts [58]. To prevent data tampering and maintain the integrity of stored information, the blockchain system is an attractive solution, particularly in power generation and distribution networks [59]. An example of this is illustrated in a diagram showing how a blockchain system can be integrated into a Single Machine Infinite Bus (SMIB) power plant and its distribution networks. In this setup, a cyberattacker could cause the generator to go out of sync by removing the load and disabling automatic voltage regulation using a proper attack strategy. However, using blockchain technology, time values of switch states and generator values can be stored in blocks, which only authorized nodes can verify and mine [60]. The smart contract of the metering device would detect any tampering and enforce Power System Stabilizer (PSS) to reduce oscillations, keeping the generator's terminal value stable, as shown in Figure 8.9 [56].

8.5.2 Peer-to-Peer Trading Infrastructure

The current trading structure of grid networks is inefficient due to the involvement of intermediaries and third parties, leading to high costs and inadequate transaction security [61]. In contrast, a blockchain-based platform for energy trading provides a peer-to-peer network for consumers and prosumers, eliminating the need for trust in intermediaries. With a decentralized platform, identity privacy and transaction security are better protected compared to the traditional system [62]. The P2P energy trading model has several uses, including in the Industrial Internet of Things (IIoT), and can

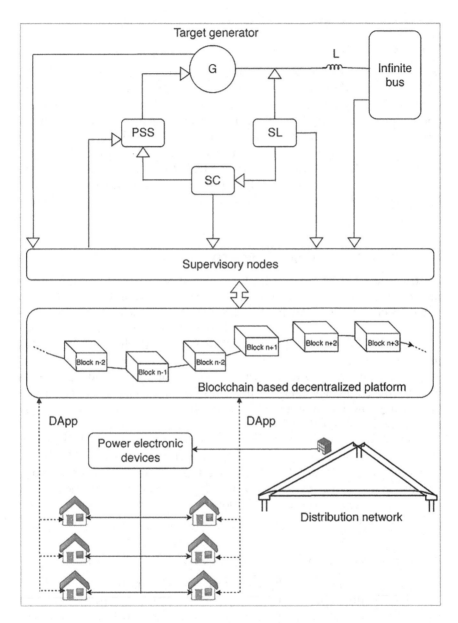

Figure 8.9 Framework for producing and distributing electrical power [56].

promote sustainable energy consumption by facilitating the establishment of microgrids.

8.5.3 Blockchain Applications in Microgrid Operations

In recent years, there has been a growing interest in the control of microgrids, especially with the increasing adoption of distributed energy resources (DERs). This has led to research on demand-based regulation and optimal operation of microgrids [63]. Blockchain technology has gained attention as a potential solution to address the challenges in this field. The use of blockchain has been proposed to create a scheduling method for DERs, ensuring the reliability and security of the system [63]. One proposed solution is a decentralized optimal power flow (OPF) model that schedules a mix of DERs, and blockchain is being explored as a platform for distributed computation and data supervision [43].

8.5.4 Energy Trading in Electric Vehicles

Electric vehicles (EVs) are a critical component of the smart grid infrastructure required to enable distributed renewable energy mobility [64]. Two potential charging sources for EVs are vehicle-to-vehicle (V2V) and vehicle-to-grid (V2G) trade. P2P V2V trading enables electric cars to exchange electricity at charging stations and parking lots, with the discharging EVs (those with excess power) supplying their energy to meet the charging EVs' electrical requirements and restoring a state of supply-demand equilibrium [65]. However, privacy concerns make discharging EVs hesitant to participate in the power trading market, leading to an uneven balance of supply and demand among EVs [66].

Blockchain technology provides several benefits for power trading, including decentralization, trust, and security. A mechanism called PETCON has been developed to ensure the safe trading of power. PETCON is more cost-effective and scalable across a network of nodes than previous methods of energy exchange between EVs. Additionally, PETCON is proven to be safe against cyberattacks [67].

8.5.5 Security and Privacy-Protecting Strategies

The real-time data collected by smart meters in a smart grid can reveal sensitive information about users' energy consumption patterns, leaving them vulnerable to privacy breaches from malicious actors. To address this issue, a blockchain-based system has been proposed in [68], which offers efficient data aggregation and privacy protection measures for smart meter data in the smart grid. Advanced cryptographic techniques such as zero-knowledge proof (ZKP), Elliptic Curve Digital Signature Algorithm (ECDSA), and linkable ring signatures can be used to enhance data privacy in blockchain systems. While blockchain technology alone cannot provide complete data privacy, integrating these cryptographic techniques can potentially safeguard the privacy of participating devices. In order to improve privacy, a privacy-preserving blockchain architecture is suggested, which utilizes ZKP in combination with pseudonyms of users and additional ZKP techniques [69].

8.6 CRYPTOGRAPHIC OVERVIEW

While cryptography is an essential part of secure communications, it should be noted that it alone is not sufficient. Cryptography, the practice of encoding information in a secret code, has been used for thousands of years. The earliest known instance of cryptography in writing dates back to around 1900 BCE, when an Egyptian scribe used nonstandard hieroglyphs in inscriptions [80]. It is believed that cryptography developed naturally after the invention of writing, for purposes such as diplomatic communication and military strategy. With the growth of computer communications, the need for new cryptographic methods also increased. Cryptography is indispensable in securing data and telecommunications, especially over untrusted networks such as the internet, which is practically every network [81]. Within the framework of any application-to-application connection, there are specific security considerations, including the need for encryption [82, 83].

i.   Authentication: This involves verifying a person's identity. Unfortunately, the most commonly used host-to-host authentication methods on the internet—name-based and address-based authentication—are not very secure [84].
ii. Privacy/confidentiality: This ensures that only the intended recipient can access the message.
iii. Integrity: This provides assurance to the recipient that the communication they received has not been altered from its original form [85].
iv. Non-repudiation: This is a way to prove that the sender did indeed send the communication.

The use of cryptography is not limited to protecting data from theft or changes; it can also serve as a means of user authentication. To achieve these goals, three types of cryptographic techniques are commonly used: private key (or symmetric) cryptography, public key (or asymmetric) cryptography, and hashing algorithms. The original data is known as plaintext, which is transformed into ciphertext through encryption and then usually decoded back into plaintext [84].

Table 8.7 Blockchain-Based Attack Detection Techniques for Cybersecurity in Smart Grids [70]

Reviews Articles	Systematic Review Search Terms	Focus Area	Review Article Gaps	Future Opportunities
[71]	Not systematic	Internet of Energy	– None identified	– Formation of rules and regulations – Networking lad – Energy use – Consideration of energy losses – Experimentation – Security and resilience
[72]	Not systematic	Power Systems	– None identified	– None presented
[73]	Not systematic	Information security	– Energy markets not mentioned – Peer-to-peer trading is not mentioned – EV scheduling techniques not explored	– None presented
[74]	Blockchain	Real-world initiatives	– Only real-world initiatives considered – Theoretical and experimental endeavors are disregarded – Research articles are disregarded	– None presented
[75]	Not systematic	Flexibility trading	– Article's primary focus is not blockchain technology	– None presented
[76]	This paper by Svetec, E., Nad, L., Pasicko, R., and Pavlin, B. provides an overview of the existing blockchain technology applied to renewable energy microgrids with the goal	Renewable energy sources	– Focus on EU and Croatian markets – Microgrids are the primary focus – Security and privacy are not taken into account	– None presented

of establishing communities that are resilient to climate change and energy-independent. The paper was presented at the 2019 16th International Conference on the European Energy Market in Ljubljana, Slovenia.

Ref	Method / Search	Topic	Limitations	Challenges / Issues
[57]	Blockchain AND Energy	Smart energy	– Only sixteen papers were evaluated Articles from conferences not considered	– Financial viability – Transaction expenses
[56]	Not systematic	Smart grid	None identified	– Scalability and cost – Contingency plan for branching and fragmentation – Self-adjusting power systems demand forecasting for the grid
[77]	Search string not provided	Start-ups and pilot Projects	– Only projects and startups systematically reviewed – Methodology not provided	– Consensus method – Lot platform development – Security and resilience – Development costs and infrastructure – Regulation and standardization
[78]	Not systematic	Renewable energy sources	– Blockchain technology is not the article's major topic	None presented
[79]	Not systematic	Smart contracts	– Concentrates only on security and dependability – Not systematic	– Scalability – Security – Performance
[21]	Not systematic	Blockchain for smart grid	– Methodology not provided	– Reliability and Safety – Scalability – Privacy – Security – Performance

Cryptographic algorithms are categorized based on the number of keys used for encryption and decryption, as well as their application and usage. One classification scheme distinguishes between Secret Key Cryptography, which uses the same key for both encryption and decryption, Public Key Cryptography, which employs different keys for encryption and decryption, and Hash Operations, which rely on a mathematical process to encrypt data irreversibly [84]. Additionally, Homomorphic Encryption allows for specific calculations to be performed on encrypted data without decryption, while methods such as these help to safeguard personal information from leakage during storage and transmission on systems [86].

8.6.1 Cryptographic ZKP

Zero-knowledge proof (ZKP) is a cryptographic technique that enables two parties, the prover and the verifier, to interact without sharing any information except for a common value. This means that ZKP allows individuals to demonstrate their knowledge of certain information without revealing that information to others, as noted by [87].

8.6.2 Zero-Knowledge Cryptography Characteristics

Three conditions must be met for a cryptographic interaction to be termed zero-knowledge proof:

i.   Completeness: Verification must let the prover continue processing the transaction after the transaction has been validated [88].
ii. Soundness: The transaction is only authorized if the prover is right; the verifier cannot be persuaded differently [89].
iii. Zero knowledge entails that the verifier has no access to any information or private data beyond the truth or falsity of the existing assertion.

8.6.3 Advantages of Zero-Knowledge Cryptography

ZKPs are noteworthy for their simplicity, as zero-knowledge cryptography necessitates somewhat less software expertise while providing superior and practical solutions [90]. It also provides an innovative alternative to standard encryption for security purposes. ZKP encryption provides a high level of security for communications and information transmission [56]. ZKPs can save time by reducing the duration of blockchain transactions. Zero-knowledge encryption safeguards users' privacy by never asking them to divulge sensitive information. Safety is another critical benefit. Users using zero-knowledge proof cryptography should avoid any firm or website that requests their personal and sensitive information without a solid justification [91].

8.6.4 Applications of Zero-Knowledge Proof Cryptography

ZKPs enable you to exchange your username and password in an open (non-encrypted) format, which may be the most immediate advantage. Zero-knowledge cryptography establishes that both you and the server know the correct password. Therefore, encryption is unnecessary [92]. ZKPs can be used to validate requests for access to sensitive information. For instance, if your bank requests your credit rating score from the credit rating authority using your SSN, it exposes that you are a client of the bank. However, suppose the bank uses your name, which is a reasonably wide identifier [93]. In that case, the interaction will only be successful if the authority has one or more records that match the necessary SSN.

8.6.5 Blockchain Technologies with Cryptography

Cryptography serves as a method for protecting information from unauthorized access, particularly in blockchain networks where it is used to secure transactions between nodes [94]. In fact, cryptography and hashing are the two fundamental concepts underlying the blockchain technology. While cryptography is used to encrypt messages in a P2P network, hashing is employed to protect block information and link blocks within a blockchain [95].

The primary aim of cryptography in the context of blockchain is to ensure the security of all parties involved in the transactions, prevent double-spending, and guarantee the confidentiality of the transaction data. As a result, it plays a crucial role in securing various transactions within a blockchain network, and only authorized individuals are able to access, read, and process the transaction data.

8.6.6 Role of Cryptography in Blockchain

A blockchain wallet, whether in the form of software or hardware, serves as a storage unit for a user's personal data and transaction details, not the actual currency itself [96]. Wallets maintain the balance of transactions and store private keys, but they only serve as a means of communication between users for transaction purposes. In contrast, the blockchain stores the actual currency or other relevant data in blocks [97].

Digital signatures are utilized by users to verify their identity as a legitimate node in the network with the authority to conduct transactions, and they are shared with the receiver and other nodes in the network to establish the authenticity of their claims [36]. Generating a unique digital signature by combining transaction data with the user's private key is a preliminary step that must be taken by users when beginning a transaction with other nodes in the blockchain network. This process guarantees that the node is legitimate and that the data has not been tampered with.

8.6.7 Cryptography Hash Function in Blockchain

The immutability of the blockchain is achieved through hashing, which is a type of encryption that does not require the use of keys [76]. Whenever a transaction is verified, the hash algorithm adds the transaction's hash to the block and generates a new, unique hash based on the original transaction. As additional hashes are combined or created, the original footprint remains accessible [98], and the resulting combined hash is known as the root hash. The hash function is instrumental in linking blocks and maintaining the data's integrity within the block, and any modification to the data in the block results in a split in the blockchain [99]. MD5 and SHA-1 are two widely used hash functions.

8.7 ADVANTAGES AND DISADVANTAGES OF BLOCKCHAIN AND CRYPTOGRAPHY IN SMART GRID

8.7.1 The Disadvantages Include the Following

The application of blockchain and cryptography in the smart grid has several advantages, according to literature:

i. Improved security: The decentralized nature of blockchain can enhance the security of the smart grid, as all transactions are checked by the entire network.
ii. Enhanced data privacy: Public blockchains with obscured node identities can protect user privacy, and all transactions are stored in the blockchain, ensuring the security of those involved.
iii. Transparency and immutability of data: All transactions and activities are transparent due to the broadcast of ledger transactions to all network nodes, and concealing individual activity from the network is difficult.
iv. Elimination of third-party control and trust: Decentralization eliminates third-party transaction control, increasing the system's dependability and stability.
v. Reduced costs: Distributed ledger technology can potentially reduce transaction fees and failed transactions, leading to cost savings.

vi. Universal solution: A distributed ledger smart grid system could be the solution to all smart energy problems.

vii. Greater data accessibility: Once recorded on the chain, data is always accessible as the blockchain structure prohibits changes or removal of a block.

8.7.2 Risks and Downsides Associated with Blockchain and Cryptography Technology

There are several risks and downsides associated with the use of blockchain and cryptography technology:

i. Limited scalability and speed: Existing blockchain technology has speed and scalability limitations that can impede its usefulness. For example, Bitcoin's proof-of-work system allows a minimum of only seven transactions per second, while Visa can handle an average of 2,000 transactions per second [100].

ii. Off-chain support requirement: Smart energy systems need physical infrastructure, and blockchain technology only improves digital recordkeeping, not data input [101]. An off-chain system must be well-designed and managed to ensure the accuracy and reliability of the system's raw data.

iii. High establishment and maintenance costs: Research shows that the initial setup and ongoing maintenance costs of blockchain technology are relatively high [102]. Since blockchain is a decentralized network that differs from most traditional systems, implementation costs can be an issue in many cases [103].

iv. High transaction costs: While some experts believe that using blockchain technology in smart energy systems may ultimately lead to lower transaction costs, others argue that it will lead to higher transaction costs [102].

8.8 CONCLUSION

The integration of blockchain technology has significant potential to enhance the functionality of the smart grid, which is a critical component of modern infrastructure. By integrating communication and control technologies, smart grids are able to increase efficiency and reliability in electricity distribution networks. However, the multitude of intelligent devices used in smart grids must be efficiently managed to maintain security and reliability. In many areas, such as energy management, power trading, microgrid management, electric car management, and security and privacy, centralized approaches to management face significant challenges.

In order for smart grid to function properly, it is essential to have a framework that is dependable and secure. This report aims to research blockchain technology with cryptographic zero-knowledge proof (ZKP) in smart grid. Despite the fact that blockchain technologies do not directly fulfill the requirement for privacy, more sophisticated cryptographic methods such as ZKP are being developed. ZKP has an extensive history spanning decades in the fields of computer science and cryptography. Currently, it is undergoing development in order to support decentralized authentication for blockchains as well as web3. ZKP is a protocol that aims to verify a fact between two parties with as little information as possible being sent as part of the verification process.

Most countries worldwide are striving to transform traditional power systems into smart grids. The traditional power grid consists of power generation plants, transmission grids, distribution grids, and power consumption. However, this system is outdated and has several issues. Power flows in a single direction, and transmission and distribution lines require frequent maintenance. Additionally, the generation plants use fossil fuels, resulting in expensive electricity. Load balancing and electricity monitoring are also challenging during peak hours. These issues can be resolved by converting to smart grids, which integrate communication, control, automation, computers, and management tools to increase efficiency, reliability, security, and sustainability.

The smart grid is more modernized and consists of many communications and automation to monitor and control the electric flow from both ends. Consumers can easily monitor their electric loads and bills. The smart grid provides easy access to point out the grid failure or any electric fault in transmission or distribution lines. This smart grid is more convenient and brings several advantages over conventional grid systems.

As the smart grid consists of communication and other devices which are more vulnerable to cyberattacks, much research has already carried out studies in this area and points out several scenarios for cyberattacks and their defense and security mechanisms. The 7D model is defined as the defense strategy in diagnosing cyberattacks and then its solution accordingly. The 7D model consists of discovery, detection, disruption, destruction, deception, and denial of attacks.

The detection is a process in cybersecurity to identify and locate sensitive data in the smart grids in order to protect the data. Detection of attacks, in the smart grid's cyber infrastructure, the cyberattacks are detected by analyzing the sensitive data and measurements of the grid's different parameters.

One of the key security measures in the smart grid is the prevention and denial of cyberattacks or threats, which involves securing the communication system through encryption methods based on symmetric and asymmetric keys. Disrupting cyberattacks is also critical for smart grid cybersecurity and is addressed through game-theory approaches. Deception of attack is another strategy that aims to alter the direction of the attack to minimize its impact on the system. Finally, the destruction of cyberattacks is achieved through techniques such as defining security metrics and distinctive modeling techniques that can modify the network topology, ensuring that the smart grid remains secure and resilient to cyber threats.

REFERENCES

[1]. Aloul, Fadi, A. R. Al-Ali, Rami Al-Dalky, Mamoun Al-Mardini, and Wassim El-Hajj. "Smart grid security: Threats, vulnerabilities and solutions." *International Journal of Smart Grid and Clean Energy* 1, no. 1 (2012): 1–6.

[2]. Khoussi, S., and A. Mattas. "A brief introduction to smart grid safety and security." In *Handbook of System Safety and Security* (pp. 225–252). Syngress, 2017.

[3]. Chopade, Pravin, and Marwan Bikdash. "Modeling for survivability of smart power grid when subject to severe emergencies and vulnerability." In *2012 Proceedings of IEEE Southeastcon* (pp. 1–6). IEEE, 2012.

[4]. Greer, Monica. *Electricity Marginal Cost Pricing: Applications in Eliciting Demand Responses.* Elsevier, 2012.

[5]. Chen, Xia, Zhao Yang Dong, Ke Meng, Yan Xu, Kit Po Wong, and H. W. Ngan. "Electricity price forecasting with extreme learning machine and bootstrapping." *IEEE Transactions on Power Systems* 27, no. 4 (2012): 2055–2062.

[6]. Chen, Po-Yu, Shusen Yang, Julie A. McCann, Jie Lin, and Xinyu Yang. "Detection of false data injection attacks in smart-grid systems." *IEEE Communications Magazine* 53, no. 2 (2015): 206–213.

[7]. Aderibole, Adedayo, Aamna Aljarwan, Muhammad Habib Ur Rehman, Hatem H. Zeineldin, Toufic Mezher, Khaled Salah, Ernesto Damiani, and Davor Svetinovic. "Blockchain technology for smart grids: Decentralized NIST conceptual model." *IEEE Access* 8 (2020): 43177–43190.

[8]. Diffie, W., and M. E. Hellman. "New directions in cryptography." In *Democratizing Cryptography: The Work of Whitfield Diffie and Martin Hellman*, IEEE (vol. IT-22, pp. 644–654), 1976.

[9]. Kakavand, Hossein, Nicolette Kost De Sevres, and Bart Chilton. "The blockchain revolution: An analysis of regulation and technology related to distributed ledger technologies." Available at SSRN 2849251 (2017).

[10]. Münsing, Eric, Mather, and Scott Moura. "Blockchains for decentralized optimization of energy resources in microgrid networks." In *2017 IEEE Conference on Control Technology and Applications* (CCTA) (pp. 2164–2171). IEEE, 2017.

[11]. Aydar, Mehmet, Salih Cemil Cetin, Serkan Ayvaz, and Betul Aygun. "Private key encryption and recovery in blockchain." arXiv preprint arXiv:1907.04156 (2019).

[12]. Azimoh, Leonard Chukwuma. *Investigation into Voltage and Angle Stability of a Hybrid HVAC-HVDC Power Network*. Master's thesis, University of Cape Town, 2010.

[13]. Metke, Anthony R., and Randy L. Ekl. "Security technology for smart grid networks." *IEEE Transactions on Smart Grid* 1, no. 1 (2010): 99–107.

[14]. Tan, Song, Debraj De, Wen-Zhan Song, Junjie Yang, and Sajal K. Das. "Survey of security advances in smart grid: A data driven approach." *IEEE Communications Surveys & Tutorials* 19, no. 1 (2016): 397–422.

[15]. Su, Yueyuan, Ping Jiang, Huan Chen, and Xiaoheng Deng. "A QoS-Guaranteed and Congestion-Controlled SDN Routing Strategy for Smart Grid." *Applied Sciences* 12, no. 15 (2022): 7629.

[16]. Otuoze, Abdulrahaman Okino, Mohd Wazir Mustafa, and Raja Masood Larik. "Smart grids security challenges: Classification by sources of threats." *Journal of Electrical Systems and Information Technology* 5, no. 3 (2018): 468–483.

[17]. McDaniel, Patrick, and Stephen McLaughlin. "Security and privacy challenges in the smart grid." *IEEE Security & Privacy* 7, no. 3 (2009): 75–77.

[18]. Delgado-Gomes, Vasco, Joao F. Martins, Celson Lima, and Paul Nicolae Borza. "Smart grid security issues." In *2015 9th International Conference on Compatibility and Power Electronics (CPE)* (pp. 534–538). IEEE, 2015.

[19]. Teixeira, André, Iman Shames, Henrik Sandberg, and Karl H. Johansson. "Revealing stealthy attacks in control systems." In *2012 50th Annual Allerton Conference on Communication, Control, and Computing (Allerton)* (pp. 1806–1813). IEEE, 2012.

[20]. Jiao, Runhai, Gangyi Xun, Xuan Liu, and Guangwei Yan. "A new AC false data injection attack method without network information." *IEEE Transactions on Smart Grid* 12, no. 6 (2021): 5280–5289.

[21]. Guo, Yihao, Zhiguo Wan, and Xiuzhen Cheng. "When Blockchain Meets Smart Grids: A Comprehensive Survey." *High-Confidence Computing* (2022): 100059.

[22]. Bekara, Chakib. "Security issues and challenges for the IoT-based smart grid." *Procedia Computer Science* 34 (2014): 532–537.

[23]. Gai, Keke, Meikang Qiu, Zhong Ming, Hui Zhao, and Longfei Qiu. "Spoofing-jamming attack strategy using optimal power distributions in wireless smart grid networks." *IEEE Transactions on Smart Grid* 8, no. 5 (2017): 2431–2439.

[24]. Sharma, Kashma, B. S. Kaith, Vijay Kumar, Susheel Kalia, Vinod Kumar, and H. C. Swart. "Water retention and dye adsorption behavior of Gg-cl-poly (acrylic acid-aniline) based conductive hydrogels." *Geoderma* 232 (2014): 45–55.

[25]. Jinhua, Gao, and Xia Kejian. "ARP spoofing detection algorithm using ICMP protocol." In *2013 International Conference on Computer Communication and Informatics* (pp. 1–6). IEEE, 2013.

[26]. Jokar Arsanjani, Jamal, Marco Helbich, Mohamed Bakillah, Julian Hagenauer, and Alexander Zipf. "Toward mapping land-use patterns from volunteered geographic information." *International Journal of Geographical Information Science* 27, no. 12 (2013): 2264–2278.

[27]. Ashok, Aditya, Adam Hahn, and Manimaran Govindarasu. "Cyber-physical security of wide-area monitoring, protection and control in a smart grid environment." *Journal of Advanced Research* 5, no. 4 (2014): 481–489.

[28]. Gritzalis, Dimitris, Marianthi Theocharidou, and George Stergiopoulos. "Critical infrastructure security and resilience." *Springer International Publishing* 10 (2019): 978–1003.

[29]. Ding, Jianguo, Attia Qammar, Zhimin Zhang, Ahmad Karim, and Huansheng Ning. "Cyber Threats to smart grids: review, taxonomy, potential solutions, and future directions." *Energies* 15, no. 18 (2022): 6799.

[30]. Bhaskar, N. "Symmetric key cryptography algorithm using complement for small data security." *International Journal of Engineering Research & Technology* 2, no. 5 (2013).

[31]. Sakhnini, Jacob, Hadis Karimipour, Ali Dehghantanha, Reza M. Parizi, and Gautam Srivastava. "Security aspects of internet of things aided smart grids: A bibliometric survey." *Internet of Things* 14 (2021): 100111.

[32]. Rituraj, Rituraj, Péter Kádár, and Annamaria R. Varkonyi-Koczy. "Smart Meter: Advantages and its Roadmap in India." In *2021 IEEE 4th International Conference and Workshop Óbuda on Electrical and Power Engineering (CANDO-EPE)* (pp. 131–138). IEEE, 2021.

[33]. Ali, Muhammad Qasim, Ehab Al-Shaer, and Qi Duan. "Randomizing AMI configuration for proactive defense in smart grid." In *2013 IEEE International Conference on Smart Grid Communications (SmartGridComm)* (pp. 618–623). IEEE, 2013.

[34]. Bhatia, Sajal, Nishchal Singh Kush, Chris Djamaludin, Ayodeji James Akande, and Ernest Foo. "Practical modbus flooding attack and detection." In *Proceedings of the Twelfth Australasian Information Security Conference (AISC 2014) [Conferences in Research and Practice in Information Technology, Volume 149]* (pp. 57–65). Australian Computer Society, 2014.

[35]. Malina, Lukas, Gautam Srivastava, Petr Dzurenda, Jan Hajny, and Radek Fujdiak. "A secure publish/subscribe protocol for internet of things." ARES'19: In *Proceedings of the 14th International Conference on Availability, Reliability and Security* (pp. 1–10), ACM Digital Library 2019. https://doi.org/10.1145/3339252.3340503.

[36]. Dwivedi, Ashutosh Dhar, Gautam Srivastava, Shalini Dhar, and Rajani Singh. "A decentralized privacy-preserving healthcare blockchain for IoT." *Sensors* 19, no. 2 (2019): 326.

[37]. Xiang, Anhao. *Design of Advanced Device Authentication Schemes for Smart Grids*. PhD Dissertation, New Mexico Institute of Mining and Technology, 2021.

[38]. Taheri, Omid, Nima Ghorbani, Michael J. Black, and Dimitrios Tzionas. "GRAB: A dataset of whole-body human grasping of objects." In *European Conference on Computer Vision* (pp. 581–600). Springer, 2020.

[39]. Wang, Yübo, Oleg Anokhin, and Reiner Anderl. "Concept and use case driven approach for mapping it security requirements on system assets and processes in industrie 4.0." *Procedia CIRP* 63 (2017): 207–212.

[40]. Hendrickx, Julien M., Karl Henrik Johansson, Raphael M. Jungers, Henrik Sandberg, and Kin Cheong Sou. "Efficient computations of a security

index for false data attacks in power networks." *IEEE Transactions on Automatic Control* 59, no. 12 (2014): 3194–3208.

[41]. Hahn, Adam. *Cyber security of the Smart Grid: Attack Exposure Analysis, Detection Algorithms, and Testbed Evaluation*. Graduate Theses and Dissertations, Iowa State University, 2013.

[42]. Hahn, Rüdiger, and Michael Kühnen. "Determinants of sustainability reporting: A review of results, trends, theory, and opportunities in an expanding field of research." *Journal of Cleaner Production* 59 (2013): 5–21.

[43]. Idika, Nwokedi, and Bharat Bhargava. "Extending attack graph-based security metrics and aggregating their application." *IEEE Transactions on Dependable and Secure Computing* 9, no. 1 (2010): 75–85.

[44]. Laszka, Aron, Abhishek Dubey, Michael Walker, and Doug Schmidt. "Providing privacy, safety, and security in IoT-based transactive energy systems using distributed ledgers." IoT'17: In *Proceedings of the Seventh International Conference on the Internet of Things* (pp. 1–8), ACM Digital Library 2017. https://doi.org/10.1145/3131542.3131562.

[45]. Sridhar, Siddharth, Manimaran Govindarasu, and Chen-Ching Liu. "Risk analysis of coordinated cyber-attacks on power grid." In *Control and Optimization Methods for Electric Smart Grids* (pp. 275–294). Springer, 2012.

[46]. Fuloria, Shailendra, Ross Anderson, Fernando Alvarez, and Kevin McGrath. "Key management for substations: Symmetric keys, public keys or no keys?." In *2011 IEEE/PES Power Systems Conference and Exposition* (pp. 1–6). IEEE, 2011.

[47]. Rathor, Sumit K., and D. Saxena. "Energy management system for smart grid: An overview and key issues." *International Journal of Energy Research* 44, no. 6 (2020): 4067–4109.

[48]. Lopes, Joao Abel Peças Andre Guimarães Madureira, and Carlos Moreira. "A view of microgrids." *Advances in Energy Systems: The Large-scale Renewable Energy Integration Challenge* (2019): 149–166.

[49]. Lind, Leandro, Rafael Cossent, José Pablo Chaves-Ávila, and Tomás Gómez San Román. "Transmission and distribution coordination in power systems with high shares of distributed energy resources providing balancing and congestion management services." *Wiley Interdisciplinary Reviews: Energy and Environment* 8, no. 6 (2019): e357.

[50]. Carlini, Enrico Maria, Robert Schroeder, Jens Møller Birkebæk, and Fabio Massaro. "EU transition in power sector: How RES affects the design and operations of transmission power systems." *Electric Power Systems Research* 169 (2019): 74–91.

[51]. Singh, A. K., and S. K. Parida. "A review on distributed generation allocation and planning in deregulated electricity market." *Renewable and Sustainable Energy Reviews*, 82 (2018): 4132–4141.

[52]. Ten, Chee-Wooi, Chen-Ching Liu, and Govindarasu Manimaran. "Vulnerability assessment of cybersecurity for SCADA systems." *IEEE Transactions on Power Systems* 23, no. 4 (2008): 1836–1846.

[53]. Manadhata, Pratyusa K., and Jeannette M. Wing. "A formal model for a system's attack surface." In *Moving Target Defense* (pp. 1–28). Springer, 2011.

[54]. Dacier, Marc, Yves Deswarte, and Mohamed Kaâniche. "Quantitative assessment of operational security: Models and tools." In *Information Systems Security*, edited by SK Katsikas and D. Gritzalis (pp. 179–86). Chapman & Hall, 1996.

[55]. Dacier, Marc, and Yves Deswarte. "Privilege graph: An extension to the typed access matrix model." In *European Symposium on Research in Computer Security* (pp. 319–334). Springer, 1994.

[56]. Alladi, Tejasvi, Vinay Chamola, Joel J. P. C. Rodrigues, and Sergei A. Kozlov. "Blockchain in smart grids: A review on different use cases." *Sensors* 19, no. 22 (2019): 4862.

[57]. Erturk, Emre, Dobrila Lopez, and Wei Yang Yu. "Benefits and risks of using blockchain in smart energy: A literature review." *Contemporary Management Research* 15, no. 3 (2019): 205–225.

[58]. Musleh, Ahmed S., Gang Yao, and S. M. Muyeen. "Blockchain applications in smart grid–review and frameworks." *IEEE Access* 7 (2019): 86746–86757.

[59]. Adeyemi, Adetomike, Mingyu Yan, Mohammad Shahidehpour, Cristina Botero, Alba Valbuena Guerra, Niroj Gurung, Liuxi Calvin Zhang, and Aleksi Paaso. "Blockchain technology applications in power distribution systems." *The Electricity Journal* 33, no. 8 (2020): 106817.

[60]. Chen, Wenzhi. *A Study of Small-Signal Stability of Multi-Machine Power Systems*. Master of Science Thesis, Department of Electrical Engineering, University of Alberta, Canada, (1995). Available at: https://scholar.google.co.in/scholar?q=A+study+of+small-signal+stability+of+multi-machine+power+systems&hl=en&as_sdt=0&as_vis=1&oi=scholart.

[61]. Yagmur, Ahmet, Beyhan Adanur Dedeturk, Ahmet Soran, Jaesung Jung, and Ahmet Onen. "Blockchain-based energy applications: The DSO perspective." *IEEE Access* 9 (2021): 145605–145625.

[62]. Tushar, Wayes, Tapan Kumar Saha, Chau Yuen, David Smith, and H. Vincent Poor. "Peer-to-peer trading in electricity networks: An overview." *IEEE Transactions on Smart Grid* 11, no. 4 (2020): 3185–3200.

[63]. Gawusu, Sidique, Xiaobing Zhang, Abubakari Ahmed, Seidu Abdulai Jamatutu, Elvis Djam Miensah, Ayesha Algade Amadu, and Frimpong Atta Junior Osei. "Renewable energy sources from the perspective of blockchain integration: From theory to application." *Sustainable Energy Technologies and Assessments* 52 (2022): 102108.

[64]. Cheng, Xiang, Xiaoya Hu, Liuqing Yang, Iqbal Husain, Koichi Inoue, Philip Krein, Russell Lefevre et al. "Electrified vehicles and the smart grid: The ITS perspective." *IEEE Transactions on Intelligent Transportation Systems* 15, no. 4 (2014): 1388–1404.

[65]. Sadiq, Ayesha, Muhammad Umar Javed, Rabiya Khalid, Ahmad Almogren, Muhammad Shafiq, and Nadeem Javaid. "Blockchain based data and energy trading in internet of electric vehicles." *IEEE Access* 9 (2020): 7000–7020.

[66]. Sree Lakshmi, G., Rubanenko Olena, G. Divya, and I. Hunko. "Electric vehicles integration with renewable energy sources and smart grids." In *Advances in Smart Grid Technology* (pp. 397–411). Springer, 2020.

[67]. Galus, Matthias D., Marina González Vayá, Thilo Krause, and Göran Andersson. "The role of electric vehicles in smart grids." *Advances in Energy Systems: The Large-scale Renewable Energy Integration Challenge* (2019): 245–264.

[68]. Erdemir, Ecenaz, Deniz Gündüz, and Pier Luigi Dragotti. "Smart meter privacy." In *Privacy in Dynamical Systems* (pp. 19–41). Springer, 2020.

[69]. Hassan, Muneeb Ul, Mubashir Husain Rehmani, and Jinjun Chen. "Differential privacy for edge computing-based smart grid operating over blockchain." In *Blockchain-enabled Fog and Edge Computing* (pp. 245–294). CRC Press, 2020.

[70]. Samy, Salma, Karim Banawan, Mohamed Azab, and Mohamed Rizk. "Smart blockchain-based control-data protection framework for trustworthy smart grid operations." In *2021 IEEE 12th Annual Information Technology, Electronics and Mobile Communication Conference (IEMCON)* (pp. 0963–0969). IEEE, 2021.

[71]. Miglani, Arzoo, Neeraj Kumar, Vinay Chamola, and Sherali Zeadally. "Blockchain for internet of energy management: Review, solutions, and challenges." *Computer Communications* 151 (2020): 395–418.

[72]. Di Silvestre, Maria Luisa, Pierluigi Gallo, Josep M. Guerrero, Rossano Musca, Eleonora Riva Sanseverino, Giuseppe Sciumè, Juan C. Vásquez, and Gaetano Zizzo. "Blockchain for power systems: Current trends and future applications." *Renewable and Sustainable Energy Reviews* 119 (2020): 109585.

[73]. Zeng, Ting, Mengying Yang, and Yifan Shen. "Fancy Bitcoin and conventional financial assets: Measuring market integration based on connectedness networks." *Economic Modelling* 90 (2020): 209–220.

[74]. O'Donovan, Peter, and Dominic T. J. O'Sullivan. "A systematic analysis of real-world energy blockchain initiatives." *Future Internet* 11, no. 8 (2019): 174.

[75]. Khajeh, Hosna, Hannu Laaksonen, Amin Shokri Gazafroudi, and Miadreza Shafie-khah. "Towards flexibility trading at TSO-DSO-customer levels: A review." *Energies* 13, no. 1 (2019): 165.

[76]. Kh-Madhloom, Jamal. "Dynamic Cryptography Integrated Secured Decentralized Applications with Blockchain Programming." *Wasit Journal of Computer and Mathematics Sciences* 1, no. 2 (2022): 21–33.

[77]. Andoni, Alexandr, Chengyu Lin, Ying Sheng, Peilin Zhong, and Ruiqi Zhong. "Subspace embedding and linear regression with Orlicz norm." In *International Conference on Machine Learning* (pp. 224–233). PMLR, 2018.

[78]. Ramnarine, Timothy J. S., Amanda Glaser-Schmitt, Ana Catalán, and John Parsch. "Population genetic and functional analysis of a cis-regulatory polymorphism in the drosophila melanogaster metallothionein a gene." *Genes* 10, no. 2 (2019): 147.

[79]. Khan, Hamzah, and Tariq Masood. "Impact of blockchain technology on smart grids." *Energies* 15, no. 19 (2022): 7189.

[80]. Meadows, Catherine. "Open issues in formal methods for cryptographic protocol analysis." In *Proceedings DARPA Information Survivability Conference and Exposition. DISCEX'00* (vol. 1, pp. 237–250). IEEE, 2000.

[81]. Rosenheim, Shawn James. *The Cryptographic Imagination: Secret Writing from Edgar Poe to the Internet.* JHU Press, 2020.

[82]. Mylrea, Michael, and Sri Nikhil Gupta Gourisetti. "Blockchain for smart grid resilience: Exchanging distributed energy at speed, scale and security." In *2017 Resilience Week (RWS)* (pp. 18–23). IEEE, 2017.

[83]. Nehai, Zeinab, and Guillaume Guérard. "Integration of the blockchain in a smart grid model." In *Proceedings of the 14th International Conference of Young Scientists on Energy Issues (CYSENI 2017)* (pp. 25–26). Kaunas, Lithuania, ACM Digital Library 2017, ISSN:1822-7554.

[84]. Devi, T. Rajani. "Importance of cryptography in network security." In *2013 International Conference on Communication Systems and Network Technologies* (pp. 462–467). IEEE, 2013.

[85]. AbuTaha, Mohammed, Mousa Farajallah, Radwan Tahboub, and M. Odeh. "Survey paper: Cryptography is the science of information security." *International Journal of Computer Science and Security (IJCSS)* 5, no. 3 (2011): 298–309. Available at: http://localhost:8080/xmlui/handle/123456789/7817.

[86]. Yang, Pan, Naixue Xiong, and Jingli Ren. "Data security and privacy protection for cloud storage: A survey." *IEEE Access* 8 (2020): 131723–131740.

[87]. Sun, Xiaoqiang, F. Richard Yu, Peng Zhang, Zhiwei Sun, Weixin Xie, and Xiang Peng. "A survey on zero-knowledge proof in blockchain." *IEEE Network* 35, no. 4 (2021): 198–205.

[88]. Feige, Uriel, Amos Fiat, and Adi Shamir. "Zero-knowledge proofs of identity." *Journal of Cryptology* 1, no. 2 (1988): 77–94.

[89]. Goldreich, Oded, and Yair Oren. "Definitions and properties of zero-knowledge proof systems." *Journal of Cryptology* 7, no. 1 (1994): 1–32.

[90]. Chander, Bhanu. "The state-of-the-art cryptography techniques for secure data transmission." In *Handbook of Research on Intrusion Detection Systems* (pp. 284–305). IGI Global, 2020.

[91]. Chander, Bhanu. "The state-of-the-art cryptography techniques for secure data transmission." In *Handbook of Research on Intrusion Detection Systems* (pp. 284–305). IGI Global, 2020.

[92]. Mainanwal, Vikash, Mansi Gupta, and Shravan Kumar Upadhayay. "Zero knowledge protocol with RSA cryptography algorithm for authentication in web browser login system (Z-RSA)." In *2015 Fifth International Conference on Communication Systems and Network Technologies* (pp. 776–780). IEEE, 2015.

[93]. Mohr, Austin. "A survey of zero-knowledge proofs with applications to cryptography." *Southern Illinois University, Carbondale* (2007): 1–12.

[94]. Al Ketbi, Maitha, Khaled Shuaib, Ezedin Barka, and Marton Gergely. "Establishing a security control framework for blockchain technology." *Interdisciplinary Journal of Information, Knowledge, and Management* 16 (2021): 307.

[95]. Rawat, B. Danda, Vijay Chaudhary, and Ronald Doku. "Blockchain technology: Emerging applications and use cases for secure and trustworthy smart systems." *Journal of Cybersecurity and Privacy* 1, no. 1 (2020): 4–18.

[96]. Fang, Weidong, Wei Chen, Wuxiong Zhang, Jun Pei, Weiwei Gao, and Guohui Wang. "Digital signature scheme for information non-repudiation in blockchain: a state of the art review." *EURASIP Journal on Wireless Communications and Networking* 2020, no. 1 (2020): 1–15.

[97]. Tabassum, Anika, Humayra Anjumee Jeba, Tasnim Kabir Mahi, SM Salim Reza, and Dilshad Ara Hossain. "Securely transfer information with RSA and digital signature by using the concept of fog computing and blockchain." In *2021 International Conference on Information and Communication Technology for Sustainable Development (ICICT4SD)* (pp. 311–315). IEEE, 2021.

[98]. Puthal, Deepak, Nisha Malik, Saraju P. Mohanty, Elias Kougianos, and Chi Yang. "The blockchain as a decentralized security framework [future directions]." *IEEE Consumer Electronics Magazine* 7, no. 2 (2018): 18–21.

[99]. Ajao, Lukman Adewale James, Agajo Emmanuel, Adewale Adedokun, and Loveth Karngong. "Crypto hash algorithm-based blockchain technology for managing decentralized ledger database in oil and gas industry." *Multidisciplinary Scientific Journal* 2, no. 3 (2019): 300–325. https://doi.org/10.3390/j2030021.

[100]. Lundqvist, Thomas, Andreas De Blanche, and H. Robert H. Andersson. "Thing-to-thing electricity micro payments using blockchain technology." In *2017 Global Internet of Things Summit* (GIoTS) (pp. 1–6). IEEE, 2017.

[101]. Liu, Chao, Kok Keong Chai, Xiaoshuai Zhang, Eng Tseng Lau, and Yue Chen. "Adaptive blockchain-based electric vehicle participation scheme in smart grid platform." *IEEE Access* 6 (2018): 25657–25665.

[102]. Pedrosa, Alejandro Ranchal, and Giovanni Pau. "ChargeItUp: On blockchain-based technologies for autonomous vehicles." CryBlock'18: In *Proceedings of the 1st Workshop on Cryptocurrencies and Blockchains for Distributed Systems* (pp. 87–92), ACM Digital Library 2018. https://doi.org/10.1145/3211933.3211949.

[103]. T. Choudhary, C. Virmani, and D. Juneja. "Convergence of Blockchain and IoT: An Edge Over Technologies." In *Toward Social Internet of Things (SIoT): Enabling Technologies, Architectures and Applications* (pp. 299–316). Springer, 2020.

Chapter 9

Big Data and Smart Grid

Implementation-Based Case Study

*Mr. Jameer Kotwal, Dr. Ramgopal Kashyap,
and Dr. Pathan Shafi*

9.1 INTRODUCTION

The adoption of massive data analysis in the banking, health-care, internet of things (IOT), communication, smart cities, and transportation industries has shown tremendous promise for innovation and commercial success during the past several years. At the moment, power grids use a variety of advancements in quantifying, control, delivery, and science of information to operate electric power systems that efficiently provide end users with inexpensive, dependable, sustainable, and high-quality energy. Globally, power grids are also implementing a sizable advanced metering infrastructure (AMI) and measurement tools like smart meters and phasor measurement units (PMUs) to gather comprehensive, high-resolution electrical measurements [1–4].

Many terabytes (TB) of new data are processed annually by a typical distribution utility [5]. As seen in Figure 9.1, these data come from a variety of sources, including sensors, meters, measuring device, social media, etc. Smart grids' big data is diverse and has a variety of resolutions, is primarily synchronous, and kept in different locations in different formats. After a time period, the consumption of energy is noted from the meter and is kept for billing process. A utility with a million smart meters deployed generates around 3,000 GB of new energy use data annually. PMUs, on the other hand, measure the voltage and current measurements with high resolution in the power grid and send reports as time-synchronized phasors to phasor data concentrators situated at the substation level or at control centers at a rate of 30 to 60 times per second. For a typical utility, PMUs produce about 40 TB of new data annually [5]. A unique information-driven control method is made possible by the big data's substantial amount of information.

At all levels, including generation, transmission, distribution, and end user, big data in smart grids enables flexibility in the way that things are now planned and operated.

Big data (BD) properties are modeled by the HACE theorem [3]. According to this statement, big proportion, diverse, independent sources are used

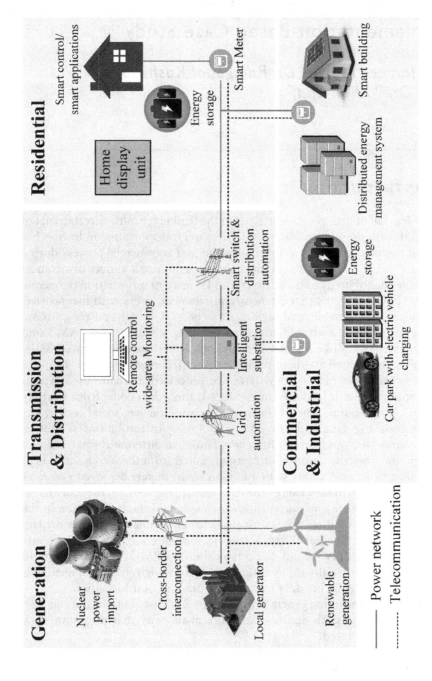

Figure 9.1 Sources of electrical and non-electrical big dataset in smart grids.

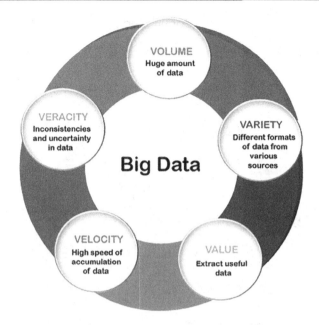

Figure 9.2 Big data characteristics.

first in BD with dispersed and disrupted control and aims to investigate intricate and changing association between data. Finding relevant information in data is quite difficult as a result of these factors.

Big data, which includes corporate processes, machines, social media platforms, networks, human interactions, and many more, are characterized by high volume in the smart grid, as shown in Figure 9.2. On Facebook, billions of people post message, how many times like button hit, daily thousands/ millions of posts is posted. So, to handle bulky data, we have to use good technology. The diversity of data is seen. Hashtag posts on Facebook are an illustration of veracity (how accurate is the data). Value (it is valuable and dependable data that we save, handle, and also evaluate). Velocity is concerned with the rate at which data comes from sources such as the corporate world, banking, social media websites, IOT, and smart devices [6–9].

9.2 UTILITY OF BIG DATA

9.2.1 Role in Social Media Analysis

As depicted in Figure 9.3, the word "social media" refers to a broad category of online platforms that let users generate and share information from social media channels. Social media can be divided into the following

Figure 9.3 Data generated from various platforms.

categories: social sites (such as Twitter), messaging services (such as Viber, WhatsApp, Telegram, etc.), scientific networks (such as Research Gate, Academia.edu, Mendeley, and ResearchID), blogs (such as Blogger and WordPress), microblogs (such as Twitter), social news sites (such as Newsvine, Prismatic), social bookmarking services (such as Pinterest and Dribble), media sharing sites (such as TikTok and Whatsapp), wikis (such as Wikipedia and Wiki Data. Centricity is the defining feature of contemporary social media, and analytics and economics are just a few of the disciplines that have done extensive research on social media analytics [10–12].

9.2.2 Role in Biological Network Analysis

Instead of spending money on costly tests, link prediction techniques are used in biology to find links or associations in biological networks (such protein–protein interaction networks). With the data flood brought on by current high throughput molecular biology studies, prominent topics like big data biology and network biology have developed. Clearly, there is a vast range of topics covered by big data and network biology. The three fundamental processes in data-intensive sciences like modern biology are capture, duration, and analysis.

Systems biology focuses on systems made up of molecular components and their interactions as opposed to bioinformatics, which focuses on individual molecules such the sequence of nucleotide acids and amino acids. Finding the best path and understanding how gene expression and regulation affect other paths are all part of the analysis of gene regulatory networks. Just a portion of each gene is expressed in a given tissue, and this expression shows some sort of pattern throughout time. Finding this temporal pattern from such a vast amount of data is the goal.

9.2.3 Role in Health Care

Medical imaging and computer-assisted image processing have advanced significantly in the last twenty years in the field of radiological sciences [13]. Health-care firms can use tried-and-true technologies to their advantage by using big data and analytics. At all levels of the health-care system, medical imaging will continue to play a role of ever-increasing importance as a fundamental component of modern health care. The data can be found in a variety of formats, including waveforms, 3D reconstructions, movies, genetic information, BCG waveforms, ultrasound photos, MRI scans, and lab results, among others. Medical photos are being stored for extended periods of time and growing by 20–40% annually [14, 15]. The causes of such expansion are plain to see. Even though there are many elderly people, the populace is wealthy. Moreover, technologies have advanced, and medications are quite protective.

9.3 BIG DATA PLATFORMS

Platforms for big data processing must work at a scale that offers very little room for error. Big data clusters must be constructed for speed, size, and efficiency [16, 17]. These platforms aid organizations in gaining insight by transforming data into high-quality information that improves comprehension of business circumstances. This essentially entails transforming raw data into potent statistics. Subsequently are a few of the platforms for managing data.

9.3.1 Microsoft Azure

Virtualization, a technology that simulates computer hardware in software, is a foundational component of Microsoft Azure. Figure 9.4 depicts the Azure dataflow as the following [18–20]:

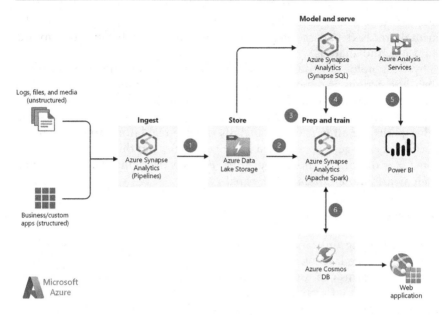

Figure 9.4 System architecture of Microsoft Azure.

1. All of your media, logs, and other structured, semi-structured, and unstructured data can be combined into Azure Data Lake Storage using Synapse Pipelines.
2. Use Apache Spark pools to clean, process, and merge the structured data from operational databases or data warehouses with the unstructured datasets.
3. To gain deeper insights from this data, use scalable machine learning/deep learning algorithms with notebook experiences in the Apache Spark pool.
4. Use Azure Synapse Analytics' Synapse Pipelines and Apache Spark pool to access and transport data at scale.
5. Use Power BI to query and report on data.
6. Use Azure Cosmos DB to store the insights from Apache Spark pools so that web and mobile apps may access them.

9.3.2 IBM Cloud Database for MongoDB

Due to the distributed system architecture of MongoDB, user data is highly available and redundant by being replicated across numerous database servers. Replica sets, the MongoDB process used to manage the multiple copies, enable this.

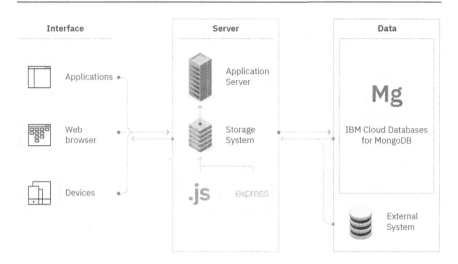

Figure 9.5 System architecture of IBM Cloud database for MongoDB.

MongoDB's design features single-master ideas, as seen in Figure 9.5. It has a single major node and up to 48 secondary nodes. All data updates to the primary node's datasets are written and read into the operation log, or oplog. The updates are applied to the datasets of the secondary nodes after they have read the original node's oplog. As a result, in the case of a primary node failure, the eligible secondary node will be selected as a primary node and handle read and write activities.

9.3.3 Hadoop HDFS Architecture

In Figure 9.6, the Name Node, the Master Daemon in the HDFS Architecture, is depicted. As we already know, this daemon maintains the metadata for each and every DataNode in the Cluster as well as the details for every block present in every single one of these DataNodes. According to the diagram, we have racks like Rack-1, which has three DataNodes, and Rack-2, which has two DataNodes. Moreover, a replication factor is used across all nodes. Now there are clients that can read data from DataNodes and clients that can write data to these DataNodes [21].

9.4 CASE STUDY OF SMART GRID

9.4.1 Identifying Linkages and Forecasting the Spread of Faults in Cyber-Physical Systems

A model to detect the interdependencies among the parts of a cyber-physical system is put out by authors Koosha Marashi et al. (2021) by employing correlation metrics and a heuristic causality analysis method. They put forth

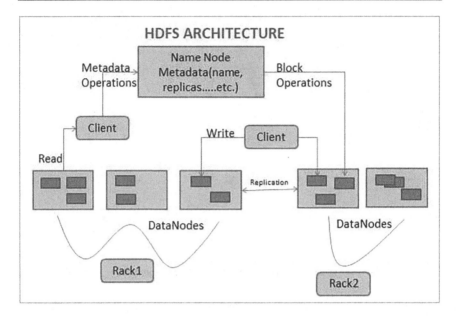

Figure 9.6 Hadoop HDFS architecture.

a prediction tool that can assist system administrators in taking prompt pre-ventive measures and minimizing the effects of unintentional failures and malicious attacks. They have examined two IEEE power-bus-based smart grid test scenarios, known as IEEE-14 and IEEE-57. Table 9.1 shows the results of accuracy, recall, and precision, and Figure 9.7 shows the actual vs. predicted values.

9.4.1.1 Results

Table 9.1 Accuracy, Recall, Precision, F-score

Step	TR-Loss	VL-Loss	Accuracy	Recall	Precision	F-Score
0	0.6919	0.6556	99.40%	0.00%	0.00%	0.00%
100	0.0120	0.0312	99.40%	100.00%	100.00%	100.00%
200	0.0009	0.0508	99.43%	71.65%	81.33%	74.46%
300	0.0002	0.0576	99.45%	70.42%	79.48%	73.26%
400	0.0002	0.0612	99.45%	71.92%	81.35%	74.81%
500	0.0002	0.0627	99.45%	71.01%	79.20%	73.44%
600	0.0002	0.0647	99.46%	72.13%	79.89%	74.43%

Step	TR-Loss	VL-Loss	Accuracy	Recall	Precision	F-Score
700	0.0001	0.0656	99.47%	73.18%	79.68%	75.08%
800	0.0001	0.0664	99.47%	74.16%	80.81%	76.12%
900	0.0001	0.0669	99.47%	74.25%	80.61%	76.07%
1000	0.0001	0.0673	99.47%	73.79%	80.52%	75.77%
1100	0.0001	0.0675	99.48%	73.83%	80.36%	75.75%
1200	0.0001	0.0676	99.48%	74.80%	81.03%	76.59%
1300	0.0011	0.0666	99.49%	75.08%	80.79%	76.64%
1400	0.0008	0.0664	99.47%	74.98%	82.19%	77.20%
1500	0.0001	0.0722	99.44%	66.79%	73.91%	68.79%
1600	0.0001	0.0654	99.47%	74.57%	80.13%	76.24%
1700	0.0001	0.0670	99.48%	75.54%	80.43%	77.00%
1800	0.0001	0.0676	99.49%	76.54%	81.25%	77.91%
1900	0.0001	0.0677	99.49%	77.88%	82.64%	79.25%
2000	0.0001	0.0676	99.49%	77.35%	81.99%	78.63%
2100	0.0001	0.0676	99.49%	78.44%	83.04%	79.73%
2200	0.0000	0.0676	99.49%	77.66%	82.26%	79.00%
2300	0.0000	0.0676	99.49%	77.61%	82.12%	78.88%
2400	0.0000	0.0679	99.50%	77.23%	82.14%	78.63%
2500	0.0000	0.0678	99.49%	77.42%	82.06%	78.72%
2600	0.0000	0.0680	99.49%	77.50%	82.10%	78.73%
2700	0.0000	0.0680	99.49%	76.88%	81.82%	78.25%
2800	0.0000	0.0683	99.49%	77.18%	82.11%	78.55%
2900	0.0000	0.0685	99.50%	77.52%	82.34%	78.79%
3000	0.0000	0.0690	99.50%	77.10%	82.37%	78.55%
3100	0.0000	0.0692	99.50%	77.51%	82.39%	78.87%
3200	0.0000	0.0698	99.50%	77.99%	82.55%	79.20%
3300	0.0673	0.1547	99.35%	51.40%	56.82%	52.68%
3400	0.0005	0.0612	99.42%	65.62%	71.94%	67.56%
3500	0.0004	0.0629	99.42%	64.28%	70.77%	66.19%
3600	0.0003	0.0655	99.42%	65.59%	72.34%	67.58%
3700	0.0004	0.0676	99.43%	66.89%	73.60%	68.84%
3800	0.0003	0.0714	99.43%	67.78%	74.27%	69.66%
3900	0.0002	0.0739	99.44%	68.00%	73.97%	69.72%
4000	0.0002	0.0758	99.44%	68.74%	74.64%	70.42%
4100	0.0002	0.0776	99.43%	68.71%	74.53%	70.36%
4200	0.0002	0.0790	99.44%	69.08%	74.75%	70.68%
4300	0.0002	0.0803	99.44%	69.52%	75.38%	71.19%
4400	0.0002	0.0814	99.44%	69.77%	75.59%	71.43%
4500	0.0001	0.0825	99.44%	70.22%	75.98%	71.87%

(Continued)

Table 9.1 Continued

Step	TR-Loss	VL-Loss	Accuracy	Recall	Precision	F-Score
4600	0.0001	0.0835	99.44%	70.93%	76.51%	72.51%
4700	0.0001	0.0845	99.44%	70.68%	76.34%	72.28%
4800	0.0001	0.0855	99.44%	69.30%	75.35%	71.00%
4900	0.0001	0.0861	99.44%	69.64%	75.64%	71.31%
5000	0.0001	0.0868	99.44%	69.98%	75.84%	71.61%
			Accuracy	Recall	Precision	F-Score
Test Dataset:			99.45%	70.29%	75.99%	72.01%
			Accuracy	Recall	Precision	F-Score
More Complex Test Dataset:			98.87%	53.56%	63.99%	55.93%

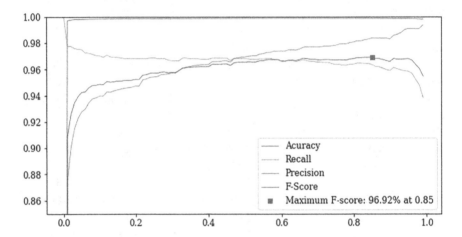

Figure 9.7 Prediction vs. actual failed components for a failure case.

9.4.2 A Sophisticated Architecture for Detecting Power Theft in a Smart Grid: EnsembleNTLDetect

Yogesh Kulkarni et al. (2021) introduce EnsembleNTLDetect in this article, a dependable and scalable framework for power theft detection. By examining client electricity usage patterns, EnsembleNTLDetect uses pre-processing techniques to process data and artificial intelligence models to identify theft. The enhanced Dynamic Time Warping Based Imputation (eDTWBI) algorithm is used in this framework to replace lacking values in the time series data while still producing balanced data using the Near-miss under-sampling

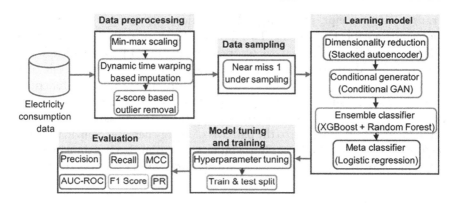

Figure 9.8 Architecture of EnsembleNTLDetect

technique. Furthermore, stacked autoencoder is implemented to reduce dimensionality and increase training effectiveness. A Conditional Generative Adversarial Network (CTGAN) is used to nourish the dataset and train the artificial model to identify the theft. A number of quality criteria were used to conduct tests on the real-time power consumption data provided by the State Grid Corporation of China (SGCC) to confirm EnsembleNTLDetect's dependability and accuracy in comparison to other state-of-the-art models for electricity theft detection.

The overall design of the EnsembleNTLDetect, the suggested model for detecting power theft, is shown in Figure 9.8. The complete EnsembleNTL-Detect working methodology, which consists of five stages (i) of data gathering and preprocessing, (ii) of data sampling, (iii) of learning models, (iv) of model tuning and training, and (v) of evaluation is made to effectively and precisely detect energy theft.

9.4.3 BI&DA for a Solar Power System

As an example, Briones et al. present a BI&DA application for a solar system (2017). Work was completed to make sure that the control panels provided quick and adaptable access to data and information. Processing the real-time data received from solar and examining past data were done in order to enable dependable and speedy decision-making. This was viewed as a key enabler for improving RE integration in a smart grid network. In order to collect, store, process, analyze, and monitor data in a solar system, the case study showed how to construct the proper "big data" infrastructure. The detail investigating of solar system through BI&DA is done. Logical layers make up the "big data" system. The steps are as follows: data collection, transmission, receipt, processing, alert verification, storage, alert notification, and analytical processing. Two different forms of analysis are displayed in the application case: analysis of operational control panels and forecast generation and analysis. The latter is essentially a descriptive analysis that illustrates how the photovoltaic system's operational procedures function. The system may show details about the solar system's efficiency, its power output, and its capacity to monitor weather-related information. As a common method of responding to the patterns of energy demand from industries, offices, buildings, and homes, photovoltaic generation also has the capability of monitoring the decrease in electricity need (see Briones et al., 2017).

9.5 CONCLUSION

With the sizable amount of data generated during the production and distribution of energy by businesses, it is increasingly important to apply data analytics to turn this information into knowledge that can be used for immediate management decision-making. Several ICT technologies are involved in this. The development of new practical knowledge for company managers is greatly aided by the use of advanced tools and techniques in smart hub. There are a number of significant software categories used in business intelligence processes, with "BI" software being one of the most popular ones for processing large amounts of data. The BI&DA technologies are successfully implemented in the energy sector. At numerous significant international companies, the block chain technology is also used to process large amount of data from energy sector which require a security and dependability in the processes of regeneration, keeping records, flow of data, and monitoring. The operation of power companies' smart grid systems, as well as processes for the collecting and management of big data in the business, commercial, and financial sectors, have all demonstrated the technical viability of this technology.

REFERENCES

[1] Aquino-Lugo, A. A., Klump, R., & Overbye, T. J. (2011). A control framework for the smart grid for voltage support using agent-based technologies. *IEEE Transactions on Smart Grid*, 2(1): 173–180. http://dx.doi.org/10.1109/TSG.2010.2096238.

[2] Arenas-Martinez, M., Herrero-Lopez, S., Sanchez, A., Williams, J. R., Roth, P., Hofmann, P., & Zeier, A. (2010). A comparative study of data storage and processing architectures for the smart grid. In

Proceedings under IEEE International Conference on Smart Grid Communications. Gaithersburg, MD (vol. 28, pp. 5–290). IEEE http://dx.doi.org/10.1109/SMARTGRID.2010.5622058.

[3]   Arzamasov, V., Böhm, K., & Jochem, P. (2018). Towards concise models of grid stability. In *Paper Presented at the 2018 IEEE International Conference on Communications, Control, and Computing Technologies for Smart Grids (SmartGridComm).* Aalborg, (pp. 1–6). http://dx.doi.org/10.1109/SmartGridComm.2018.8587498.

[4]   Asad, Z., & Chaudhry, M. A. R. (2017). A two-way street: Green big data processing for a greener smart grid. *IEEE Systems Journal*, 11(2): 784–795. http://dx.doi.org/10.1109/JSYST.2015.2498639.

[5]   Chen, M., Mao, S., & Liu, Y. (2014). Big data: A survey. *Mobile Networks and Applications*, 19: 171–209. http://dx.doi.org/10.1007/s11036-013-0489-0.

[6]   Avgerinou, M., Bertoldi, P., & Castellazzi, L. (2017). Trends in data centre energy consumption under the European code of conduct for data centre energy efficiency. *Energies*, 10, Article 1470. http://dx.doi.org/10.3390/en10101470.

[7]   Baker, T., Al-Dawsari, B., Tawfik, H., Reid, D., & Ngoko, Y. (2015). GreeDi: An energy efficient routing algorithm for big data on cloud. *Ad Hoc Networks*, 35: 83–96. http://dx.doi.org/10.1016/j.adhoc.2015.06.008.

[8]   Banerjee, P., Patel, C., Bash, C., Shah, A., & Arlitt, M. (2012). Towards a net-zero data center. *ACM Journal on Emerging Technologies in Computing Systems*, 8(4), Article 27. http://dx.doi.org/10.1145/2367736.2367738.

[9]   Barbeito, I., Zaragoza, S., Tarrío-Saavedra, J., & Naya, S. (2017). Assessing thermal comfort and energy efficiency in buildings by statistical quality control for autocorrelated data. *Applied Energy*, 190: 1–17. http://dx.doi.org/10.1016/j.apenergy.2016.12.100.

[10]   Berral, J., Gojri, I., Nguyen, T., Gavalda, R., Torres, J., & Bianchini, R. (2014). Building green cloud services at low cost. In 34th *IEEE International Conference on Distributed Computing Systems.* Madrid (vol. 44, pp. 449–460). IEEE Digital Library http://dx.doi.org/10.1109/ICDCS.2014.53.

[11]   Bhattarai, B. P. (2019). Big data analytics in smart grids: state-of-the-art, challenges, opportunities, and future directions. *IET Smart Grid.* http://dx.doi.org/10.1049/ietstg.2018.0261.

[12]   Billinton, R., & Gao, Y. (2008). Multistate wind energy conversion system models for adequacy assessment of generating systems incorporating wind energy. *IEEE Transactions on Energy Conversion*, 23: 163–170. http://dx.doi.org/10.1109/TEC.2006.882415.

[13]   Chen, M., Hao, Y., Hwang, K., Wang, L., & Wang, L. (2017). Disease prediction by machine learning over big data from healthcare communities. *IEEE Access*, 5: 8869–8879. http://dx.doi.org/10.1109/ACCESS.2017.2694446.

[14]   Bisong, E. (2019). Google colaboratory. In *Building Machine Learning and Deep Learning Models on Google Cloud Platform.* Berkeley, CA: APress, http://dx.doi.org/10.1007/978-1-4842-4470-8_7.

[15]   Chandarana, P., & Vijayalakshmi, M. (2014). Big data analytics frameworks. In *Proceedings under IEEE International Conference on Electronics, Circuits and Systems, Information and Communication Technology Applications*, 43: 0–434. http://dx.doi.org/10.1109/CSCITA.2014.6839299.

[16]   Al-Ali, A. R., & Aburukba, R. (2015). Role of internet of things in the smart grid technology. *Journal of Computer and Communications*, 3(5): 229–233. http://dx.doi.org/10.4236/jcc.2015.35029.

[17]   Albawi, S., Mohammed, T. A., & Al-Zawi, S. (2017). Understanding of a convolution neural network. In *Paper Presented at the 2017 International Conference on Engineering and Technology (ICET)*, Antalya (pp. 1–6). IEEE Digital Library http://dx.doi.org/10.1109/ICEngTechnol.2017.8308186.

[18]   Diamantoulakis, P. D., Kapinas, V. M., & Karagiannidis, G. (2015). Big data analytics for dynamic energy management in smart grids. *Big Data Research*, 2: 94–101. http://dx.doi.org/10.1016/j.bdr.2015.03.003.

[19]   Gencer, K., & Başçiftçi, F. (2021). Time series forecast modeling of vulnerabilities in the android operating system using ARIMA and deep learning methods. *Sustainable Computing: Informatics and Systems*, 30, Article 100515. http://dx.doi.org/10.1016/j.suscom.2021.100515.

[20]   Goiri, I., Beauchea, R., Le, K., Nguyen, T., Haque, M., Guitart, J., Torres, J., & Bianchini, R. (2011). GreenSlot: Scheduling energy consumption in green datacenters. In *SC'11: Proceedings of 2011 International Conference for High Performance Computing, Networking, Storage and Analysis*. (pp. 1–11). IEEE Digital Library http://dx.doi.org/10.1145/2063384.2063411.

[21]   Goiri, I., Le, K., Nguyen, T., Guitart, J., Torres, J., & Bianchini, R. (2012). Green Hadoop: Leveraging Green Energy in Data-Processing Frameworks. In *Proceedings of the 7th ACM European Conference on Computer Systems*. EuroSys'12 (pp. 57–70). http://dx.doi.org/10.1145/2168836.2168843.

Chapter 10

Big Data Analytics

A Holistic Assessment of Paradigm Shift Challenges and Opportunities for Future Smart Grid

Divya Asija and R. K. Viral

10.1 INTRODUCTION: SMART GRID

Today's traditional power sources can be split into separate components for power generation, transmission, substations, distribution, and most of the customers. These broad features count as the following [1, 2]:

- Centralized power generation.
- One-way energy flow from source to customer.
- Passive Customer Participation: Customer knowledge of power consumption is limited to monthly invoices received in arrears at the end of the month.
- Real-time monitoring and control are primarily limited to power generation and transmission.
- And only in some utilities it extends to the distribution system.
- The inflexibility of this system makes it difficult to inject power from alternative power sources at every point in the grid and to efficiently manage the new services demanded by power users.

Three key factors are affecting the world's future electrical systems. Government regulations, customer efficiency requirements, and new intelligent computer software and hardware technology. Environmental worries are also pouring the entire energy system towards efficiency, economic, and renewable energy sources. Customers will be more proactive and will be able to participate in energy consumption decisions that affect their daily lives.

The advancement of the power grid is an imperative long-term effort over decades. New requirements for renewable portfolio standards, greenhouse gas reservoir limits, demand response, and energy conservation concern put environmental issues at the forefront of the utility venture [2].

Some of the key challenges of today's power grids evolving towards smart grids can be summarized as follows [3, 4]:

- Incorporation of renewable energy resources into the primary grid.
- Renewable energy resources are situated far away from load centers.
- Traditional energy sources are obsolete.
- Introducing a power electronics converter to the grid.
- Increased global electricity demand, etc.

Figure 10.1 shows the conceptual model of the planned future smart grid (SG) and the traditional grid [3]. The smart grids and existing grids can be distinguished based on several aspects, as outlined in Table 10.1 [4–6]. The power grid is expected to evolve from electromechanical control systems to electronically controlled grids over the next 20 years.

The smart grid consists of two interconnected and integrated subsystems:

- Information infrastructure through which data flows in the cyber part of the smart grid. For example, measurement data and control signals are communicated over a computer network.
- A power infrastructure that powers the physical parts of the smart grid, which consists of smart meters and power devices such as generators, towers, and transformers [4, 7]. The IT components of an information infrastructure include modeling, analytics, commerce, information exchange, and management [8].

The National Institute of Standards and Technology (NIST) stated the smart grid definition as follows [9]:

"A state-of-the-art grid that enables bidirectional energy flow and uses bidirectional communication and control capabilities to enable a variety of new features and applications. Various new features and applications." Figure 10.2 represents the infrastructure, consisting of information and electrical infrastructure [10]. As depicted in Figure 10.2, some of the major components of a smart grid can be described at the physical level [10]:

Innovative Grid Components: DG, Combined heat and power (CHP), plug-in hybrid electric vehicle (PHEVs), photovoltaic (PV) cells, wind turbine (WT), etc.

Detecting and Control Devices: Sensors, intelligent electronic devices (IEDs), smart meters

Communications Infrastructure: Communication networks based on fiber optics, µwave, infrared radiation (IR), PLCC, GSM, and CDMA etc.

Automation and IT Back End: High-end servers, middleware, data-storage unit, and data management systems

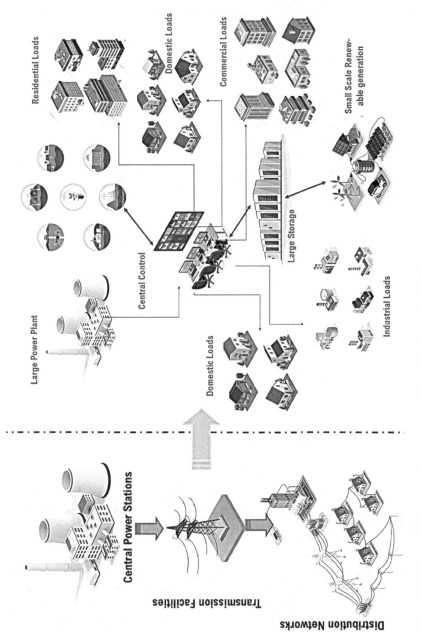

Figure 10.1 Smart grid data analytics structure with application analytics [3].

Table 10.1 Comparison of Power Grid and Smart Grid

S. No.	Existing Grid	Smart Grid
1	Electromechanical	Completely digital
2	One-way communication	Bidirectional communication
3	Conventional generation	Embedded generation
4	Failures and blackouts	Adaptive and islanding
5	Few sensors	Sensors all over
6	Blind	Self-healing Capability
7	Manual restoration	Self-monitoring
8	Physical check/test	Remotely check/test
9	Hierarchical	Network
10	Restricted control	Persistent control

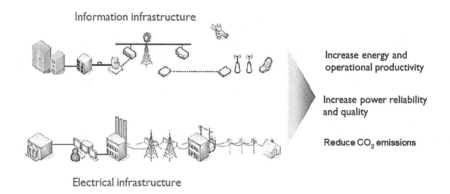

Figure 10.2 Smart grid broad infrastructure.

Advanced Analytics: Advanced applications based on the available components. Figure 10.3 illustrates the example from a smart building to smart grid [4, 10]. Figure 10.4 (a and b) show the different technologies used in smart grid [4, 10–12].

Figure 10.4 (a) depicts smart-grid advanced technologies for integration of renewable energy resources in reference to demand control. Further, 10.4 (b) represents smart-grid advanced technologies for Geographical Information System (GIS) reflecting big data management and machine learning.

From these figures, it is clear that in order to introduce a smart grid system in place of the existing grid, many devices are required from the field to the information infrastructure, and it is necessary to monitor and control in real time the normal operation of the entire system. As a result, smart grids generate large amounts of data. The next section describes smart grid data and its importance.

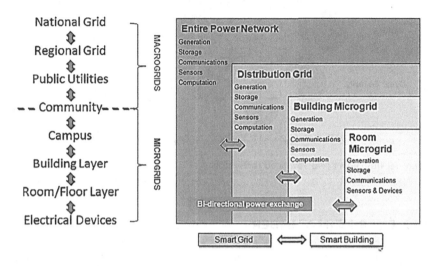

Figure 10.3 Example showing bidirectional power exchange beginning a smart building towards smart grid [4, 10].

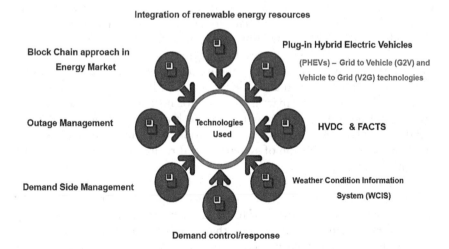

Figure 10.4(a) Smart grid advanced technologies control.

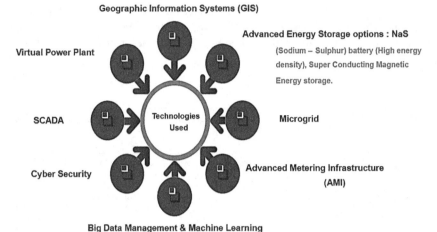

Figure 10.4(b) Smart grid advanced technologies.

10.2 ENERGY IN NUMBERS

The ever-increasing amount of data generated is the reality we live in. Recent advances in technology are generating large amounts of data from different domains such as social networks, scientific sensors, smart cities, and the Internet. The amount of data in the world is expected to increase 300 times from 2005 to 2020, from 130 exabytes to 40,000 exabytes. This is equivalent to doubling every two years [13]. SGs operations and future energy management are becoming increasingly data intensive. For example, smart metering produces data with higher time resolution. There is no doubt that the increased particle size and the resulting increase in quantity will allow for deeper analysis, thus better understanding of energy consumption and better management on the demand side [13]. The ability to process big data is a prerequisite for mining smart meter data for insightful knowledge. Power System Big Data (BD) brings new features such as providing feedback loops that do not exist otherwise, taking actions to modify and improve plans, and enabling accurate realization of system state. It realizes operation based on a lot of information.

The term "big data" is self-explanatory, but it can still cause confusion and controversy. For example, what a utility might consider as a BD might be considered medium-sized data for a data-centric business. The relativity of BD to the system that manipulates that data is also recognized within the IT community [14, 15]. Nonetheless, a commonly used definition in BD is "a large amount, rapid, that requires cost-effective and innovative forms of information gathering, storage, and processing to enhance insights and decision making. It is a diverse information asset." [16].

Today, smart cities are increasing the amount of data they can collect and use. Recent advances in hardware and software technologies such as social media, the Internet of Things, wearable sensors, mobile technology, data storage and cloud computing, data mining technology, and machine learning algorithms make it easy to collect and analyze large amounts of data. When saved, you can collect datasets from a variety of quantitative and qualitative domain-specific data sources. One of the biggest challenges for smart grids is managing and analyzing big data.

10.3   CORE COMPONENTS OF BIG DATA

Big data analysis refers to the techniques used to investigate, process, discover, and discover hidden underlying patterns, interesting relationships, and other insights into the application context under investigation. Big data can be defined as a huge dataset with a structure that increases diversity and complexity. The inherent difficulty of processing these large amounts of data leads to major challenges in storing and analyzing them and providing results in a cost- and time-efficient manner. In addition, the information should be provided in an interpretable and easily visible way [17].

Big data in smart grids comes from a variety of sources. An analog SCADA (monitoring control and data collection) system implemented in the power network at sampling rates per 2–4 seconds for decades. Due to the limited sampling rate, it is not possible to observe the transient stability and vibration of the power grid. Therefore, a much faster sampling rate (30–60 samples per second) phasor measurement unit (PMU) can directly generate time-stamped voltage/current magnitudes and phase angles [18, 19]. In addition to the PMU, an Advanced Meter Read (AMR) with a 15-minute read interval was also used instead of the traditional monthly read meter. A huge amount of data is powered by the proliferation of PMUs, AMRs, and other advanced measurement devices such as intelligent electronic devices (IEDs), digital fault recorders (DFRs), and event recorders (SERs) [20, 21] which is supplied to a system for preservation, hardening, mining, sharing, and visualization. The EPRI study concluded that the three major domains of big data are (i) visualization, (ii) situational awareness, and (iii) predictive prediction. Figure 10.5 shows the exponential data growth pattern of SG data. This shows that a single device and entity can generate thousands of terabytes of data per year [22].

Components of Big Data – At the same time, there is much debate about what big data really means [2, 14, 15]. However, the most common definition in literature is the definition of "Vs" [19, 20], which includes some features of big data that start with the letter "V." This white paper is limited to

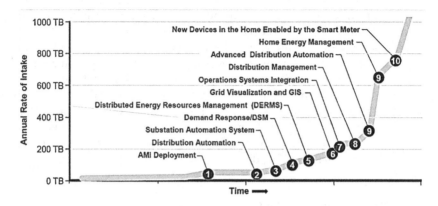

Figure 10.5 Exponential data evolution trend of data in SG [22].

the definition of "5V" [18] (volume, speed, variety, credibility/effectiveness, and value) described subsequently (Figure 10.6).

Volume: Big data volumes define the "amount" of data generated. The value of the data also depends on the extent of the data. Currently, data is generated from different sources in diverse formats (structured and unstructured). These data formats comprise media content such as Word and Excel documents, PDFs and reports, images, and videos. Along with this, Table 10.2 gives an overview of the various data classes, data sources, and corresponding volumes generated by SG [12, 13, 17, 20].

Velocity: Speed refers to the speed at which data is produced, composed, and evaluated. Data incessantly drifts through numerous channels, for example, computer systems, networks, social media, and mobile phones. In today's data-driven commercial environment, the stride of data growth is best defined as "rapid" and "unprecedented." This data should also be recorded as close to real time as probable so that the correct data is accessible at the right time. The speed with which you have direct access to your data directly influences your timely and correct business verdicts. Even the restricted amount of data accessible in real-time produces better business results than the huge amount of data that takes a long time to collect and examine. Along with this, Table 10.3 outlines the various SG-generated data classes, data sources, and corresponding speeds [12, 13, 17, 20].

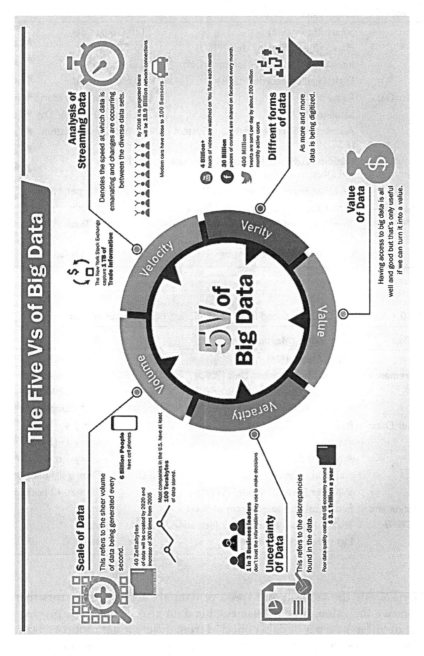

Figure 10.6 5 Vs of big data [12, 13, 17, 20].

Table 10.2 Volume of Data Produced in SG for Different Data Classes and Sources

Data Class	Data Source (Measurement)	Volume
Utility Measurements	Smart Meter (SM)	120 GB per day
	Phasor Measurement Unit (PMU)	30 GB per day
	Intelligent Condition Monitor (ICM)	5 GB per day
	Digital Fault Recorder (DFR)	10 MB per fault
Weather Data	Radar	612 MB/day per radar Scan
	Satellite	At least 10 GB per Day
	Automated Surface Observing System (ASOS)	10 MB/day per station
	National Lightning Detection Network (NLDN)	40 MB/day
	Weather Forecast Model (WFM)	5–10 GB/day per Model
Vegetation and Topography	Ecological Mapping System of Texas	2.7 GB for Texas
	Texas National Resources Information System	300 GB for Texas
	Light Detection and Ranging	7 GB for Harris Co.

Table 10.3 Velocity of Data Produced in SG for Different Data Classes and Sources

Data Class	Data Source (Measurement)	Velocity
Utility Measurements	Smart Meter (SM)	Every 5–15 min
	Phasor Measurement Unit (PMU)	240 samples/sec
	Intelligent Condition Monitor (ICM)	250 samples/sec
	Digital Fault Recorder (DFR)	1600 samples/sec
Weather Data	Radar	Every 4–10 min
	Satellite	Every 1–15 min
	Automated Surface Observing System (ASOS)	Every 1 min
	National Lightning Detection Network (NLDN)	During lightning
	Weather Forecast Model (WFM)	15 min–12 hours
Vegetation and Topography	Ecological Mapping System of Texas	static
	Texas National Resources Information System	static
	Light Detection and Ranging	static

Variety: While the amount and speed of data are significant factors that improve the value of your business, big data also includes the processing of different types of data collected from different data sources. Data sources can include both external sources and internal business units. In general, big data is divided into structured data, semi-structured data, and unstructured data. Structured data is data that has a well-defined format, length, and quantity, while semi-structured data is data that is partially compliant with a particular data format. Unstructured data, on the other hand, is unstructured data and does not conform to traditional data formats. Data generated via digital and social media (images, videos, tweets, etc.) can be classified as unstructured data. Along with this, Table 10.4 outlines the diversity of different data classes, data sources, and corresponding variety in SGs [12, 13, 17, 20].

Veracity/Validity: The Veracity of big data, or Validity, as it is more commonly known, is a guarantee of the quality or reliability of the data collected. Can you trust the data collected from you? Is this data reliable enough to gain insight? Do you need to make business decisions based on the insights from this data? Once you know the accuracy of your data, you can answer all these and more questions. Along with this, Table 10.5 outlines the various data classes, data sources, and corresponding veracity in SG. [12, 13, 17, 20].

Value: Today, data is being generated in large quantities, but simply collecting data is not useful. Instead, data that drives business insights creates "value" for the organization. In the context of big data, value is how valuable data is in having a positive impact on a company's business. This is where big data analysis comes in handy. Many companies are investing in establishing data aggregation and storage infrastructure within their

Table 10.4 Variety of Data Produced in SG for Different Data Classes and Sources

Data Class		Data Source (Measurement)
Variety	Utility Measurements	Smart Meter (SM)
		Phasor Measurement Unit (PMU)
		Intelligent Condition Monitor (ICM)
		Digital Fault Recorder (DFR)
	Weather Data	Radar
		Satellite
		Automated Surface Observing System (ASOS)
		National Lightning Detection Network (NLDN)
		Weather Forecast Model (WFM)
	Vegetation and Topography	Ecological Mapping System of Texas
		Texas National Resources Information System
		Light Detection and Ranging

Table 10.5 Veracity of Data in SG by Different Data Classes and Sources

Data Class	Data Source (Measurement)	Veracity (Accuracy)
Utility Measurements	Smart Meter (SM)	Error <2.5%
	Phasor Measurement Unit (PMU)	Error <1%
	Intelligent Condition Monitor (ICM)	Error <1%
	Digital Fault Recorder (DFR)	Error <0.2%
Weather Data	Radar	1–2 dB; ms' 1
	Satellite	VIS<2% IR <1–2K
	Automated Surface Observing System (ASOS)	T. 1.8°F, P<1%, Wind speed: 5%, RR. 4% Precipitation
	Weather Forecast Model (WFM)	Varies by parameter

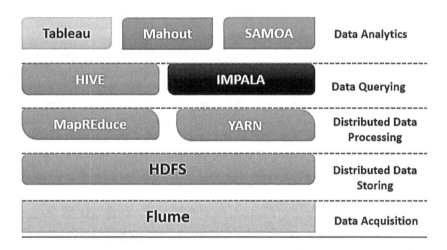

Figure 10.7 Hierarchical architecture of core components of smart grid big data.

organizations, but they do not understand that data aggregation is not the same as value creation. The important thing is how to handle the collected data. With the help of advanced data analysis, you can derive useful insights from the collected data. These insights, in turn, enrich the decision-making process.

Figure 10.7 shows the architecture of the core components of smart grid big data, including data acquisition, data storage, data processing, data acquisition, and data analysis components [2, 17–21].

Today's energy data comes from different sources, covering different locations, types, and applications. In addition, many formats of mesh data are generated at high speed.

10.4 SMART GRID: BIG DATA APPLICATIONS

Network big data applications offer new possibilities in terms of intelligent energy management and cover multiple operational functions. The generated and transmitted datasets are used to perform monitoring, optimization, forecasting, planning, and management tasks. Big data analytics techniques play an important role in managing and processing large amounts of data generated by smart grid infrastructure. It provides rapid failure detection, dynamic system recovery, and rapid response to load and source fluctuations, improving the reliability and flexibility of the entire network [20]. Therefore, big data and data analytics methods can leverage the advances in smart grids by providing a variety of opportunities for load planning, demand management, forecasting, and data analytics. Figure 10.8 shows a smart grid application and data analysis based on large-scale data processing operations [22].

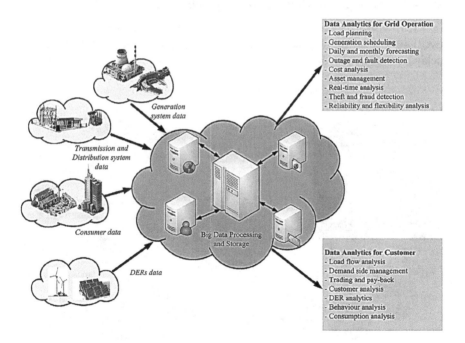

Figure 10.8 Big data analytics in the smart grid.

Data analysis for smart grids can be divided into two basic aspects, such as grid operations and customer operations. Data analysis required for grid operations includes load planning, power generation planning, daily and monthly forecasts of energy demand, outage and failure detection, cost analysis, asset management, real-time analysis, theft and fraud detection, reliability, and measurement of flexibility. Data analysis from customer-side applications is required to detect load flow, demand management, transaction and refund operations, customer behavior analysis, customer DER monitoring, and consumption analytics [22].

Key concerns relate to efficient data collection, storage and management, analysis and mining of collected data, acquisition of meaningful results, and protection from vulnerabilities and privacy breaches. The types of data that can eventually form a BD in a power system can be categorized into domain data and off-domain data, as seen in Figure 10.9.

The next section provides a comprehensive overview of the applications leveraged by smart grid big data. This includes some new applications that use the latest big data technologies. Figure 10.10 shows the wide range of uses for BD in smart grids [5, 8–12, 17, 19, 21, 22].

10.4.1 Wide area situational awareness

In a real-world scenario for a wide area situational awareness application, two issues need to be resolved. The limits of the installed PMU and the delay caused by the decision algorithm. Here are some examples of WASA

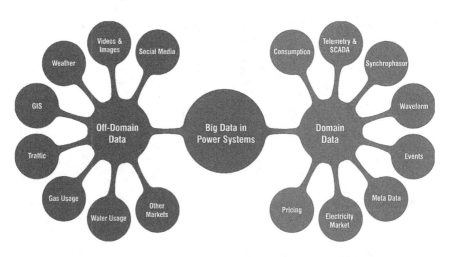

Figure 10.9 Big data type classification and examples in power systems

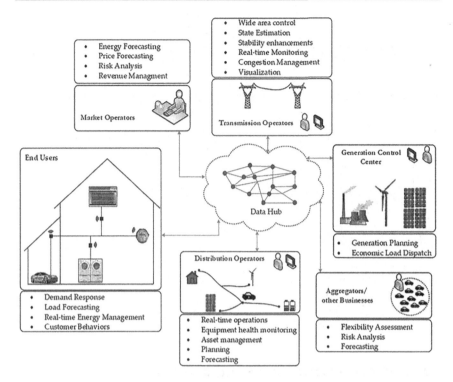

Figure 10.10 Potential applications of big data analytics in smart grids.

applications. The location information system SMDA (ver5.0) was used for large-scale monitoring and event detection of Hydro-Quebec [18]. NYISO used real-time and offline data to display information on the dashboard. The dashboard alerts the operator of abnormalities such as low voltage, temporary vibrations, and line trips [17].

10.4.2 State estimation

Traditional state estimation problems are repeatedly solved by nonlinear measurements made by SCADA systems. This is quite inefficient, and bad data is intolerable. Motivated by the advent of big data and smart grids, new algorithms and techniques have been developed and used.

In reality, there are many causes for "bad data" (BD), such as metering devices failure and electromagnetic interferences. The latest methods of BD detection can be divided into two categories: pre-estimation and post-estimation [22].

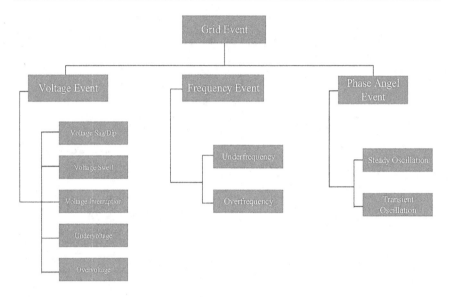

Figure 10.11 Hierarchical event classification in grids.

10.4.3 Event classification and detections

Power system failures include many types, such as faults, line trip, load limit, loss of generation, oscillation, etc. Traditional event detection is model/topology-based post-event analysis. With large amounts of data and information, smart grids can use a data-driven approach to perform real-time event classification and detection. Event classification/classification is event detection and location preparation. Cowardly. Figure 10.11 shows a hierarchical approach for classifying catastrophic events [8, 19–21]. This is a functional specification of a particular disturbance event, and all voltage and frequency events can be classified as either vibrating or non-oscillating.

- Other Applications [4, 6, 11–13, 17, 19–22]

10.4.3.1 Power plant models validation and calibration

Verification and calibration of power plant models has long confused energy suppliers and operators. A new data-driven approach has been developed to validate power plant models based on large-scale measurement data measured by PMUs, IEDs, and FDRs.

10.4.3.2 Short-term load forecasting

Utilising historical load and environmental data, smart metering data associations, clustering analysis, and recently acquired temperature, humidity, and precipitation data are all part of a method for short-term load prediction in large databases.

10.4.3.3 Distribution network verification

Big data analysis is useful for checking the distribution network topology of smart grids, especially for recently used underground feeds.

10.4.3.4 Big data–driven demand response

Big data is also used for demand response management and seems to have the effect of reducing the load during rush hours, but the traditional approach is inflexible because it turns off a given load.

10.4.3.5 Parameter estimation for distribution system

Implementing a large number of sensors on the smart grid proposes a new method for parameter estimation of the secondary network of the distribution system. Big data from AMIs and other sensors provides the secondary system with the opportunity to achieve line impedance calibration.

10.4.3.6 System security and protection

Cyberattacks are considered one of the greatest threats to smart grid systems due to their component and network connectivity and interoperability. Many security solutions have been developed for smart grids, but most are not based on big data. Currently, big data security and privacy have three typical outcomes: (i) big data–oriented cryptosystems, (ii) big data–oriented Anomaly Detection, and (iii) big data–oriented intelligent applications.

10.5 CLASSIFICATION OF TECHNIQUES USED FOR BIG DATA ANALYTICS IN SMART GRID

In contrast to the big data approach in the IT industry, most of the measured data in power systems are meant to be used near to the point of generation and were never planned to be transferred to an enterprise data center [23]. It is somewhat due to the distinct design and development requirements in the power sector since no centralized data storage solution has traditionally matched the objectives of controller having specified low latency rate systems in many actual power applications.

In accordance with many newly deployed or upcoming power data measurement systems which fits in to the criteria of big Data, some of the managerial systems do not perfectly meet the essence and goal of it. When such concealed data has been collected, maintained, and evaluated, it will become the true big data in power systems. Big data is merely seen in power systems so far, but soon it would certainly become the most promising alternative for data measurements and collection.

Domain data and off-domain data are the two types of data that can eventually constitute the part of big data in power systems. Additionally, details of intended data are shown in Figure 10.12.

Classification of the domain data as per the type of sources:

- Telemetry and SCADA data
- Oscillograph and synchrophasor data
- Consumption data or smart meter data
- Asynchronous event data (embedded processors enabled devices producing data in the form of output signals or messages under diversified conditions)
- Metadata (grid metadata is usually diverse and can be comprised of calibration data, internal sensor data, and other information specifically related to a kind of device)
- Financial data (data associated with electrical market such as bilateral transactions, retail rates, day-ahead and real-time market bids, and price data.

Power grid operation has traditionally relied on various types of off-domain data, that is, data which is out of the range of the power sector and related to other subsidiary domains. Secondary data such as weather data, GIS data, and National Lightning Detection Network data are currently employed for the improvement of power system operations at multitude levels and time [24–26]. Further, several existing or new off-domain data are still to be utilized for different assignments covering power grid and energy industry. Most pertinent examples of such data include image and video feeds, social media data, traffic data, trading indexes, etc. [27, 28]. Effectively, there are no boundaries to the intelligence given to power systems via data sources, which can together eventually develop big data.

10.5.1 Categorization of smart grid data analytics

Data analytics associated with smart grid has been categorized into four main categories which are demonstrated in Figure 10.13.

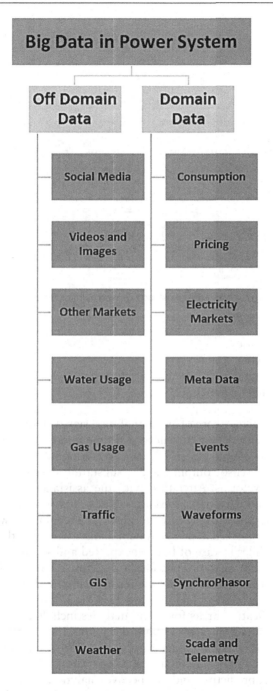

Figure 10.12 Big data types in power system area.

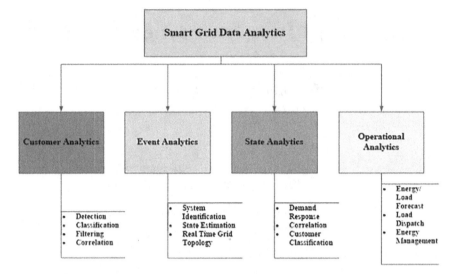

Figure 10.13 Smart grid data analytics structure with application analytics.

- Event analytics
- State analytics
- Customer analytics
- Operational analytics

Under preliminary phase of event analytics, signal analytics is being done. Signal analytics utilizes the current or real-time status of the signals retrieved from the sensors coupled in an advanced metering infrastructure. It fetches the meters data, sensor output signals, substation devices waveforms, and Line sensor waveforms. After this, with the assistance of event analytics, identification and detection of events such as outage or malfunctioning of devices or independent system connected via common networks or links [29–35] is accomplished in power system domain. It allows the organization of energy schedules in case of both unexpected and scheduled occurrences. Furthermore, event analytics includes a descriptive study of former power system events using various approaches (for example, identification, categorization, event correlation, and filtering) [29–31, 35]. Apart from that, some of the key application areas for event analytics include detection of abnormal operating situations such as fault detection [29–31] detection of malicious assaults [30], system outage detection [32–34], and power theft [35].

The primary components of state and operational analytics are descriptive, diagnostic, predictive, and perspective analytics. It necessitates diverse studies and assessments of the grid's status geographically that includes electrical states, parametric identification, topology identification, and asset utilization. There is also cognitive analytics, which is a relatively new technology that integrates several functionalities. State analytics, as shown in Figure 13, comprises state estimation [29, 36], system identification [32, 37, 38], and real-time grid topology identification [39–41]. In the same manner, the key power system applications for operational analytics include energy management and dispatch of resources [27, 28, 36, 40], energy/load forecast [42–46].

Moving to the third category, customer analytics. It utilizes customers' operational data, their demand, and reactions. It also includes one or more of the descriptive, diagnostic, predictive, and perspective analytics depending on the specific applications and use cases. The key power system applications that fall under the customer analytics include customer classification/ categorization [41, 47], sentiment analysis, home energy management, utility communication, enhanced billing, nonlinear load parameters, the correlation between consumer behavior and energy consumption patterns [35, 43, 45, 48], and demand profile [49, 50]. The last category is mainly concerned with enterprise/operational analytics. This examines the overall grid management system's business expectations and economic values. It encompasses the procedures such as demand response, dynamic pricing analysis, asset management, energy forecasting, and energy analytics. Application areas of operational analytics are load forecasting, load dispatch, and energy management.

10.5.2 Big data analytics platforms

Predictive, prescriptive, descriptive, diagnostic, corrective, adaptive, and distributed analytics are some of the intelligent big data analytics methods that are intended to improve knowledge or decision-making for the power industry [23, 50]. Work on many of these intelligent methods has already started, and it is anticipated that they will become more widespread in the power community.

Cloud storage and computing, a recently emerging technology, is gaining a lot of attention and appeal owing to its numerous benefits. Chang et al. [51] compared cloud and non-cloud large data storage, and the results reveal that on the cloud, real execution time is a lot less, although reliability and system efficacy are greater on the non-cloud foundation. Functioning of smart grid involves various online and offline parameters. Analytics of this data would certainly lead to execution and performance of grid in a smarter way. There are various data analytics platforms which become the backbone of application-specific smart grid analytics.

10.5.2.1 Map Reduce Platform

MapReduce, created by Google in 2004, is the most widely used software development model for processing and implementation of big or large volume of data. It has numerous implementations, including Dryad, Hadoop, Mars, Phoenix, and Sector/Sphere. Due to its automated failed restoration procedures, fault resistance, and scalability, Mache Hadoop is considered as the most compliant application software. It was created in 2005 [34] by Doug Cutting and Mike Cafarella and is extensively utilized by IT behemoths such as Facebook, Google, IBM, Microsoft, Yahoo, and YouTube.

Figure 10.14 depicts the architecture of Hadoop MapReduce framework which processes high volume of data constituting of multiple datasets of terabytes parallelly existing on thousands of nodes. Its execution is being done in a reliable and fault-tolerant manner without any unnecessary ambiguities. The design and architecture of Hadoop MapReduce is comprised of two primary components [52–54]:

- MapReduce
- The Hadoop Distributed File System (HDFS)

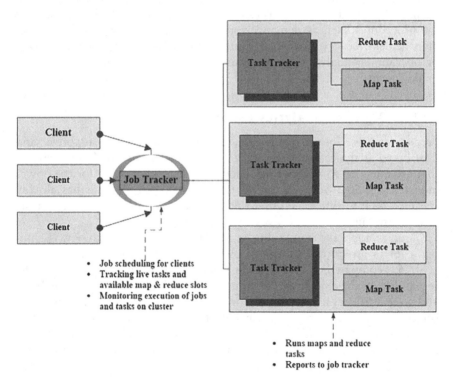

Figure 10.14 Architecture of Hadoop MapReduce Framework.

The platform developed by information science can be adapted and employed in the power system because of the distinctive feature of energy big data. Thus, to execute key-value pair level incremental processing and to facilitate more complex iterative computing in power systems, Zhang et al. presented a new incremental MapReduce and called it i2 MapReduce [35]. Further, Xing et al. [36] introduced the Petuum platform for comprehensive machine learning. By contrasting this all-purpose framework with MapReduce, the experimentation's effectiveness was also confirmed.

10.5.2.2 Apache Spark Platform

Big data processing may be done in one of three ways: batch, iterative, or stream. Hadoop Map-Reduce is good for the assessment of empirical and static data, but it is not ideal for the assessment of real-time and stream data as described in [37]. On the contrary, Apache Spark can process online and streaming data more effectively than Hadoop. It is an open-source big data processing platform which was first created at the University of California, Berkeley's AMPLab. Spark can perform applications up to 100 times quicker in memory or 10 times faster on disc as compared to Hadoop MapReduce [38].

Structured query language (SQL) and data frames, MLlib for machine learning, GraphX, and Spark streaming are just a few of the libraries that are powered by the Spark framework. An example of a Spark implementation in a smart grid is the North American Power Grid Frequency Monitoring Network (FNET/GridEye) [39], which is run by Yilu Liu. Architecture design of this system comprises of the open PDC for real-time applications, the distributed analytics cluster for near-real-time applications, and Apache Spark for post-event and statistical analysis. It employs 150 frequency disturbance recorders in the United States and roughly 50 ones globally. Hence, contemplating some power system incidents, such as the generators outage at James A. Fitzpatrick power plant during Hurricane Sandy in 2012 [39], can be identified quickly owing to the high speed, extensively monitored data, and decentralized data analytics platform.

10.5.2.3 SQL Platform

SQL has also been considered a potential choice for power system data analytics. Its advanced variant, which is associated with post-relational database systems, not only SQL (NoSQL) database, enables innovative data management solutions that are easier to scale and operate optimally than their alternatives. The main drawback is that they do not support SQL-style queries. Many NoSQL databases have grown with SQL-like interfaces (Contextual Query Language (CQL) of Cassandra, Hive, Pig, and others) to simplify querying SQL-like. There have been advancements in the form of SQL interfaces that can directly connect to NoSQL databases (such as PrestoDB, etc.). NewSQL refers to SQL-like interfaced NoSQL databases that have the intrinsic power of structuring massive-scale data and categorizing to ensure efficient offline analytics (H-Store, Google Spanner, etc.) [40]. Cassandra, Elastic Search, MongoDB, and Hbase are examples of NoSQL open-source database types. Hbase and Cassandra are both column stores based on the BigTable idea. Hbase, on the other hand, is built on Apache Hadoop, whereas Cassandra is built on DynamoDB. Further, Figure 10.15 depicts the big data analytics architecture with different platforms like Hadoop, Storm, and Spark.

10.5.2.4 Application of Data Analytics Platforms in Case of Smart Grid Customer Data Analytics

Big data analytics of consumer data has become a must rather than an option for electricity businesses. Consumers participate in smart grids as an

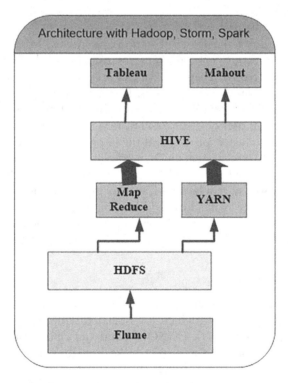

Figure 10.15 Architecture for big data analytics platforms.

ultimate user through smart meters that provide them with greater control over their own usage. Customers' data is in the terabyte range and comes in several forms. Consequently, high velocity, scalability, and fault tolerance are required in data handling, storing, and visualization. Several technologies may be used to deploy big data, but analytics tools are the most important in business outcomes. Figure 10.16 depicts multiple big data tools for managing smart grid data. Due to the sheer multiplicity of consumer datasets like smart meters, gadgets, historical information, etc., data uniformity demands use of such unified deployments. Because messaging technologies are highly effective for integration of raw data, they may also be utilized for integration of consumer data.

Big data analytics may be performed in numerous ways:

- **Batch processing tools**: Big data analytics provides a wide range of data processing methods, beginning with batch handling. Hadoop [27] is a wise option for cluster analytics in smart grids.
- **Real time processing tools**: Real-time processing is faster than batch processing in terms of implementation since it tackles data with high velocity demands utilizing stream processing or complicated event

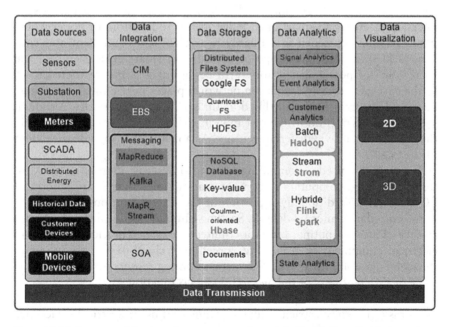

Figure 10.16 Future architecture for customer data analytics. Tools utilized depend on customer data analytics.

processing systems. Several systems, including Storm, Splunk, S4 and others, may be used to execute real-time processing.

- **Hybrid processing tools**: Hybrid processing tools are capable of handling both real-time and batch processing. A platform for batch processing called Spark [30] also provides a real-time processing option called Spark streaming. Large-scale data processing is handled by Spark, which also includes supportive tools like GraphX., Spark SQL, a machine learning framework, and Spark Streaming. Another configuration that can process data in both batch and stream modes is Apache Flink [32]. Flink is constructed on a foundation of massive APIs, including transformation functions (such as mapping and reduction, grouping, etc.), which make it scalable, simple to install, fault tolerant, and quick to execute. Flink is effective in machine learning since it uses its own machine learning library, FlinkML. Flink already contains libraries for accessing HDFS; therefore, it can be utilized to process information using HDFS.

10.6 EDGE COMPUTING AND SMART GRID: A WAY FORWARD

Edge computing delivers and employs computer resources near data suppliers. In reference to smart grid, "edge" refers to locations or nodes where data is available, which is probably near electrical equipment and consumers [13]. Indeed, the scope of the edge in smart grids includes "the final mile" of power distribution/grid edge, but it is not restricted to it. In the case of power transmission network, places near data sources must be included for inclusion in this domain e.g., system operators. Although substations do not fall in the last mile in electricity distribution network, they produce data via different sensors. As a result, they include the extent of the edge.

The concept of edge computing must also describe its role in SG. C4s, that is, caching, computation, communication, and control, are all critical EC tasks [10]. Traditionally, a portion of these C4 operations is conducted in the core data center by default. Sending out 4Cs in edge domain will not replace cloud computing, but is a counterpart of it. The cloud, edge, and electrical equipment resources are pooled as a cloud-to-things continuum through edge computing [16]. Distinct computing resources, whether in the same or different tiers of the hierarchy, can co-function.

Even though edge computing is relatively new in the communication business, it is old in the electricity industry. Some prevailing electrical devices are already installed with features close to edge computing. Consider a traditional relay protection scheme. In this scheme, relay protection equipment may collect data from electrical meters via possible communication channels.

Further, computation and caching are done based on the relay settings, and then appropriate control signals are communicated to line breakers which are located near power lines. Thus, all 4Cs are already there in relay protection scheme. However, the power grid is normally organized in a top-down hierarchical structure. A single substation or power plant has the lowest hierarchical structure [55, 56].

With the rising requirement for smart grids to interact with millions of distributed energy resources and electrical consumers in the coming years, the relevance of embedding edge computing in smart grids will become enormously apparent. This is especially valid for the power distribution network, which is currently an unprotected, uncontrolled, and non-communicated area in the power system.

The primary features of edge computing that assist smart grid are mentioned as follows:

- Low latency: Less hops, less middleware
- Cognition: Similar environment with smart grid agents, acquainted with user end information
- Flexibility: On-demand or plug and play, intercommunity distributed tasks
- Reliability: Resistant to N-1 failure, cybersecurity, and privacy

The introduction of edge computing in smart grids will be accompanied by the proliferation of huge data very soon in the coming information system scenario. The smart grid data flow may have a growing impact on the functioning of SG operations and services, making smart grid data management increasingly important. The current data management plan is disconnected from SG applications, and feedback is not provided to "application unaware" data management plan.

10.6.1 Tier-Based Edge Computing Architecture for Smart Grids

Three tier-based edge computing architecture is utilized for smooth functioning of smart grid. All these tiers can communicate in a horizontal and vertical direction within the architecture. It encompasses intra thing links that includes devices which can be wired or wireless.

Three tiers are namely thing tier, edge tier, and cloud tier. Each layer would function independently [57, 58].

- Thing tier – It is an IOT-based layer that includes all electrical equipment and provides communication access with smart grid.
- Edge tier – This layer involves intermediate storing along with computing resources between the smart grid control center and things.

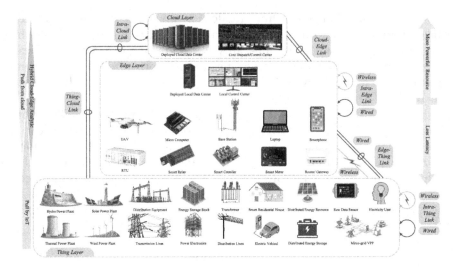

Figure 10.17 Implementation of edge computing in smart grids via three tier-based architecture.

- Cloud tier – This layer is like a conventionally existing layer in communication and IOT industries. It consists of control, computing, and storage devices.

Figure 10.17 presents implementation of edge computing in smart grids via three tier-based architecture.

10.7 CHALLENGES AND OPPORTUNITIES

Big data from multiple sources carries valuable data relevant to smart grids, and cross-pollination of the diverse data sources that unravel several innovative solutions advantageous to all stakeholders, such as clients, electric utilities, grid personals, and so on. It is primarily intended for planning and operational decisions. Big data has the potential to (i) increase power grid stability and resiliency, (ii) deliver optimal resource management and operations, (iii) enhance decision-making through information or data distribution, and (iv) facilitate quick assessment of massive datasets for improving performance.

However, as per the current scenario of energy big data, data analytics is being utilized for smart meters coupled with smart grid. Other functionalities include baseline estimation, load forecasting, and load clustering applications [59–62]. PMU big data products are primarily focused on dynamic model

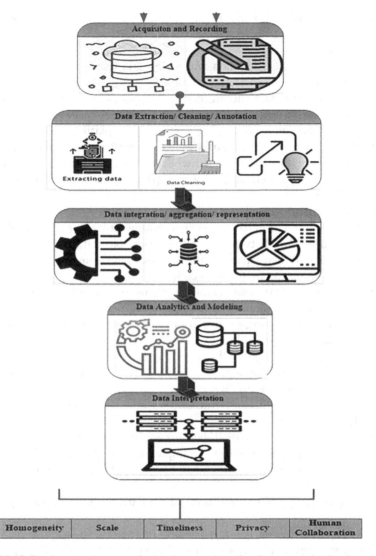

Figure 10.18 Big data requirements for implementation of tasks at complex level.

calibration, transmission grid visualization, and state estimation [63–65]. With the ongoing development of data analytics in smart grid, we are more concerned about certain challenges or barriers which are linked with the processes starting from data acquisition, recording at initial stage. The continual process progress leads to interpretation at the last stage. Figure 10.18 shows the different challenges encountered during the energy data analytics.

Barriers or challenges which are encountered by implementation of big data analytics in smart grid are mentioned as follows:

- Addressing discarded data and siloed data which is usually present in the system at different nodal points.
- Real-time big data intelligence for supporting real-time analytics by incorporating real-time-based control structure producing physical signals with smart energy big data analytics platform.
- Coexistence of distributed as well as centralized data management.
- Building or developing worthwhile distributed intelligence algorithm with solid theoretical base for approximating overall performance indicators.
- Balancing integrated and disintegrated systems.
- Scalable and interoperable computing infrastructure leading to interoperability between several devises, big data architectures, network operability, various data analytics platforms, information models, and repositories for data collection.
- Custom-built data management systems to cope with fast data.
- Codesign of big data analytics–based smart energy system and tolerant security mechanism, leading to a rigid integrated framework capable of reducing security risks.
- Necessity of holistic and modular data analytics–based platform for data sharing and intelligence, precise system monitoring, and financial/ economic domain intelligence.
- Demand for regulatory frameworks and standards for sharing and deployment of big data.
- Deployment of diversified data for avoiding interdependencies among the critical infrastructure. Examples include GE Data Lake, Pecan Street Data port, etc., which can be utilized for this purpose.

a. Opportunities and applications of big data analytics in smart grid

Big data analytics is being harnessed in smart grid, leading to several opportunities and applications. Some of the probable applications are mentioned as follows.

- Applications relating to energy management
- Remarkable upgradation in smart grid reliability and stability
- Visualization
- Parameter and state estimation techniques
- Application of cyber-physical system

10.8 CONCLUSION

Even though data in the electricity sector has been rapidly increasing, the major data present in the power system has yet to be utilized. Many traditional energy domain measuring equipment and data management systems are based on the old concept of corporate data warehousing, although some of its essential elements have been revisited underneath the Big Data Analytic approach. This chapter examines the notable characteristics of big data analytics advancements in power systems. The ideas, needs, and technology involved are underlined through a review of the literature on big data analytics in smart grids. Additionally, the current study examines big data analytics in the smart grid and how they are employed in conjunction with grid visualization as a future technology for successful accomplishment of several distributed generations. The following is a summary of the present review's conclusion: (i) an exhaustive overview and comparison of existing smart grid infrastructure, its core components, and technologies utilized; (ii) the need for BD in smart grid, SG core components, various applications of BD in SG operation, classifications; and (iii) concise discussions on technical approaches, edge computing (EG) in SG, and challenges and opportunities in BD implementation in SG. Based on a comprehensive study, certain recommendations for future smart grid are suggested.

REFERENCES

[1] Gharavi H., and Ghafurian R. Smart grid: The electric energy system of the future. *The Proceedings of the IEEE* 99 (6) (2011): 917–921.

[2] Divya A., and Viral R. K. Renewable energy integration in modern deregulated power system: challenges, driving forces, and lessons for future road map. In *Advances in Smart Grid Power System*. Academic Press, 2020, pp. 365–384 (e-ISBN 9780128243374).

[3] R. K. V., and Khatod D. K. Optimal planning of distributed generation systems in distribution system: A review. *Renewable and Sustainable Energy Reviews* 16 (7) (2012): 5146–5165.

[4] Jarrah M., Jaradat M., Jararweh Y., Al-Ayyoub M., and Bousselham A. A hierarchical optimization model for energy data flow in smart grid power systems. *Information Systems* 53 (2015): 190–200.

[5] Kim Y. J., Thottan M., Kolesnikov V., and Lee W. A secure decentralized data-centric information infrastructure for smart grid. *Communications Magazine, IEEE* 48 (11) (2010): 58–65.

[6] Nabeel M., Ding X., Seo S.-H., and Bertino E. Scalable end-to-end security for advanced metering infrastructures. *Information Systems* 53 (2015): 213–223.

[7]   Gungor V., Sahin D., Kocak T., Ergut S., Buccella C., Cecati C., and Hancke G. A survey on smart grid potential applications and communication requirements. *Industrial Informatics, IEEE Transactions* 9 (1) (2013): 28–42.

[8]   Mondragon A. E. C., Coronado E. S., and Mondragon C. E. C. Defining a convergence network platform framework for smart grid and intelligent transport systems. *Energy* 89 (2015): 402–409.

[9]   *National Institute of Standards and Technology (NIST)*, 2021. www.nist. gov/el/smart-grid.

[10] Panda D. K., and Das S. Smart grid architecture model for control, optimization and data analytics of future power networks with more renewable energy. *Journal of Cleaner Production* 301 (2021): 126877.

[11] Alagoz B., Kaygusuz A., and Karabiber A. A user-mode distributed energy management architecture for smart grid applications. *Energy* 44 (1) (2012): 167–177.

[12] Tu C., He X., Shuai Z., and Jiang F. Big data issues in smart grid a review. *Renewable and Sustainable Energy Reviews* 79 (2017): 1099–1107.

[13] Gantz J., and Reinsel D. The digital universe in 2020: Big data, bigger digital shadows, and biggest growth in the far east. *IDC iView: IDC Analyze the Future* (2012):1–16.

[14] Chen Y., Xie L., and Kumar P.R. 2014. Power system event classification via dimensionality reduction of synchrophasor data. In *Sensor Array and Multichannel Signal Processing Workshop (SAM)* (IEEE 8th). IEEE, 2014, pp. 57–60.

[15] Russom P. Big data analytics. *TDWI Best Practices Report* (Fourth Quarter), 2011, pp. 1–35.

[16] De Mauro A., Greco M., and Grimaldi M. A formal definition of big data based on its essential features. *Library Review* 65 (3) (2016): 122–135.

[17] Sagiroglu S., and Sinanc D. Big data: A review. In *Collaboration Technologies and Systems (CTS), 2013 International Conference*. IEEE, 2013, May, pp. 42–47.

[18] DOE. *Advancement of Synchrophasor Technology in ARRA Projects*, 2016. www.smartgrid.gov/recovery_act/program_publications.html.

[19] Yang B., and Yamazaki J. Big data analytic empowered grid applications-Is PMU a big data issue? In *Proceedings of the 2015 12th International Conference on the European Energy Market (EEM)*. IEEE, 2015, p. 1–4.

[20] Depuru S. S. S. R., Wang L., and Devabhaktuni V. Smart meters for power grid: Challenges, issues, advantages and status. *Renewable and Sustainable Energy Reviews* 15 (6) (2011): 2736–2742.

[21] Kabalci Y. A survey on smart metering and smart grid communication. *Renewable and Sustainable Energy Reviews* 57 (2016): 302–318.

[22] Asad Z., and Rehman Chaudhry, M. A. A two-way street: Green big data processing for a greener smart grid. *IEEE Systems Journal* 11 (2017): 784–795.

[23] Stimmel C. L. *Big Data Analytics Strategies for the Smart Grid*. Auerbach Publications, 2014.

[24] Chow C. W., Urquhart B., Lave M., Dominguez A., Kleissl J., Shields J., and Washom B. Intra-hour forecasting with a total sky imager at the UC San Diego solar energy testbed. *Solar Energy* 85 (11) (2011): 2881–2893 (ISSN 0038–092X). https://doi.org/10.1016/j.solener.2011.08.025.

[25] Paoli C., Voyant C., Muselli M., and Nivet M.-L. Forecasting of pre-processed daily solar radiation time series using neural networks. *Solar Energy* 84 (12) (2010): 2146–2160.

[26] Cummins K. L., Krider E. P., and Malone M. D. The us national lightning detection network/sup tm/and applications of cloud-to-ground lightning data by electric power utilities. *EEE Transactions on Electromagnetic Compatibility* 40 (4) (1998): 465–480.

[27] Huang Y., Warnier M., Brazier F., and Miorandi D. Social network-ing for smart grid users. In *2015 IEEE 12th International Conference on Networking*. Sensing and Control, 2015, pp. 438–443. https://doi.org/10.1109/ICNSC.2015.7116077.

[28] Moreno-Munoz A., Bellido-Outeirino F. J., Siano P., and Gomez-Nieto M. A. Mobile social media for smart grids customer engagement: Emerging trends and challenges. *Renewable and Sustainable Energy Reviews* 53 (2016): 1611–1616. https://doi.org/10.1016/j.rser.2015.09.077.

[29] Pignati M., Zanni L., Romano P., et al. Fault detection and faulted line identification in active distribution networks using synchro phasors-based real time state estimation. *IEEE Transactions on Power Delivery* 32 (1) (2017): 381–392.

[30] Jiang H., Dai X., Gao D. W., et al. Spatial-temporal synchro phasor data characterization and analytics in smart grid fault detection, identification, and impact causal analysis. *IEEE Transactions on Smart Grid* 7 (5) (2016): 2525–2536.

[31] Usman M. U., and Faruque M. O. Validation of a PMU-based fault location identification method for smart distribution network with photovoltaics using real-time data. *IET Generation, Transmission & Distribution* 12 (21) (2018): 5824–5833.

[32] Hosseini Z. S., Mahoor M., and Khodaei A. AMI-enabled distribution network line outage identification via multi-label SVM. *IEEE Transactions on Smart Grid* 9 (5) (2018): 5470–5472.

[33] Ahmed A., Awais M., Naeem M., et al. Multiple power line outage detection in smart grids: probabilistic Bayesian approach. *IEEE Access* 6 (2018): 10650–10661.

[34] Jiang Y., Liu C.-C., Diedesch M., et al. Outage management of distribution systems incorporating information from smart meters. *IEEE Transactions on Power Systems* 31 (5) (2016): 4144–4154.

[35] Jokar P., Arianpoo N., and Leung V. C. Electricity theft detection in AMI using customers' consumption patterns. *IEEE Transactions on Smart Grid* 7 (1) (2016): 216–226.

[36] Prostejovsky A. M., Gehrke O., Kosek A. M., et al. Distribution line parameter estimation under consideration of measurement tolerances. *IEEE Transactions on Industrial Informatics* 12 (2) (2016): 726–735.

[37] Azzouz M. A., and El-Saadany E. F. Multivariable grid admittance identification for impedance stabilization of active distribution networks. *IEEE Transactions on Smart Grid* 8 (3) (2017): 1116–1128.

[38] Wenli F., Xuemin Z., Shengwei M., et al. Vulnerable transmission line identification using ISH theory in power grids. *IET Generation, Transmission & Distribution* 12 (4) (2017): 1014–1020.

[39] Babakmehr M., Simões M. G., Wakin M. B., et al. Compressive sensing-based topology identification for smart grids. *IEEE Transactions on Industrial Informatics* 12 (2) (2016): 532–543.

[40] Cavraro G., and Kekatos V. Graph algorithms for topology identification using power grid probing. *arXiv preprint arXiv*:1803.04506, 2018.

[41] Pappu S. J., Bhatt N., Pasumarthy R., et al. Identifying topology of low voltage distribution networks based on smart meter data. *IEEE Transactions on Smart Grid* 9 (5) (2018): 5113–5122.

[42] Weng Y., Liao Y., and Rajagopal R. Distributed energy resources topology identification via graphical modeling. *IEEE Transactions on Power Systems* 32 (4) (2017): 2682–2694.

[43] Chaouch M. Clustering-based improvement of nonparametric functional time series forecasting application to intra-day household-level load curves. *IEEE Transactions on Smart Grid* 5 (1) (2014): 411–419.

[44] Shi H., Xu M., and Li R. Deep learning for household load forecasting – A novel pooling deep RNN. *IEEE Transactions on Smart Grid* 9 (5) (2018): 5271–5280.

[45] Gulbinas R., Khosrowpour A., and Taylor J. Segmentation and classification of commercial building occupants by energy-use efficiency and predictability. *IEEE Transactions on Smart Grid* 6 (3) (2015): 1414–1424.

[46] Naeem A., Shabbir A., Hassan N. U., et al. Understanding customer behavior in multi-tier demand response management program. *IEEE Access* 3 (2015): 2613–2625.

[47] He D., Du L., Yang Y., et al. Front-end electronic circuit topology analysis for model-driven classification and monitoring of appliance loads in smart buildings. *IEEE Transactions on Smart Grid* 3 (4) (2012): 2286–2293.

[48] Wang Y., Chen Q., Kang C., et al. Sparse and redundant representation based smart meter data mmm compression and pattern extraction. *IEEE Transactions on Power Systems* 32 (3) (2017): 2142–2151.

[49] Sui Z., Niedermeier M., de meer H. TAI: A threshold-based anonymous identification scheme for demand-response in smart grids. *IEEE Transactions on Smart Grid* 9 (4) (2018): 3496–3506.

[50] Kezunovic M., Xie L., and Grijalva S. The role of big data in improving power system operation and protection. In *Bulk Power System Dynamics and Control Optimization, Security and Control of the Emerging Power Grid (IREP), 2013 IREP Symposium*. IEEE, 2013, pp. 1–9.

[51] Chang V. I., and Wills G. B. A model to compare cloud and non-cloud storage of Big Data. *Future Generation Computer Systems* 57 (2016): 56–76.

[52] *Apache Hadoop*, 2016. http://hadoop.apache.org/.

[53] Zhang Y., Chen S., Wang Q., et al. i2 MapReduce: Incremental MapReduce for mining evolving big data. *IEEE Transactions on Knowledge and Data Engineering* 27 (7) (2015): 1.

[54] Xing E. P., Ho Q., Dai W., et al. Petuum: A new platform for distributed machine learning on big data. In *Proceedings of the ACM SIGKDD International Conference on Knowledge Discovery and Data Mining*. ACM, 2015, p. 1.

[55] Shyam R., Bharathi G. H. B., Sachin K. S., et al. Apache spark a big data analytics platform for smart grid. *Procedia Technology* 21 (2015): 171–178.

[56] *Apache Spark*, 2016. http://spark.apache.org/.

[57] Zhou D., Guo J., Zhang Y., et al. Distributed data analytics platform for wide area synchrophasor measurement systems. *IEEE Transactions on Smart Grid* 7 (5) (2016): 2397–2405.

[58] Meier R., Cotilla-Sanchez E., Mccamish B., et al. Power system data management and analysis using synchrophasor data. *Technologies for Sustainability IEEE* (2014): 225–231.

[59] Maharjan S., Zhu Q., Zhang Y., et al. Dependable demand response management in the smart grid: a Stackelberg game approach. *IEEE Transactions on Smart Grid* 4 (1) (2013): 120–132 ([147] Kwac J., and Rajagopal R. Demand response targeting using big data analytics. *Proceedings of IEEE International Conference on Big Data* (2013): 683–690).

[60] Wang Y., Chen Q., Hong T., et al. Review of smart meter data analytics: Applications, methodologies, and challenges. *IEEE Transactions on Smart Grid* (2018): 1

[61] Fallah S. N., Deo R. C., Shojafar M., et al. Computational intelligence approaches for energy load forecasting in smart energy management grids: State of the art, future challenges, and research directions. *Energies* 11 (3) (2018): 596.

[62] Tureczek A., Nielsen P. S., and Madsen H. Electricity consumption clustering using smart meter data. *Energies* 11 (4) (2018): 859.

[63] Zhao J., Zhang G., Das K., et al. Power system real-time monitoring by using PMU-based robust state estimation method. *IEEE Transactions on Smart Grid* 7 (1) (2016): 300–309.

[64] Pignati M., Zanni L., Romano P., et al. Fault detection and faulted line identification in active distribution networks using synchrophasors-based realtime state estimation. *IEEE Transactions on Power Delivery* 32 (1) (2017): 381–392 IEEE Digital Library.

[65] Agarwal A., Balance J., Bhargava B., et al. Real time dynamics monitoring system (RTDMS) for use with synchrophasor technology in power systems. In *Proceedings of IEEE Power & Energy Society General Meeting*, Detroit, MI, 2011, pp. 1–8.

Index

Printed in the United States
by Baker & Taylor Publisher Services